The Sciences Po Series in International Relations and Political Economy focuses on the transformations of the international arena and of political societies, in a world where the state keeps reinventing itself and appears resilient in many ways, though its sovereignty is increasingly questioned. The series publishes books that have two main objectives: explore the various aspects of contemporary international/transnational relations, from a theoretical and an empirical perspective; and analyze the transformations of political societies through comparative lenses. Evolution in world affairs sustains a variety of networks from the ideological to the criminal or terrorist that impact both on international relations and local societies. Besides the geopolitical transformations of the globalized planet, the new political economy of the world has a decided impact on its destiny as well, and this series hopes to uncover what that is.

The series consists of works emanating from the foremost French researchers from Sciences Po, Paris. It also welcomes works by academics who share our methods and philosophy of research in an open-minded perspective of what academic research in social sciences allows for and should aim for. Sciences Po was founded in 1872 and is today one of the most prestigious universities for teaching and research in social sciences in France, recognized worldwide.

More information about this series at
http://www.palgrave.com/gp/series/14411

Bayram Balci · Nicolas Monceau
Editors

Turkey, Russia and Iran in the Middle East

Establishing a New Regional Order

Editors
Bayram Balci
CERI Sciences Po
Paris, France

Nicolas Monceau
University of Bordeaux
Bordeaux, France

The Sciences Po Series in International Relations and Political Economy
ISBN 978-3-030-80290-5   ISBN 978-3-030-80291-2   (eBook)
https://doi.org/10.1007/978-3-030-80291-2

This Palgrave Macmillan imprint is published by the registered company Springer Nature Switzerland AG
The registered company address is: Gewerbestrasse 11, 6330 Cham, Switzerland

CONTENTS

Notes on Contributors

Khalid Almezaini is an Assistant Professor of Politics and International Relations, Zayed University, Abu Dhabi. He completed his Ph.D. in 2009 from the University of Exeter (UK). He has taught in several universities such as the University of Cambridge, University of Exeter, the University of Edinburgh, Qatar University, and Sciences Po in Paris, France. Almezaini has also worked as a researcher at the London School of Economics and Political Science. His teaching and research interests include Politics and IR, with particular focus on the politics of the Gulf, Foreign Policy, Foreign Aid and development in the Middle East. He is the author of *The UAE and Foreign Policy. Foreign Aid, Identities and Interests* (Routledge, 2012).

Bertrand Badie (Ph.D. in political science, Institut d'Etudes Politiques, 1975) is Emeritus Professor at Sciences Po Paris. Full Professor of political science since 1982 he was Director of the Presses de Sciences Po (1994 to 2003) and of the Rotary Center for International Studies in Peace and Conflict Resolution at Sciences Po (2001–2005). He has authored numerous books among which, *New Perspectives on the International Order No Longer Alone in This World* (Palgrave Macmillan, 2019), *Diplomacy of Connivance* (Palgrave Macmillan, 2012) and *Rethinking International relations,* Elgar, 2020.

Joseph Bahout is the Director of the Issam Fares Institute for Public Policy and International Affairs, American University of Beirut, where he is also an Associate Professor of Politics. Prior to that, he was a Research Fellow at the Carnegie Endowment. An expert in Middle East politics, both in the academic and policy-consultancy fields, Joseph Bahout holds a Ph.D. in Political Science from Sciences Po Paris. He is the Author of two books, on Syria's business community and its political outlook (1994), and on Lebanon's political reconstruction (1998), in addition to numerous articles and book chapters.

Bayram Balci holds a Ph.D. in political science, on Turkish Islamist movements and their missionary activities in post-Soviet Central Asia. His current research focuses on the relationship between Islam and politics in the post-Soviet era and Turkey in its regional environment, the Caucasus, Central Asia, the Middle East. Bayram Balci is currently on secondment in Istanbul as the director of Institut français d'études anatoliennes (IFEA).

Mitat Çelikpala is Professor of International Relations and the Dean of Faculty of Economics, Administrative and Social Sciences at Kadir Has University, Istanbul. He teaches graduate and undergraduate courses on Eurasian security, Turkish foreign and domestic policy, Turkish-Russian relations. He also contributed many conference papers on Turkish foreign policy, Turkish-Russian relations, Eurasianism and Turkish geopolitics.

Igor Delanoë (Ph.D. in history, Université Côte d'Azur) is the Deputy Director of Observatoire franco-russe (CCI France-Russie, Moscow). He is an Associate Researcher at the Center for International and European Studies (Kadir Has University, Istanbul), at the Centre de la Méditerranée Moderne et Contemporaine (CMMC) and at Laboratoire de Droit international et Européen (LADIE), Université Côte d'Azur.

Michel Duclos a career diplomat, is Special Advisor to Institut Montaigne (Paris). He was Ambassador of France to Syria from 2006 to 2009. He is the Author of *La Longue Nuit Syrienne* (Les Éditions de l'Observatoire, 2019). A frequent Contributor to various press media, Michel Duclos is also a non-resident fellow at the Atlantic Council (Washington).

Nicolas Monceau is Associate Professor in Political Science at the University of Bordeaux, France. He is a Researcher at Institut de recherche Montesquieu (Bordeaux) and a research associate at IFEA-Georges Dumézil (Istanbul). His research focuses on Turkish politics and Turkey in its regional and international environment. He has recently co-edited *Rising Powers, Institutions and Elites. Brazil, China, Russia, Turkey* (Presses Universitaires de Bordeaux, 2018) and published several books on Turkey and the EU as well as the Turkish elite.

Thomas Pierret is a Senior Researcher at CNRS-IREMAM, Aix-en-Provence, France. He holds a Ph.D. in Political science from Sciences Po Paris and the University of Louvain. He was a Senior Lecturer at the University of Edinburgh (2011–2017) and a Postdoctoral Research Associate at Princeton University. He is the Author of *Religion and State in Syria. The Sunni Ulama from Coup to Revolution* (Cambridge University Press, 2013) and *Islam in Post-Ottoman Syria* (Oxford Bibliographies, 2016). He has published extensively on the Syrian insurgency.

Bayram Sinkaya (Ph.D. from Middle East Technical University, Ankara) is Assistant Professor in the Department of International Relations, Faculty of Political Science at Ankara Yıldırım Beyazıt University. A Visiting Researcher at Tehran University (2003) and Columbia University (2007–2008), his research interests include Iranian politics, Middle Eastern politics and the Turkish foreign policy. He is the Author of *The Revolutionary Guards in Iranian Politics: Elites and Shifting Relations* (NY: Routledge, 2015).

Ömer Taspinar is Professor at the National Defense University and a non-resident senior fellow at the Brookings Institution in Washington, D.C. His areas of expertise include Turkey, Kurdish nationalism, Political Islam, American Foreign Policy, the Middle East, the European Union and Muslims in Europe. He is the Author of three books: *Kurdish Nationalism and Political Islam: Kemalist Identity in Transition* (Routledge, 2005) and *Winning Turkey: How the EU and the US can restore a fading partnership* (with Philip Gordon, Brookings, 2008) and *What the West is Getting Wrong About the Middle East: Why Islam is not the Problem* (I.B. Tauris, 2020).

Clément Therme is an Associate Fellow with the Regional Security Initiative at the Middle East Directions Programme of the Robert Schuman Centre for Advanced Studies at the European University Institute (EUI). He is also a Research Associate at the School for Advanced Studies in Social Sciences (EHESS) in Paris. Previously, he was a Research Fellow for Iran at the International Institute for Strategic Studies (IISS) and Lecturer at the National Institute for Oriental Languages and Civilizations (INALCO) in Paris. His articles have appeared in *Iranian*

Studies, The Middle East Journal, Survival, Politique étrangère, Maghreb-Machrek, Politique américaine. He recently edited *Iran and its Rivals,* Paris, Passés Composés, 2020.

LIST OF TABLES

CHAPTER 1

Introduction: Turkey, Russia, and Iran—New Dominant Powers in the Middle East?

Bayram Balci and Nicolas Monceau

The Arab Spring and the resulting conflicts, particularly the Syrian crisis that erupted in 2011, have ushered in a new era of domination and influence in the Middle East. As a former province of the Ottoman Empire, to which Turkey is the principal heir, as a French mandate before becoming independent and integrating Moscow's sphere of influence during the Cold War, and as an immediate neighbor of Israel where security is threatened by Iran but assured by the United States, Bashar al-Assad's Syria is the scene of a conflict that has a decisive influence on the Middle East and more broadly on the international order as a whole. Many actors, local, regional, and international, are involved in this conflict: forces loyal to the Syrian regime, rebel groups (Free Syrian Army, Kurds, and jihadists), international and regional organizations (the United Nations and the

B. Balci (✉)
CERI Sciences Po, Paris, France

N. Monceau
University of Bordeaux, Bordeaux, France
e-mail: nicolas.monceau@u-bordeaux.fr

© The Author(s), under exclusive license to Springer Nature Switzerland AG 2021
B. Balci and N. Monceau (eds.), *Turkey, Russia and Iran in the Middle East*, The Sciences Po Series in International Relations and Political Economy, https://doi.org/10.1007/978-3-030-80291-2_1

1

European Union), and Western countries (United States) as well as several regional powers, with Turkey, Iran, and Russia in the forefront.

This book attempts to examine and explain the effects of the Syrian conflict on the new governance of the Middle East region by these three political regimes: Russia, Turkey, and Iran. What is their role in the Syrian conflict? What do their role and influence show about the new governance of the Middle East? What are the dynamics at work, which would make it possible to envisage a three-way governance? What are this triumvirate's chances of success in acting as a lever for transformation in the Middle East? These are some of the major questions this edited volume aims to address. The main hypothesis of this book is that the Syrian conflict has had a major effect on the regional order in the Middle East. Syria has become a territory where the rivalry between Russia and Iran against Western powers is being played out, and where the contradictions and tensions between Turkey and its Western partners are brought to light. In recent years, with the Western countries' gradual withdrawal from the region, the conflict will doubtless have lasting effects on the regional and international order.

Many studies have been published on the relations between Turkey, Russia, and Iran, but most of these works mainly study relations between two regional powers, some of them with an emphasis on historical dimensions, such as Turkey-Russia (Kurban 2017), Turkey-Iran (Elik 2012; Kumral 2020), or Russia-Iran (Moore 2014). Concerning the Syrian conflict, many articles and a number of books have been written on this topic that has lasted over ten years. Among a growing literature, five books may be cited or indicated which focus on the internal and external dynamics of the conflict (Baczko et al. 2020; al-Haj Saleh 2017; Khen et al. 2020; Hetou 2018; Hinnebusch and Imady 2018).

Nevertheless, no publication has examined simultaneously and comparatively *how* these three states are participating in the shared management of the Syrian conflict. There are no academic works which study, in the same volume, the foreign policies and strategies of the three regional powers (Turkey, Russia, and Iran) both in the Syrian conflict and more widely in the Middle East. Most of the sources for this topic are research notes and think tank reports which do not examine the three powers either together or comparatively. The rare examples of studies comparing the three powers appeared before the conflict in Syria, in a totally different regional context, marked by the collapse of the USSR (Rubinstein and Smolansky 1995; Criss and Güner 1999, 365–376), or at the very start of the conflict (Brannen 2013; Flanagan 2013, 163–178). Those works which concentrate on the relations—rivalries and cooperation—between the three powers focus on the regions which for several decades or even centuries have been the field for their competition, in particular in Eurasia—the Caucasus, Central Asia, the Caspian basin—(Mesbahi 2010, 164–192) and more modestly the Middle East. Finally, much of the recent literature on Syria has focused on the role of a single power, such as Russia (Cooper 2018; Lovotti et al. 2020) or Turkey (Hinnebusch and Tür 2013; Şenbaş 2018), as well as the role and relations of two powers in the conflict: Turkey-Russia (Kelkitli 2017) or Turkey-Iran (Hetou 2018; Larrabee and Nader 2013). Two recent publications offer an approach similar to this study by analyzing the internationalization of the conflict in Syria (Khatib 2021) or the involvement of external powers in the Syrian conflict and the impact of events as much at regional as at international level (Hinnebusch and Saouli 2019).

While taking into account the international dimension of the fighting and the parts played by local as well as international powers, our study proposes a different approach by focusing on the role of regional powers in their attempt to resolve the Syrian question, an effort which seems to make them the "administrators" of a future Syria or even of the Middle East. The approach developed in this book does not aim to understand relations between Turkey, Iran, and Russia or to take an interest in the role played by all the external actors in Syria but to contribute elements for reflection on the causes which led to the Syrian war rendering obsolete all the classic mechanisms for resolution conflict by external actors, like the United Nations, or traditional powers—the United States or the EU—leading to the emergence of the Turkey-Russia-Iran triumvirate.

In other words, it is not about explaining the reasons, processes, or blockages in the settlement of the Syrian crisis—questions which have been widely analyzed by the earlier works mentioned—but of taking a more particular interest in the role of Russia, Turkey, and Iran in the Syrian conflict. The Syrian conflict had in fact led the three regional powers, whose relationships with the West were already tense and who had already displayed belligerent attitudes in the regional context, to grow closer despite their differences and to thereby transform Syria into a shared condominium, thus forming a kind of bloc which was certainly fragile but able to challenge the West. This attitude existed before the Syrian crisis but was materialized *by* and *through* the conflict. In the Syrian context, these three regional powers were competitors to the traditional powers which regulated the Middle East and, for many observers, they also supplanted them in order to become themselves the new key players.

In order to understand this process of "collaboration in divergence" between the three states, we need to go back over the regional context in Syria and then to examine the prospects and the conditions for the emergence of a new regional order. The intervention by the three powers brought about a relative calm in the fighting on the ground, leading some analysts to begin talking of a "low intensity conflict" which would lead the way to a search for a political solution. And yet, would the Turkey-Russia-Iran axis, formed at the time of the Syrian conflict, herald an in-depth reshaping of the Middle East region marked by the new dominance of these three regional powers?

THE REGIONAL CONTEXT: THE SYRIAN CONFLICT

The Syrian regional context is characterized by the authoritarian power of a dictatorial dynasty that has run the country since it was seized by force in 1970 by Hafez al-Assad, the father of the current president, Bashar al-Assad (Lesch 2005, 20–56). In principle inspired by Arab socialism, in fact, over time, power has been concentrated in the hands of a group from the Alawite minority. However, support for the regime went beyond this religious minority, with representatives of other community groups also associating with it. Bashar al-Assad's regime had rather cordial relations with its neighbors, in particular Turkey and Iran, and no excessive tension with Israel but it did not avoid the Arab Spring in the early 2010s. While the popular uprisings managed to topple the leaders in Tunisia, Egypt, Libya, and even Yemen, they did not have the same effect in Syria although demonstrations for freedom there were just as strong, from 2011 onwards (Lynch et al. 2014, 1–7). How should the fact that Bashar al-Assad's regime held on to power be explained? Although there are multiple causes, it is necessary to re-examine the two Syrian contexts—internal and external—in order to understand this "Syrian exception."

The internal reasons which helped the Syrian regime to survive, that is, the local resources from which it benefited, are to be found in Syria's particularities, in its population and the character of the regime. Once part of the Ottoman Empire, Syria has retained certain characteristics such as its multi-ethnic and multi-faith character which is more developed than in other countries affected by the Arab Spring. Syrian society allowed

Bashar's regime to better exploit this mosaic in order to defend his grip on power. Although most of the population are Sunni Arabs, there are sizeable ethno-religious minorities, such as the Kurds, the Christians, the Druze, and of course the Alawites (Valter 2018). Bashar's regime manipulated and instrumentalized the religious and ethnic groups that made up society in order to stay in power. Similarly, in order to divide the opposition and discredit it in the eyes of the international community, the Syrian regime freed many jihadist prisoners who had fought in Iraq so that they could join the protest movements against his power. Seeking therefore to establish a link between the Syrian revolution and jihadism, the regime caused growing concern among Western countries which quickly identified DAESH/ISIS as the priority in their intervention in the region (Becker 2015, 95–103).

The international context, or more specifically, Syria's position on the regional and international chessboard, also allows us to partly understand the Syrian regime's resilience and its grip on power. Unlike Libya, Egypt, and Tunisia, Syria finds itself at the meeting point of several geopolitical blocs that are intense rivals. Syria is a close neighbor of Israel, whose security is paramount for the United States, and it occupies a major strategic position for the regime in Tehran (notably for the continuation of a "Shi'ite arc" allowing access to the Mediterranean and to supply Hezbollah in Lebanon). Syria shares a 900 km border with Turkey and in the north of its territory has a large Kurdish population whose political and military organizations—PYD (Partiya Yekîtiya Demokrat, Democratic Union Party), YPG (Yekîneyên Parastina Gel, People's Protection Units)—are classed as terrorists by Ankara because they are under the orders of the PKK (Partiya Karkerên Kurdistan, Kurdistan Workers' Party) which Ankara has been fighting for decades. Largely based on a fear of Kurdish irredentism, Turkey launched three military operations in northern Syria between 2017 and 2019 in order to secure its borders, to fight the Kurdish organizations, and to establish a buffer zone in the north of Syria. In this configuration, the Syrian regime polarized and stoked rivalries and tensions among the various stakeholders in the region. Despite the opposition of several states in the Arab League, of Turkey and Western countries which called for the departure of Bashar al-Assad, the Syrian regime managed to stay in place thanks to actions by Russia and Iran. Russia vetoed all initiatives by the UN Security Council, with China's support, and along with Iran and Hezbollah, it supplied diplomatic, military, and financial help to Syria. Russia's military intervention in Syria from September 2015 proved to be decisive because of its successes in the field, ensuring the survival of the Syrian regime in the face of rebellion.

These two Syrian particularities—ethno-religious and position at the crossroads of several rival geopolitical blocs—also partly explain the prolongation of fighting and the division of its territory as well as the absence of any solution to this day. However, the context which would help in understanding the emergence of the Turkish-Russian-Iranian nexus on the regional scale is more complex. Changes in the international order, marked by the failures of meetings set up in Geneva by the UN and the Astana peace process, must also be taken into consideration. In fact, the Syrian conflict has shed light on profound changes in the international order. World governance was long dominated by the bipolar logic of the Cold War, and then by the single pole logic in the post-Cold War period. These logics are now hotly contested by the emergence of new powers which aspire to a multipolar order. The analysis of the rise in power of countries such as India and Brazil as well as Turkey, Iran, and others must bear this in mind (Prantl 2012, 39–56). In the case of Syria, the United Nations quickly revealed its inability to resolve the conflict through concertation. This paralysis in UN diplomacy has been accompanied by questioning from new actors on the scene, including Russia, Turkey, and Iran, the architects of the "Astana peace process" whose implications and effects raise the possibility of a new regional order being founded.

Establishing a New Regional Order

Turkey, Russia, and Iran are certainly not the only states in the region to be pursuing ambitious foreign policies. Other actors—Saudi Arabia, the Emirates, Qatar, Israel, and Egypt—also have interests and ambitions in the region.

However, reflecting this new governance in the region, these three powers, which sponsored the Astana and Sochi processes for the resolution of the conflict, are at the same time the main actors with real influence on the three dominant military actors in the Syrian field: namely, the Bashar regime, the Sunni Islamist rebels, and the Syrian Democratic Forces dominated by the Kurds of the PYD. Despite their divisions, the three states now seem able to lay the foundations for the future of Syria as a prelude to the establishment of a new order in the Middle East.

Turkey, Russia, and Iran also have several points in common and seek to exert an influence over the new global governance, either as a global power committed to restoring this status (Russia) or as major regional actors (Iran and Turkey). However, one of the main characteristics that unite them is the fact that these three states are each the heir to a great empire and are driven by the same wish to reclaim an imperial past or, at least, to be a part of its heritage even if this stance can be seen as a discourse of legitimization. Thus, this close link between imperial past and the ambition to become a new power must be remembered when interpreting the current diplomatic orientations of these three countries and even their military engagement in the conflict in Syria.

In the context of the Syrian conflict, and more generally in that of the Arab Spring, Russia opposed the support of Western countries and the United States in particular, for revolutionary processes acting in the name of democracy and freedoms which sowed chaos and instability in countries which had been stable up to that point. For Moscow, the Arab Spring can be compared to the "Color Revolutions" which erupted in its vicinity, in Ukraine, Georgia, and Kirghizstan (Nikitina 2014, 87–104). Through these revolutions, the Western countries aimed to extend their domination in order to maintain a unipolar international order to which Russia was opposed. In the context of the Arab Spring, this divergence between Russia and the West erupted in Libya in 2011. France and Britain's intervention, with no UN mandate but with the United States' assent, led to the toppling of the Libyan regime which was a close ally of Russia. Keeping the Libyan affair in mind, Russia showed the greatest intransigeance in Syria to ensure the survival of one of its oldest allies in the Arab world. In this demand for a new international order not dominated by Western countries, Russia is "joined" by the other major players in the Syrian conflict: Turkey and Iran.

The Syrian question remains paradoxical for Turkey. In 2011, this country enjoyed great popularity in the Arab countries in the region and relations between Turkish and Syrian authorities blossomed in the political, commercial, and security fields. During the first months of demonstrations in Syria, Turkey tried to act as a mediator with the Syrian regime. In the face of the violence of the repression, Turkey decided abruptly to break with the Syrian regime and called for Bashar to stand down. After that, Turkey provided the rebels with material help and welcomed the headquarters of the Free Syrian Army and then the Syrian National Council onto its territory. Developments in the Syrian conflict, in particular Turkey's Western partners' strategies in favor of Kurdish organizations close to or linked to the PKK in the north of Syria, seeing them as allies on the ground, shed light on an evolution observed since the end of the Cold War: the geostrategic interests of Turkey, a member of NATO, no longer necessarily converge in the region with those of its traditional Western partners (EU and United States).

Turkey had benefited from dizzying economic growth in the early 2010s as well as political stability, unprecedented for decades, and it aspired to a reorientation of its foreign policy, under the guidance of the Minister for Foreign Affairs, Ahmet Davutoğlu, in order to gain further autonomy regarding Western powers (Taspinar 2011, 11–17). Seeking a new position on the regional and international scene, Turkey sided with the positions defended by Russia in favor of an international system which would not be headed by one single power. This opposition to the domination of the major powers was expressed by President Erdoğan beginning in 2013 and repeated, notably during the 74th session of the United Nations General Assembly in September 2019 when he declared that "the world is bigger than five," referring to the five permanent members of the Security Council (Duran 2017; United Nations 2019; Aral 2019, 71–96).

As for Iran, it has deployed a foreign policy of opposition to the international order since the Islamic Revolution of 1979 (Hunter 2010). One of the latest examples of this foreign policy at odds with the majority positions in the international community is the handling of the Iranian nuclear crisis since the mid-2000s, which nevertheless concluded with the Vienna agreement in July 2015 (Ehteshami and Molavi 2012). When the fighting broke out in Syria, Tehran chose to back Bashar's regime in a steady and determined fashion so that he could pursue his autonomous policies and defend his interests while still being allowed to impose himself as a major player in the Middle East. Thousands of Hezbollah combatants are supported by Iran, and Iranian advisers present in Syria also enjoy financial aid from the Iranian regime.

With interests and points of view that are simultaneously held in common and differing, Turkey, Russia, and Iran are involved in the Syrian conflict supporting different camps—the Assad regime or rebel groups. These divergences do not prevent them from forming an "alliance" or a "partnership" through the Astana peace process which competes with and short-circuits the official talks in Geneva, carried out under the auspices of the UN (Heller 2017). In January 2017, the meeting in

Astana (Kazakhstan) between the "sponsors"—Turkey, Russia, and Iran—and representatives of the Syrian regime and rebel groups, launched the "Astana peace process" to find a political solution to the strife. Several meetings have been organized there since January 2017, followed by others at Sochi. This rapprochement between the three powers is also fostered by the chance offered by the progressive withdrawal of the United States ground forces, announced in October 2019 by President Trump who said he wanted to put an end to American forces involvement in "endless wars," and by the EU's relatively low profile on the terrain.

This rapprochement of the three powers in the framework of the Astana Process, and particularly between Turkey and Russia which belong to opposing security blocs or to rival alliances, raises a number of questions (Köstem 2020). This closeness between them is all the more striking since the states that share the same values—the United State and European countries—were not themselves committed to a deepening cooperation to resolve the Syrian crisis because they had different perceptions of the threats involved. The risks posed by refugees or terrorism were not framed in the same terms for European countries, geographically closer to Syria, as they did for their American ally.

Turkey is an ally of the United States and a partner of the EU and it has enjoyed a certain margin of maneuver in the Syrian conflict by adopting a strategy of alliance with Russia and Iran in the Astana Process. Despite several points of difference, these discussions with other regional powers have procured more security for the country rather than its being subordinated to its American ally. In the Turkish view of the regional issues, the United States' strategy of relying on the Kurdish organizations linked to the PKK in Syria might eventually lead to the forming of a Kurdish state and that would present a threat to Turkey's security. Moreover, the unpredictable nature of American foreign policy in northern Syria during the Trump administration reinforced Turkey's concerns. Consequently, Turkey—the United States' close ally and a member of NATO—turned to Russia and Iran whose Syrian agenda seemed to pose fewer threats to its national security. The Astana Process might thus be interpreted as the wish to represent a balanced force, with the aggregation of several regional powers, and to neutralize the risks of potential threats represented by United States policies in the region in its role as a great power. In other words, the "Astana spirit" is not a translation of the convergence of the three partners' viewpoints but is their common perception of the potential menace represented by the United States as an outside actor dominating the Syrian crisis (Cengiz 2020, 200–214; Namli and Farasin 2021, 123–144).

This alignment of the three regional powers in the Astana Process nevertheless raises several questions. The change in administration in the United States is the first uncertainty or unknown. At present, there is nothing to indicate that Joe Biden will carry on his predecessor Trump's policy of American troop withdrawal, even though the American president confirmed in spring 2021 that American forces would leave Afghanistan. Also, the Astana partnership remains shaky as it was built on common adversity to the United States and not on a united vision over the Syrian issue. Lastly, this alliance was forged on interpersonal relations between the leaders of the three powers, in particular Putin and Erdoğan. However, there could be government change in Turkey after the next presidential and legislative elections in 2023 and the AKP party has lost support over the past few years. Should there be a change in power, then Turkey might revise its policy in Syria thereby casting doubt on the partnership founded by the Astana Process.

Structure and Contents of the Book

This edited volume has been written by academics and experts who specialize in the region and the three powers at play (Russia, Iran, and Turkey). Most of the chapters were presented at an international conference which took place at the University of Bordeaux (France) on November 23, 2018, organized by the University of Bordeaux, the French Institute of Anatolian Research (IFEA) in Istanbul, CERI (Sciences Po Paris), and the Institut Montaigne. The two editors of this book were the scientific co-organizers of the international conference, jointly responsible with Michel Duclos (Institut Montaigne). Other authors were later invited to contribute in order to complete this book.

The volume is divided into two parts. The first part of the book focuses on the Syrian crisis and the role of the three regional powers in it. The functioning of the Russia-Turkey-Iran triumvirate and its ability to resolve the Syrian crisis are addressed in six chapters which aim at studying the motivations, logics, and strategies implemented by the three states to put an end to the Syrian crisis. The chapters look at the means and resources deployed by each of these actors, as well as their mutual relations, to achieve stabilization or even a final settlement of the Syrian crisis. In this perspective, Mitat Çelikpala examines the relations between Turkey and Russia during the Syrian conflict while Bayram Balci analyzes the impact of the Syrian crisis on Turkey's domestic and foreign policies. Igor Delanoë examines the part played by Russia in post-conflict Syria, in particular with regard to reconstruction projects in the country. Bayram Sinkaya analyzes Iran's role in the Syrian conflict while Khaled Almezaini looks at relations between the United Arab Emirates and Syria to highlight their converging and diverging interests. To have a better understanding of the failure of the Syrian revolution, this first part also deals with two other major facts—the emergence of the Kurdish issue as a regional geopolitical event and the "Islamic State" phenomenon which quickly occupied a central place in the Syrian crisis, and the contribution of Thomas Pierret focuses on the relations between Turkey and the rebel Syrian groups, in particular jihadists.

By expanding it to the regional level beyond the Syrian case, the second part of the book, composed of five chapters, aims at analyzing the influence of Russia, Iran, and Turkey in the changes occurring in the Middle East. Bertrand Badie offers some thoughts on the idea of regional powers and the evolution of their status and influence in the Middle East since the end of the Cold War. The two following chapters then examine the relations between these three powers and in particular between Iran and Russia in the Middle East (Clément Therme) and the multidimensional relations between Turkey and Russia (Nicolas Monceau). Russia, Turkey, and Iran do not act alone or without considering their Western partners or rivals (the European Union and the United States). Two chapters focus on an examination of United States policy in the Middle East (Joseph Bahout) or on the development of relations between the United States and Turkey in the light of the Syrian conflict and the Kurdish question (Ömer Taspinar). Finally, as a conclusion, Michel Duclos offers some elements of reflection on the present situation and the future of relations between the three regional powers after ten years of strife in Syria.

Bibliography

Aral, Berdal. 2019. "'The World Is Bigger Than Five': A Salutary Manifesto of Turkey's New International Outlook." *Insight Turkey* 21 (4): 71–96.
Baczko, Adam, Gilles Dorronsoro, and Arthur Quesnay. 2020. *Syrie. Anatomie d'une guerre civile*. Biblis, Paris: CNRS Éditions.

Becker, Michael. 2015. "When Terrorists and Target Governments Cooperate: The Case of Syria." *Perspectives on Terrorism* 9 (1) (February): 95–103.

Brannen, Samuel, ed. 2013. *The Turkey, Russia, Iran Nexus: Evolving Power Dynamics in the Middle East, the Caucasus, and Central Asia*. Center for Strategic & International Studies, 12 November. Lanham: Rowman & Littlefield.

Cengiz, Sinem. 2020. "Assessing the Astana Peace Process for Syria: Actors, Approaches, and Differences." *Contemporary Review of the Middle East* 7 (2) (June): 200–214. https://doi.org/10.1177/2347798920901876.

Cooper, Tom. 2018. *Moscow's Game of Poker: Russian Military Intervention in Syria, 2015–2017*. Warwick: Helion & Company.

Criss, Nur Bilge, and Serdar Güner. 1999. "Geopolitical Configurations: The Russia-Turkey-Iran Triangle." *Security Dialogue* 30 (3) (September): 365–376.

Duran, Burhanettin. 2017. "Erdogan in India, the World Is Bigger Than Five." *SETA*, May 3. https://www.setav.org/en/erdogan-in-india-the-world-is-bigger-than-five/.

Ehteshami, Anoushiravan, and Reza Molavi, eds. 2012. *Iran and the International System*. London: Routledge. https://doi.org/10.4324/9780203809136.

Elik, Süleyman. 2012. *Iran-Turkey Relations, 1979–2011: Conceptualizing the Dynamics of Politics, Conceptualizing the Dynamics of Politics, Religion and Security in the Middle-Power States*. London: Routledge.

Flanagan, Stephen J. 2013. "The Turkey–Russia–Iran Nexus: Eurasian Power Dynamic." *The Washington Quarterly* 36 (1): 163–178.

al-Haj Saleh, Yassin. 2017. *The Impossible Revolution: Making Sense of the Syrian Tragedy*. London: Hurst & Co.

Heller, Sam. 2017. "Geneva Peace Talks Won't Solve Syria—So Why Have Them?" *The Century Foundation*, June 30. https://tcf.org/content/report/geneva-peace-talks-wont-solve-syria/.

Hetou, Ghaidaa. 2018. *The Syrian Conflict: The Role of Russia, Iran and the US in a Global Crisis*. London: Routledge.

Hinnebusch, Raymond, and Adham Saouli, eds. 2019. *The War for Syria: Regional and International Dimensions of the Syrian Uprising*. London: Routledge.

Hinnebusch, Raymond, and Omar Imady, eds. 2018. *The Syrian Uprising: Domestic Origins and Early Trajectory*. London: Routledge.

Hinnebusch, Raymond, and Özlem Tür, eds. 2013. *Turkey-Syria Relations Between Enmity and Amity*. Farnham: Ashgate.

Hunter, Shireen T. 2010. *Iran's Foreign Policy in the Post-Soviet Era: Resisting the New International Order*. Santa Barbara, CA: Praeger.

Kelkitli, Fatma Asli. 2017. *Turkish-Russian Relations: Competition and Cooperation in Eurasia*. London: Routledge.

Khatib, Dania Koleilat, ed. 2021. *The Syrian Crisis: Effects on the Regional and International Relations*. Springer. https://doi.org/10.1007/978-981-15-5050-8.

Köstem, Seçkin. 2020. "Russian-Turkish Cooperation in Syria: Geopolitical Alignment with Limits." *Cambridge Review of International Affairs*. https://doi.org/10.1080/09557571.2020.1719040.

Kumral, Mehmet Akif. 2020. *Exploring Emotions in Turkey-Iran Relations: Affective Politics of Partnership and Rivalry*. Palgrave Macmillan. https://doi.org/10.1007/978-3-030-39029-7.

Kurban, Vefa. 2017. *Russian-Turkish Relations from the First World War to the Present*. Newcastle upon Tyne: Cambridge Scholars Publishing.

Larrabee, F. Stephen, and Alireza Nader. 2013. *Turkish-Iranian Relations in a Changing Middle East*. Santa Monica, CA: Rand Corporation.

Lesch, David W. 2005. *The New Lion of Damascus: Bashar al-Assad and Modern Syria*. Yale University Press.

Lovotti, Chiara, Eleonora Tafuro Ambrosetti, Christopher Hartwell, and Aleksandra Chmielewska, eds. 2020. *Russia in the Middle East and North Africa: Continuity and Change*. London: Routledge.

Lynch, Marc, Deen Freelon, and Sean Aday. 2014. "Syria in the Arab Spring: The Integration of Syria's Conflict with the Arab Uprisings, 2011–2013." *Research and Politics* 1 (3) (October–December): 1–7.

Mesbahi, Mohiaddin. 2010. "Eurasia Between Russia, Turkey, and Iran." In *Key Players and Regional Dynamics in Eurasia*, edited by Maria Raquel Freire and Roger. E. Kanet, 164–192. Palgrave Macmillan. https://doi.org/10.1057/9780230290754.

Moodrick-Even Khen, Hilly, Nir T. Boms, and Sareta Ashraph, eds. 2020. *The Syrian War: Between Justice and Political Reality*. Cambridge: Cambridge University Press.

Moore, Eric D. 2014. *Russia-Iran Relations Since the End of the Cold War*. London: Routledge.

Namli, Kaan, and Fadi Farasin. 2021. "ASTANA: The Rise of a New Alliance and Its Implications for the International Relations." In *The Syrian Crisis Effects on the Regional and International Relations*, edited by Dania Koleilat Khatib, 123–144. Springer. https://doi.org/10.1007/978-981-15-5050-8.

Nikitina, Yulia. 2014. "The 'Color Revolutions' and 'Arab Spring' in Russian Official Discourse." *Connections* 14 (1): 87–104.

Prantl, Jochen. 2012. "Les mutations de la gouvernance mondiale: pays émergents et groupes 'G'." *Critique internationale* 56 (3): 39–56.

Rubinstein, Alvin Z., and Oles M. Smolansky, eds. 1995. *Regional Power Rivalries in the New Eurasia: Russia, Turkey and Iran*. London: Routledge.

Şenbaş, Demet. 2018. *Post-Cold War Relations Between Turkey and Syria.* London: Transnational Press.

Taspinar, Ömer. 2011. "The Rise of Turkish Gaullism: Getting Turkish-American Relations Right." *Insight Turkey* 13 (1): 11–17.

United Nations. 2019. "General Debate. General Assembly of the United Nations." Meeting on September 24–30, 2019. https://www.un.org/en/ga/69/meetings/gadebate/24sep/turkey.shtml.

Valter, Stéphane. 2018. "The Dynamics of Power in Syria: Generalized Corruption and Sectarianism." In *The Syrian Uprising, Domestic Origins and Early Trajectory,* edited by Raymond Hinnebusch and Omar Imady. London: Routledge.

CHAPTER 2

Situating 'New Turkey' in the Middle East Within a Competition-Cooperation Spiral of Turkish-Russian Relations

Mitat Çelikpala

Due to the spiral of competition and cooperation that shaped their history, Turkey and Russia have failed to establish stable bilateral relations since the end of the Cold War. The two countries' unbalanced bilateral relations influence a wide geography—almost all Eurasian territories that cover not just the immediate surroundings of both countries from the Black Sea to the Caucasus but Central Asia and the Middle East as well. Consequently, it is not sufficient to label Turkish-Russian relations only as bilateral relations. A comprehensive assessment of Turkish-Russian relations can only be done in the context of regional and global developments and with an eye on the realities of the two countries' history with one another.

M. Çelikpala (✉)
Kadir Has University, Istanbul, Turkey
e-mail: mitat@khas.edu.tr

B. Balci and N. Monceau (eds.), *Turkey, Russia and Iran in the Middle East*, The Sciences Po Series in International Relations and Political Economy, https://doi.org/10.1007/978-3-030-80291-2_2

Both states' relations with Western actors also play a significant role in shaping their foreign and security policies as well as their bilateral relations. The Turkish authorities have always considered Russia to be a counterweight to the West and have played the Russia card in their negotiations with Western actors on different issues. Similarly, Russian authorities consider Turkey as either the locomotive of cooperation or an adversary blocking the advancement of Russian interests in its neighborhood.

Turkish-Russian bilateral relations in the modern era went through a rapid transformation beginning in the mid-1990s. While considering each other rivals in almost all neighboring regions in the early 1990s, Ankara and Moscow have changed their perceptions of each other with the aim of establishing a 'new strategic partnership in the new century' with a special focus on Eurasia (Balta and Çelikpala 2020; Marcou and Çelikpala 2020). They preferred to focus on prospective areas of cooperation and leave the traditional issues of contention to hibernate. Thus, the two parties reframed their relations based on the principle of 'compartmentalization' of issues. Through this compartmentalization policy, Ankara and Moscow managed to segregate geopolitical and economic issues from one another, especially in Eurasian regions, namely the Caucasus, Central Asia, and very lately the Middle East. Such a downgrading of geopolitics looks strange when one considers the strategic cultures and history of both parties, that are heavily laden with grand geopolitical narratives. In such an environment where geopolitics can always return to the top of the agenda, the level of actualization of Eurasia-centered cooperation discourse necessitates the establishment of a realistic connection between discourse and action. To that effect, both countries have managed to institutionalize their initiatives and have implemented several fundamental changes in their own geopolitical and security cultures during the last decades. Nevertheless, the increasing disagreements, competition, and insecurity in those Eurasian sub-regions put any improvements in the political, economic, and security-related arenas into a tight spot.

The ebbs and flows of events in Syria since 2012 and their reflections on Turkish-Russian relations are worth studying in order to analyze the unsteady nature of Turkish-Russian bilateral relations. The agenda of bilateral relations especially after the Russian-Georgian War was restricted to matters such as the changing balance in the Black Sea and the Caucasus, which required more effort compared to the past, as well as the Arab Spring and security issues focusing on the developments in Syria and

Libya. Here came a fragile juncture that required further efforts by both sides in order for any progress or positive considerations to be possible. In other words, a highly challenging process to sustain multidimensional relations in the context of differing national interests and security threats was imminent. The aggressive regional and global policies Russia started to pursue toward its neighbors revealed that Turkey's various policies such as 'zero problems with neighbors' or 'precious loneliness' failed to bring the parties together around similar visions and interests as opposed to the past (Köstem 2018). So, this chapter seeks to analyze the ebbs and flows of Turkish-Russian relations with a special reference to the Syrian war and the Middle East.

THE SYRIAN WAR

It was Syria that underlined the fundamental divergence of the expectations and interests of the two countries since the end of the Cold War. Regarding Syria, Ankara pursued an active policy that aimed at regime change in Damascus and favored explicit support for the anti-regime opposition forces along the border, while Russia extended its all-out support for al-Assad and focused on preventing a new Libya case as a result of Western-led policies (Aydın-Düzgit et al. 2020). Indeed, Russia apparently deemed the 2011 incidents in Libya as the result of a neglect of Russia's global role as well as a blow to its reputation in the Arab world. Therefore, it started to pursue an active policy in Syria, Russia's ally since the Cold War era, to ensure its weight in the Middle East was acknowledged by both the regional players and the Western world (Karasik and Blank 2018).

The first signals that Turkish-Russian relations were headed toward a difficult period because of Syria had indeed come up in June 2015. The increase in the frequency of news reports that Turkey would intervene in Syria coincided with Russia's deciding on a direct military intervention in Syria (Özcan 2017; Aydıntaşbaş 2016). The process had already led to a point of no return when international news reports showed in September 2015 that the Russian Air Force had started to build up at *Hmeimim* air base, the former *Bassel al-Assad* Airport (Crilly 2015). After Turkey allowed the anti-ISIL coalition the use of Incirlik base, Sergey Lavrov, the Russian Foreign Minister, and Feridun Sinirlioglu, the then Turkish Foreign Minister, had a meeting in Sochi on September 17, 2015. Following the meeting, Lavrov's statements showed that Russia was not happy with Turkey's anti-ISIL coalition, another indication that the political differences between the two countries had grown deeper (The Ministry of Foreign Affairs of the Russian Federation 2015).

Starting from early October, especially around the province of Hatay, Russian warplanes deployed in Syria from September 2015 began violating the rules of engagement declared by Turkey in 2012 after the downing of a Turkish fighter jet by the Syrian air force. The agenda for bilateral relations was quickly transformed once Russia's airborne operations started to target groups explicitly supported by Turkey. President Erdogan's ensuing statement in early October openly pointed to an imminent transformation in bilateral relations:

> For Turkey, Russia's operations in Syria are in no way acceptable. Such an attitude will ultimately lead Russia into loneliness in the region. Such steps as Russia took despite Turkey have upset and bothered us. Russia has no borders with Syria. I wonder what Russia intends to achieve this way. They claim the Syrian regime demanded such operations. It is not necessary to launch such operations just because the regime demanded them. (NTV Haber 2015)

Following an increased number of breaches by Russian jets despite such warnings by Erdogan, the defense ministers of NATO member countries met in Brussels on October 8 at Turkey's request to discuss Russian air strikes in Syria. After the meeting, NATO Secretary General Jens Stoltenberg declared that 'The recent violations of Turkish airspace are unacceptable. NATO will continue to follow the developments closely. And we stand in strong solidarity with Turkey' (NATO 2015). So, it was a clear-cut declaration that the alliance was ready to protect Turkey and send troops in support if necessary and it emphasized that NATO was in solidarity with Turkey, which was a relief for Turkey. These developments suggested that, when vital interests were concerned, Turkey prioritized its traditional alliance relations with its Western allies against Russia and Iran, which were considered a resurgent threat. Responding to media questions upon his return from Brussels, President Erdogan said Russia's statements about the breaches were far from being serious. The key message from these statements was that Turkey had considered suspending its relations with Russia in the aftermath of the developments in Syria. During the process, Turkey highlighted its NATO membership and sided with NATO, moving away from Russia.

The culmination of the rapidly rising tension was reached on November 24, 2015, when an F-16 fighter jet of the Turkish Air Force shot down a Russian warplane that had violated Turkish airspace to the south of the Turkish city of Hatay. This was the incident that put an end to the cooperative spirit that had governed the previous 15 years of Turkish-Russian bilateral relations. The downing was followed by a period of about nine months that was dubbed the 'Horrible Year' or '*annus horribilis*' in bilateral relations. This period was proof that bilateral relations were indeed very sensitive and quickly influenced by external developments (Çelikpala 2018).

The jet shoot-down was important for Russia in the sense that it was the first after a long period of time, from 1953 to 2015. The disappointment was much greater because that recent incident had occurred with Turkey, a NATO member, which had lately been considered 'a close friend'.

The peak of the Syria-focused tension was the downing of the Russian fighter jet, which coincided with a period when domestic political problems in Turkey heavily impacted on the country's stability. In 2013, all of Turkey was the scene for *Gezi* Protests resembling the Arab Spring in the Middle East, which Erdogan supported right from the beginning.

In such a severe political atmosphere, Erdogan secured about 52percent of votes during the presidential election on August 10, 2014, a bid that he made to eliminate the instability caused by the graft probes in 2013 as well as the local elections. The political environment emerging after Erdogan's election as the president forced the country into two successive general elections in 2015, one on June 7 and the other on November 1. The Justice and Development Party's (AKP) failure in the June 7 elections to gain a majority required for maintaining single-party rule, coupled with the rise of the Peoples' Democratic Party (HDP) as a political actor based on a claim to be 'Turkey's party', gave rise to a political atmosphere where domestic political balances were essentially altered. This interim period also marked the end of the government's 'Kurdish Initiative', that had been launched to seek a moderate and constructive solution to the Kurdish issue after the Kurdistan Workers' Party's (PKK) July 2015 decision to resume terrorist activities by engaging in 'trench and barricade warfare'. As a result, the determined fight launched by the Turkish Armed Forces against the PKK in the entire south-eastern Anatolia region, chiefly in Sur, Silopi, and Cizre, re-militarized the Kurdish issue and rapidly related it to Syria. The battlefront in Turkey's fight against terrorism broadened, instantly making any developments in Syria a domestic issue for Turkey. Turkey expected its allies to recognize the PYD/Peoples' Protection Units (YPG) as a terrorist organization just like Islamic State (ISIL) and to engage in a fight in Syria within the same understanding but failed to get the support it wanted from the USA, and Russia, also failing to launch land and air operations in Syria. These all drove Turkish decision makers into nervousness. The argument of nationalist and conservative cliques in Turkey that external powers conspired to divide Turkey was actually resurrected and influenced the public during that period. Discussions of a 'Sèvres Syndrome' that focused on protecting Turkey's territorial integrity once again became an item on the agenda. Thus emerged an atmosphere that combined domestic developments with external factors that mutually fed and fueled each other.

In addition to the international attitude adopted against Turkey's interests and expectations in the aftermath of the developments in Egypt and Syria, Russia's indifference/negligence in this matter coincided with a time when Ibrahim Kalın, Erdogan's chief advisor, suggested the concept of 'Precious Loneliness' (*Hürriyet Daily News* 2013). That was a key statement to understanding the psychology that influenced the Turkish decision makers during that period. Russia's attitude meant a *cul-de-sac* for Turkey's foreign policy, which focused on ousting al-Assad, as well as for its security policies within the context of the fight against the PKK. Due to Russia's attitude, the expected end of the al-Assad regime was not coming any nearer. This resulted in Turkey's reducing its Syrian policy down to almost only the fight against the PYD/YPG. Yet that struggle was being hampered by the Russian bombings. Russia was destroying not only Turkey's investments but also the opposition elements that Turkey had been training under great difficulties. The downing of the jet against such a background thus coincided with a moment when things were far from being acceptable for Turkey.

It may also be asserted that Russia was not able to interpret the developments in Turkey and the impact thereof on bilateral relations in a realistic manner. Furthermore, it may be assumed that Russia favored and prioritized its global interests over its bilateral relations with Turkey, and thought the issues could be sorted out through a kind of appeasement initiative toward Turkey.

The Ice Age in Relations

Considering what happened between November 24, 2015, and Erdogan's visit to St. Petersburg on August 9, 2016, it is evident that Russia, and Putin in person, attempted to isolate and pressurize Turkey. Russia's rapid and efficient reaction was to put into effect sanctions against Turkey that resembled the EU sanctions against Russia after the annexation of Crimea. Starting from January 2016, Russia began to enforce the sanctions consisting of six articles. These were deliberately selected in a way to harm Turkey's economic and trade interests. The sanctions mainly included prohibiting any security-related operations in Russia by Turkey-based firms that were legally bound by Russian laws, prohibiting the recruitment of Turkish nationals in Russia, banning certain Turkish-made products from entering Russia, applying a very strict control and audit process for vehicles carrying commodities into Russia, suspending all charter flights except for scheduled flights between the two countries, instructing Russian tour operators to avoid selling tours to Turkey, and suspending the visa-free travel regime (Özdal 2015).

Throughout that period, Russia did not hesitate to re-employ certain conventional tools against Turkey in a way that recalled the competition period of the 1990s. Aware of Turkey's anti-terrorism priorities and the impact of developments in Syria on those priorities, Russia increased its interaction with the YPG/PYD in Syria and established open connections with the Kurdish opposition elements within Turkey. This was also the end of the policy of not meddling with the likes of Kurdish and Chechen issues, which the two countries mutually included on their agenda in the early period of cooperation. In January 2016, Maria Zakharova, the spokesperson for the Russian Foreign Ministry, shifted from the traditional Russian attitude and strikingly declared Russia's support for the petition signed by a group of academics that demanded Turkey stop human rights violations in the fight against the PKK, a petition that dominated domestic politics in Turkey back then. In a similar vein, Selahattin Demirtas, the chairman of the HDP, was invited to Moscow by the Russian Foreign Minister Lavrov in December to discuss the Kurdish issue and Turkey's operations. That meeting paved the way for subsequent meetings between Russian officials and different Kurdish groups, which re-opened political bureaus in Moscow and Yerevan. At that point,

Turkey was hamstrung regarding Russia, unable to issue any other political response than diplomatic reprimands against the steps Russia had taken.

RAPPROCHEMENT ANEW: JULY 15 AND A NEW DIRECTION IN RELATIONS

After the calming down of a fierce period full of accusations, both parties evaluated the consequences of the recent developments and felt that a 15-year effort had been shelved overnight. 2016 was a year of loss in bilateral relations for both sides. The Turkish side was more harshly and rapidly impacted by the process. It may be asserted that the parties were forced by the economic and security issues created by the situation in Syria to question their positions as well as the recent developments. The fight against terrorism was intertwined with the cross-border developments, specifically with those in Syria, making a significant impact on Turkey's security policies. Things turned more problematic for Ankara when Turkey was isolated from what was going on in Syria due to the tension with Russia.

It was the Turkish side that took the first steps toward normalizing bilateral relations under the severe impact of all the foregoing developments. President Erdogan's new political initiative called the '2023 Goals' included a different series of economic, trade and political measures. That was a period when Erdogan prioritized the fight against terrorism, converged with the nationalist faction and engaged in a struggle against the Gulenist elements, the recent threat that was called the 'parallel structure' back then, in addition to continuing the existing fight against the PKK. In May 2016, there was a change in the government as required by the need to support the domestic struggle with foreign relations. Ahmet Davutoglu was replaced by Binali Yıldırım as the prime minister. The new government began by introducing some basic changes to Turkey's foreign policy in relation to Russia, Israel, and Syria in a discourse of 'increasing the number of friends, decreasing the number of foes' (Milliyet 2016). Letters by President Erdogan and the new Prime Minister Yıldırım to their Russian counterparts on June 12, 2016, on the occasion of Russia Day about a month before the coup attempt, were the first signals of the intention to improve relations. The letters were followed by the Turkish government's launching a series of new measures to improve relations with Russia. Those measures meant the practical implementation stage had started. It was declared that a series of measures would be undertaken including re-establishing high-level diplomatic relations between the two countries, actively involving the media and civil society organizations in the process of improving relations, and setting up a working group for normalization (Çetin 2016). President Erdogan sent a letter to Putin on June 27, 2016, in which he assumed, although in indirect expressions, the responsibility for the downing of the Russian warplane and stated the family of the Russian pilot who died in the incident would be paid damages. This was the first fruit of the détente period between the countries (TRT Haber 2016).

The coup attempt of July 15, 2016 was what transformed the initial warm-up laps into a rapid normalization process. The nine-month break in bilateral relations came to an end after Russia issued a rapid reaction to the July 15 coup attempt and President Erdogan paid his first official visit after the coup attempt to St. Petersburg on August 9 in a bid to 'return to the pre-November period'. Subsequently, the two leaders were accompanied by a large delegation of ministers including the economy and energy ministers during the meeting held in Hangzhou, China, on September 3, 2016, for the G-20 Summit. The meeting increased the expectations that relations could be rapidly normalized in the new period.

The extraordinary developments in Turkey's domestic and foreign politics within a period of about nine months between November 24, 2015, and August 9, 2016, could be deemed as the main reason that rapprochement was reinstated at an undoubtedly unexpected pace. Back then, as a result of domestic developments, Turkey was unable to receive the interest it expected from its Western allies in foreign politics, thus leaving it feeling isolated and alone. That was a decisive factor. Turkish decision makers believed that their Western allies, chiefly the USA, did not want to understand their priorities in the fight against terrorism that for them was considered a matter of survival. Adding the new threat perception, emerging after the rupture of bilateral relations with Russia, it was concluded that Turkish foreign policy was facing serious bottlenecks despite great success in the previous decade. Russia's failure to improve its relations with Western countries, coupled with its unilateral international operations falling short of winning international legitimacy, enabled Russia to conclude that none of the parties in Syria would benefit from Russia's sustained tension with the Turkish side at least on certain key matters. Furthermore, as can be inferred from subsequent developments, it may be asserted that Russia needed Turkey in the game it wanted to set up in order to eliminate the long-bothersome Ukraine and establish new transport routes, and thus have safer access to the European market.

Bilateral relations recovered at a surprisingly quick pace during the year that followed President Erdogan's visit on August 9. Considering the developments in Syria, both sides needed each other, a main reason why recovery was so quick. The fact that Turkey was unable to receive the attention it expected from its traditional allies, chiefly the USA was a major contributing factor. The Turkish-Russian convergence was directly fueled by the increased cooperation of American forces with the PYD/YPG to the east of the Euphrates, a security priority for Turkey, by the US weapons and ammunition support for the PYD/YPG, and also by the visual media reports that American soldiers were conducting a joint operation with those elements, not to mention the belief that the Gulenist Movement was supported by the USA (and that the USA was the secret power behind the coup attempt). To that end, Operation Euphrates Shield launched on August 24, 2016, marked Turkey's return to Syria for the sake of actively fighting terrorism and establishing a new room for alliance including not only Russia but also Iran. The operation aimed to ensure Turkey's border security and start a fight against both ISIL and the PYD/YPG, an extension of the PKK, within the framework of the UN Treaty. Moreover, it acted as the driver for the normalization of Turkish-Russian relations and, to put it even more ambitiously, for the reinvigoration of the relations in line with a vision that pursued certain political goals (Anadolu Agency 2017).

The Turkish-Russian cooperation not only opened Syrian airspace and territories for military operations by the Turkish Armed Forces but also created a new diplomatic space for Turkey, Russia, and Iran, and enabled Turkey to communicate with the Syrian regime, albeit indirectly. The operation served as a means to issue a public message that the Turkish Armed Forces maintained their strength in the aftermath of the coup attempt and a tactical depth was secured abroad on Syrian soil in order to ensure the permanence of the success in domestic anti-terrorism initiatives.

THE ASTANA PROCESS

Turkey and Russia used Euphrates Shield as a means to re-establish bilateral relations within the framework of military cooperation unlike past initiatives, and transposed this effort to diplomatic and political domains under the Astana Process, an initiative for cooperation among Turkey, Russia, and Iran.

On December 20, 2016, the Moscow Declaration was issued after the meeting of the foreign ministers of Iran, Russia, and Turkey in Moscow. The document signaled the intention to transfer the efforts of the trio of countries, which were conducting military activities and the fight against terrorism on Syrian soil, onto the political arena in a bid to find a solution to the Syrian issue (Republic of Turkey, Ministry of Foreign Affairs 2016). The key step deserving attention in Syria after 2012 was that the three countries defined themselves as 'facilitators', or guarantors, in the negotiations for a potential agreement between the Syrian Government and the opposition.

Responding to the invitation from the president of Kazakhstan, the first meeting was held in Astana, hence the name the Astana Process. Both the declaration and the process turned the trio into active and legitimate players determining and bringing together the parties concerned by the quest for a solution to the Syrian issue. The talks during that period enabled certain steps that served the priorities of delivering an active fight against the PYD/YPG, an item to which Turkey had paid much attention since the beginning; protecting civilians and moderate opposition elements; establishing de-escalation zones; maintaining the issue of immigration on the agenda, and securing a permanent solution in Syria. Just as had been the case in the Astana Process, the expectation was to render Turkey an active and efficient player in finding a solution in Syria under the Geneva Process, a more comprehensive initiative including Western powers.

Through the Astana Process, the parties addressed a myriad of matters such as facilitating talks between the Syrian government and the armed opposition, ensuring the permanence of the ceasefire declared and establishing monitoring mechanisms, identifying and drawing the borders of de-escalation zones and leaving them to the control of guarantors, establishing coordination between them, identifying the elements that would contribute to the drafting of a new constitution to shape Syria's future, and developing trust-building measures between the parties.

It may be deemed that the process enabled the parties to shift to a mindset for compromise regarding the developments in and the future of Syria. It revealed different and similar approaches and encouraged positive steps toward targeting a solution. Making an impact on bilateral relations in the process, the issue of fighting against the PKK/PYD/YPG was also an occasional highlight in the Astana Process. Although Turkey was usually supported by Russia to that end, there were times when uncertainties prevailed, for instance, on what attitude Russia would adopt against the PYD within the framework of the plan to gather a 'public congress' that was made up of all the relevant ethnic groups. Turkey's priority was to 'exclude the terrorist groups from the process' while Russia wanted to 'hold a meeting in which all factions in Syria would be represented'. This led to a short-lived tension that came to an end when the parties quickly addressed and solved the matter without covering it, unlike what they had done in the past. The solution was brought along by Turkey, which submitted to Russia a list of Kurdish groups that could attend the congress excluding the PYD. At that point, it is possible to say that Russia carefully and accurately interpreted Turkey's sensitivities and issued the desired responses to expectations. Where the Syrian issue was concerned, the Astana Process acted as an assurance that supported bilateral cooperation.

Idlib Conundrum

The most powerful outcomes of Turkey's cooperation with Russia and Iran in Syria were that Idlib was established as a de-escalation zone and left to Turkey as the guarantor, and Turkish military troops were subsequently deployed in Idlib. Operation Olive Branch was launched by the Turkish Armed Forces in coordination with the Free Syrian Army (FSA) on Afrin on January 20, 2018, in order to put an end to terrorist activities originating from the north of Syria. It was regarded as a military operation and was concluded successfully in a short space of time. Linking the Syrian issue with its own fight against terrorism, Turkey enjoyed the success it achieved during that operation, which led to consequences such as proving Turkey's military capacity, establishing an efficient strategy in the fight against the US-backed YPG, which moved its troops to the east of Manbij and the Euphrates controlled by the USA, and reviewing relations specifically with the USA.

In 2018, the Astana Process was gradually progressing toward the end of armed conflict and the subsequent step of restructuring Syria. That also marked a period when a challenging phase had been reached in Turkish-Russian bilateral relations, and discussions had prevailed on whether it was possible for the Astana Process to survive. However, it was at the Tehran Summit in September 2018 when disagreements among the parties became noticeable and expectations started to differ (Hürriyet 2018).

It may be asserted that the Astana Process presented a certain convergence between Russia and Turkey (and Iran, definitely) in cognizance of the priorities and expectations of the parties and in order to improve the ability to manage a regional cooperation initiative that had the capacity to sort out a regional issue. It was critical that the two countries be able to agree on Syria, on which they had had almost fully opposing views and expectations in 2015, and to establish common interests to set up a basis to support bilateral cooperation. However, it goes without saying that challenging issues loomed on the horizon for the parties.

As the most striking example of those challenges, we may give the example of an airstrike on Turkish military personnel in Idlib on February 27, 2020, that killed 34 soldiers and wounded more. It was the deadliest incident for Turkey since the start of the Syrian conflict. Ankara blamed both Syrian and Russian forces in the field and retaliated by attacking more than 200 Syrian targets in Idlib. This worrisome incident occurred despite the existence of an active coordination mechanism between Turkish and Russian military authorities acting in the field. The incident caused much tension between Turkey and Russia and showed the fragility of bilateral relations in the Syrian field (Hughes 2020). All the warring parties in Syria announced a ceasefire after a week accompanying with the intervention of both leaders, Putin and Erdoğan in March 2020. Despite the fact that the March 2020 memorandum by the leaders of both parties included a commitment to eliminate all terrorist groups in Idlib, it is the most crucial challenge facing the parties over the presence of terrorist groups still located there (Aydın-Düzgit et al. 2020).

In brief, Turkish-Russian bilateral relations pursued an unstable path under the direct impact of the expectations and interests of both parties and these occasionally differed radically when faced with the inevitable pressure from global and regional developments. The parties are now trying to eliminate mutual distrust, a legacy of geopolitical and historical competition, and develop a permanent and common perspective on regional and global matters. This effort has produced some positive outcomes in Syria, albeit to a limited extent, as can be inferred from how things have progressed.

The parties had come to the brink of war in 2015 but, as of end 2018, they were seeking a collaborative, peaceful and permanent solution for the Syrian issue through diplomatic means. Although the success of that process was not directly dependent on bilateral relations, friendly and cooperation-focused relations apparently made a great contribution to the success of the solution process. In other words, the two players cultivated a common belief that acting in cooperation was the only way to find success against the considerable global issues they faced. Furthermore, it is possible to state that the restrictions and obstacles such cooperation faced in terms of providing a result led the parties to a point where they focused on the process itself. To that end, process orientation formed the main axis of recent Turkish-Russian relations.

Considering the importance and priorities of such rapprochement for Turkey and in a context of domestic political developments, another point to stress is the conviction of the Turkish decision makers that it was the powers backed by the USA, which Turkey called 'the mastermind', which were behind the domestic and regional problems Turkey has faced lately. Despite that, Russia was still deemed a reliable partner for the highly emphasized 'New Turkey', which meant the restructuring of public agencies and bodies under the state of emergency conditions and the presidential system. There was a move away from individual liberties as well as liberal values including the freedom of the press, within the framework of a discourse on anti-terrorism and on the need to reinstate stability in the country. An illiberal government system was being carved out that almost took Russia as a role model. Under such circumstances, in which the Turkish political system almost entirely evolved into that in Russia, the new political system held the Western world, chiefly the USA, as the threat or the Other, under the terms of the ongoing 'national struggle'. The Gulenist military officers backed by the USA were held responsible for the jet shoot-down incident that had driven a wedge between Turkey and Russia. This represented an entirely different perspective than that observed in November 2015 in terms of explaining and understanding the causes and consequences of the incidents. On a similar note, in December 2016, Andrei Karlov, the Russian ambassador to Ankara, was assassinated by a police officer who was related to the Gulenist movement at a time when Turkey and Russia had started to agree on certain security issues including Syria. Unlike the jet shoot-down, this abominable incident was calmly handled by both parties from the very beginning and was regarded as an act of provocation intended to hinder the progress in bilateral relations. It was implied that behind the perpetrator of the provocation were Western players, naturally.

It is ironic that what happened in Syria since 2012 was the reason why the parties had caught an actual wave of clash and rapprochement. The developments in Syria first brought the relations between Turkey and Russia to a point of rupture due to the jet shoot-down but then the parties converged within an initiative for a common fight against terrorism and to establish order in the Middle East. However, the factor that forced such cooperation to focus on the process rather than the outcome is the unstable relations the parties, each known historically as a European power, have with the Euro-Atlantic world.

Conclusion

Despite the achievements and ongoing cooperation in the last three years, bilateral political relations have had an extremely fragile basis in terms of the developments in the Middle East, chiefly in Syria, due to the different and imbalanced perspectives of the parties that are easily impacted by daily developments. To that end, it is possible that the imbalanced US policies on Syria, coupled with the EU's giving up on its indifferent approach to the matter, will evolve to prioritize cooperation with Turkey. This would bear the potential to directly influence Turkish-Russian relations in the future. It may be asserted that Turkey will need its Western allies in the upcoming period in order to balance, as a minimum, the increasing influence of Iran and Russia specifically in the Middle East. Furthermore, we will apparently witness a difficult process in the future, considering that Russia has given the green light to cooperation with players with regional influence such as Israel in addition to its need to keep Turkey as a partner, in order to balance the occasionally increasing Iranian influence.

On the other hand, the foregoing elements have kept the parties from building visionary, permanent, and stable relations and led to competition. Ironically, they have also emerged as the major points pushing the parties to cooperate as well. Regional and global developments created by geopolitical competition, coupled with the disagreements with the Western countries, force the parties to engage in permanent political relations and diplomatic cooperation. It is a fact that bilateral relations between Turkey and Russia assumed a different tactic, even a strategic dimension, following recent developments in Syria. It is critical that the parties have been able to find some common ground despite radically differing expectations and interests when they established the Astana Trio together with Iran. In addition to regional developments, the fact that Turkey did not get the interest and support it expected from its Western allies after the military coup attempt in Turkey resulted in its re-positioning Russia as a partner with whom it could cooperate in terms of regional and global issues including security. The construction of the TurkStream natural gas pipeline, the ongoing cooperation for constructing a nuclear power plant, and, most importantly, Turkey's purchasing of air defense systems from Russia despite objections from its NATO allies are construed as concrete signs that cooperation between the two countries has set sail for new horizons.

References

Anadolu Agency. 2017. "Operation Euphrates Shield: Aims and Gains." January 19. https://www.aa.com.tr/en/analysis-news/operation-euphrates-shield-aims-and-gains/730531. Accessed on 7 April 2021.

Aydıntaşbaş, Aslı. 2016. "With Friends Like These: Turkey, Russia, and the End of an Unlikely Alliance." ECFR Policy Brief, June.

Aydın-Düzgit, Senem, Evren Balta, and Andrew O'Donohue. 2020. *Turkey, Russia, and the West: Reassessing Persistent Volatility, Asymmetric Interdependence, and the Syria Conflict*. Istanbul: IPC.

Balta, Evren, and Mitat Çelikpala. 2020. "Turkey and Russia: Historical Patterns and Contemporary Trends in Bilateral Relations." In *The Oxford Handbook of Turkish Politics*, edited by Güneş Murat Tezcür. https://doi.org/10.1093/oxfordhb/9780190064891.013.12.

Crilly, Rob. 2015. "Russia is Building Military Base in Syria." *Daily Telegraph*, September 5.

Çelikpala, Mitat. 2018. "Russia's Policies in the Middle East and the Pendulum of Turkish-Russian Relations." In *Russia in the Middle East*, edited by Theodore Karasik and Stephen Blank, 105–130. Washington, DC: The Jamestown Foundation.

Çetin, Çetiner. 2016. "Dokuz Adımda Normalleşme." *Yeni Şafak*, June 17. https://www.yenisafak.com/gundem/dokuz-adimda-normallesme-2481662. Accessed on 7 April 2021.

Hughes, Lindsay. 2020. "Russia and Turkey in Syria: The Erosion of the Friendship?" Future Directions International: Strategic Analysis Paper, March 10.

Hürriyet. 2018. "Son Dakika: Tahran'da Tarihi İdlib Zirvesi." September 7. http://www.hurriyet.com.tr/dunya/son-dakika-tahranda-tarihi-idlib-zirvesi-40949318. Accessed on 7 April 2021.

Hürriyet Daily News. 2013. "Turkey Not 'Lonely' but Dares to Do So for Its Values and Principles, Says PM Adviser." August 26. http://www.hurriyetd

ailynews.com/turkey-not-lonely-but-dares-to-do-so-for-its-values-and-princi
ples-says-pm-adviser--53244. Accessed on 7 April 2021.
Karasik, Theodore, and Stephen Blank, eds. 2018. *Russia in the Middle East.*
Washington, DC: The Jamestown Foundation.
Köstem, Seçkin. 2018. "Different Paths to Regional Hegemony: National Iden-
tity Contestation and Foreign Economic Strategy in Russia and Turkey."
Review of International Political Economy 25 (5): 726–752.
Marcou, Jean, Mitat Çelikpala. 2020. "Regard sur les relations turco-russes: De la
rivalité dans un monde bipolaire à la coopération dans un espace eurasiatique?"
La Turquie aujourd'hui. Istanbul: Institut français d'études anatoliennes.
Milliyet. 2016. "Binali Yıldırım'dan Dış Politika Mesajı." *Milliyet*, Haziran
16. http://www.milliyet.com.tr/binali-yildirim-dan-dis-politika-gundem-226
3739/. Accessed on 7 April 2021.
NATO. 2015. "Press Conference by NATO Secretary General Jens Stoltenberg
Following the Meeting of the North Atlantic Council in Defence Ministers
Session." Press Conference, Brussels, Belgium, October 8. https://www.nato.
int/cps/en/natohq/opinions_123522.htm?selectedLocale=en.Accessed on 7
April 2021.
NTV Haber. 2015. "Cumhurbaşkanı Erdoğan'dan Rusya Açıklaması." October
4. https://www.ntv.com.tr/turkiye/erdogandan-rusya-aciklamasi,EehEaasyy
Ei9WiwXpJWurw. Accessed on 7 April 2021.
Özcan, Gencer. 2017. "Rusya'nın Suriye Bunalımına Müdahalesi ve Türkiye." In
Kuşku ile Komşuluk, Türkiye ve Rusya İlişkilerinde Değişen Dinamikler, edited
by Gencer Özcan, Evren Balta, and Burç Beşgül, 269–288. Istanbul: İletişim.
Özdal, Habibe. 2015. "Türk-Rus İlişkilerinin En Zorlu Sınavı." *Analist* 58: 100–
101.
Republic of Turkey, Ministry of Foreign Affairs. 2016. "Joint Statement by the
Foreign Ministers of the Islamic Republic of Iran, the Russian Federation
and the Republic of Turkey on agreed steps to revitalize the political process
to end the Syrian conflict." Joint Declaration, Moscow, Russia, December
20. http://www.mfa.gov.tr/joint-statement-by-the-foreign-ministers-of-the-
islamic-republic-of-iran_-the-russian-federation-and-the-republic-of-turkey-
on-agreed-steps-to-revitalize-the-political-process-to-end-the-syrian-conflict_-
20-december-2016_-moscow.en.mfa. Accessed on 7 April 2021.
The Ministry of Foreign Affairs of the Russian Federation. 2015. "Foreign
Minister Sergey Lavrov's comments and answers to media questions following
talks with Turkish Foreign Minister Feridun Sinirlioğlu, Sochi, September
15, 2015." Press Release, September 15. https://www.mid.ru/en/press_ser
vice/minister_speeches/-/asset_publisher/7OvQR5KJWVmR/content/id/
1756594. Accessed on 7 April 2021.

TRT Haber. 2016. "Cumhurbaşkanı Erdoğan, Putin'e mektup gönderdi." June 27. https://www.trthaber.com/haber/gundem/cumhurbaskani-erdogan-putine-mektup-gonderdi-258503.html. Accessed on 7 April 2021.

CHAPTER 3

The Syrian Crisis and Its Contribution to Authoritarian Transformation of Turkish Domestic and Foreign Policy Identities

Bayram Balci

The humanitarian, political, and geopolitical crisis in Syria is one of the most serious crises, if not the most serious, that the world has known since the end of the Second World War, and its effect on the whole of the Middle East and the international order is not yet over since the new "Cold War" between Vladimir Putin's Russia and a large part of the Western bloc is focused around it. Beyond its borders, it is neighboring Turkey which is the most affected, as much by the diversity as by the intensity of each of its effects.

In fact, Turkey is not a bland neighbor. Under the Ottoman Empire, Turkey and Syria did not exist as such, as nations and independent states, but they formed the binding material of the Empire. When this was dismantled, modern Turkey emerged in 1923. Syria had to wait until 1946 to gain independence. Turkey and Syria then found themselves

B. Balci (✉)
CERI Sciences Po, Paris, France

© The Author(s), under exclusive license to Springer Nature Switzerland AG 2021
B. Balci and N. Monceau (eds.), *Turkey, Russia and Iran in the Middle East*, The Sciences Po Series in International Relations and Political Economy, https://doi.org/10.1007/978-3-030-80291-2_3

33

separated by a new border 900 kilometers long, whereas they shared a rich, common past that was historical, religious, and cultural. Thus, because of their current geopolitical and geo-economic configuration, the Syrian crisis affects Turkey more than any other neighbor. The aim of this chapter is not to list the consequences, which would be exacting and would not help much in understanding the current state of Turkey, but rather to show that the Syrian crisis has had and will continue to have a major effect on what many Turkey observers called the authoritarian drift of the Turkish government, both nationally and internationally. We therefore propose several points of analysis to show how this crisis has triggered an underlying authoritarianism that was thought to be gone. In parallel, and the two are linked, the crisis has revived the Turkish elites' obsession with security to the point that Turkey has moved away from its traditional allies, the democratic and liberal West, and got closer to a new, more authoritarian axis composed of Russia, China, and even Iran.

In order to better understand the way in which the Syrian crisis has had negative effects on Turkish democracy, we propose to examine the impacts of this crisis on the internal and external political life in Turkey. Concerning domestic politics, light will be shown on the weaknesses and gaps in Turkish democracy. At the same time that the first Justice and Development Party (AKP) governments in the years 2002–2010 were trying to shore up the democratization of institutions and when the Alevi and Kurdish questions were the object of a new political openness, the Syrian shambles largely contributed to the failure of these attempts and revealed their weaknesses. Concerning external policies, the Syrian crisis aggravated tensions within Turkish society and also transformed Turkey's foreign policy, and lines of alliance were re-drawn. In order to demonstrate the way in which Syria contributed to the Turkish authoritarian drift, this article is presented in three parts. Firstly, a brief reminder of how Turkey, on the eve of the crisis, was still a model of development for a good number of Muslim countries, in particular those who had just begun their revolutions, known as the Arab Springs. Secondly, we shall see how the religious aspect of the Syrian crisis affected Turkish society, by examining the Alevi and Kurdish questions. Finally, we will demonstrate the manner in which the crisis has accompanied the Turkish political shift regarding the West and its democratic model, leaving Turkey to drift between democracy and autocracy, between East and West, for an indefinite period which will probably be long, and is a reflection of the difficult evolution of the international order.

DEBATES ABOUT DEMOCRACY, TURKEY, AND THE MUSLIM WORLD

More than once in its history, Turkey has been seen as a model for political development by other countries in the Muslim world. The first time was when it was founded in 1923 on the ruins of the Ottoman Empire. In fact, the secular and pro-Western Republic, founded by Mustafa Kemal Atatürk, was the model for a number of Muslim states seeking political modernization, such as Afghanistan, Iran, and other states in Africa and Asia, in the context of decolonization (Mango 1993, 726–757). The second time was at the collapse of the Soviet Union when Turkish-speaking and Muslim countries in the Caucasus and Central Asia gained independence and intended to free themselves from the model imposed by the Russians and the Soviets. Once again, the West promoted the "Turkish model" because of its economic virtues and its open policies which would be able to help these new states to find their place on the international stage and to resist the siren song of political Islam, whose Iranian and Saudi versions worried world governments (Aras and Fidan 2009, 193, 215). Then, the 2000s saw the first Erdoğan government in power in Turkey in a context of openness and an exceptional economic expansion. When, from 2010 onward, Arab peoples attempted to rise up against the autocratic regimes which oppressed them, events remembered in history books as the Arab Springs, Arab countries saw democratic elections vote into power new political groupings arising out of political Islam. Turkey was once again praised by its Western allies as a political, economic, and social model to be copied. Thus, in Tunisia, Egypt, Libya, and, to a lesser extent, Morocco—which was hardly affected by the Arab Spring movements but was obliged to introduce reforms in order not to suffer the same fate—local and international political elites and intellectuals preached the Turkish experience. This was notably because Turkey was seen as being able to help new political groups with Islamist roots reconcile their electoral victory with the principles of secularism already present in the former regimes (Duran and Yılmaz 2011). Of course, the Turkish example was not appreciated unanimously, or rather, not everybody believed in the possible transposition of the Turkish model into the Arab experiences. But the merit of these discussions was that they questioned the model of the compatibility of Islam and democracy, and the recent history of Turkey thus was proof that a government arising from political Islam could be reconciled with a democratic political system, a prosperous economy, an efficient diplomacy, and a vibrant civil society. Just before the Arab Springs and during the first years of this process, unheard of and unprecedented in the Muslim world, including in Syria, Turkey basked in a positive image throughout the Middle East and beyond, reinforced by considerable soft power (Çevik 2019, 50–71). However, at the time of writing, summer 2020, almost nothing remains of this idyllic picture postcard. The Turkish model failed for many Arab countries and Muslims. Today, the authoritarian nature of power in Ankara can be measured by the number of people imprisoned for their opinions, the number of media muzzled, and the strict control over the legal system.

Today, there are still 160 journalists in prison, deprived of all rights and freedoms, as well as Kurdish militants, those from the Gülen movement and also intellectuals and journalists defending various causes that irk those in power. Among the most well-known figures held prisoner is Osman Kavala, a famous businessman and philanthropist who supports civil society in Turkey and a number of initiatives in favor of peace and democracy. The case of the liberty of the press is not glorious either. Turkey ranks 157th out of 180 in the press freedom classification drawn up by *Reporters Sans Frontières*. About 150 media outlets, television channels, newspapers, and associations have been banned and subsequently shut down after the failed coup d'état of July 15, 2016 (Human Rights Watch 2016). Opposition media are rare these days and most of the authorized media are careful not to criticize the government's policies. Previously known for its liberal character, the Turkish political system is now among the most authoritarian in the world, at least in wider Europe. Since the move to a presidential system through the constitutional reform approved by referendum in April 2017 and the victory in the June 2018 presidential elections, parliament carries virtually no weight and the political regime is becoming a "Turkish Bonapartism," to use Hamit Bozarslan's expression (2021). On the international stage, Turkey has fallen from its pedestal and no longer enjoys the prestige of the past, finding itself, euphemistically, out of step with the liberal Western bloc to such an extent that it is clearly growing closer to more authoritarian countries such as Russia, or even China and Iran.

It is plain, the AKP and its president, Recep Tayyip Erdoğan, are clearly responsible for this authoritarian drift by Turkey and the starting point might be placed before the Syrian crisis. But at the same time, because of its multiple effects, the war in Syria has acted as an accelerator and a factor seriously aggravating the authoritarian Turkish reaction, as much inside the country as on the international scene.

THE SYRIAN CRISIS AS A SOURCE OF AGGRAVATION OF INTERNAL TENSIONS IN TURKISH SOCIETY

The Syrian crisis is entering its tenth year. A decade of crimes and horrors, of power games and vested interests with contradictory objectives, which has led to us forgetting what happened before the crisis. Up until 2011, Turkish diplomacy, in the hands of the AKP for nearly ten years, boasted of having established a bilateral agreement with Damascus which was mutually beneficial and friendly. This success was all the more significant because until then the two states had maintained extremely complicated and tense relations since their very foundation, the motives being old territorial disputes, ideological antagonism, and Syrian support for separatist movements in Turkey. Ankara had managed to make Syria its best neighbor and relations were excellent at every level, to such a point that the two countries' parliaments had even had joint cabinet meetings for bold projects such as the creation of a common economic area, called *Shamgen*, which would also include Jordan and Lebanon (Aras and Polat 2008, 495–515; Çakmak 2016, 695–717). Two vital questions might have contented Ankara in this good relationship with Damascus: the Kurdish question and the Alevi issue. In fact, while Damascus had long supported the separatist Partiya Karkerên Kurdistan in Kurdish, Workers Party of Kurdistan (PKK), this support had ceased in 1989 and the Kurdish separatist organization had become seriously weakened. And though the Muslim world had long been divided by the Shi'ite/Sunni split, Turkey and Syria seemed to have got over this issue. Turkey, mostly Sunni and led by a government arising from Sunni political Islam, had been able to build up a good relationship with the powers in Syria which, although not admitting it openly, had sprung from the Alawite branch of Shi'ism, considered as a deviant branch by the Sunnites. However, the bilateral political and economic issues went well beyond the cultural and religious differences. This good relationship was too precious to be disturbed and Turkish power acted cautiously during the first months of the Syrian crisis for there was a lot to lose if this relationship deteriorated. Thus, the first popular protests in Damascus, encouraged by the examples in Tunisia, Libya, and Egypt, were based on demands for social and democratic reforms and they took place peacefully. The Turkish government in Ankara, bolstered by the personal friendship between Tayyip Erdoğan and Bashar al-Assad, acted as mediator to persuade Damascus to undertake some reforms in order to calm the demonstrators in the streets (Bishku 2012, 36–53). Thus, it was that between March and October 2011 the Turkish Foreign Minister Ahmet Davutoglu made no fewer than 19 trips to Damascus to try to reason with the Syrian authorities (interview with Lakhdaar Brahimi[1]). But his efforts were useless and in vain, and when the revolt stepped up and the dynamics of the Arab Springs toppled numerous Arab dictators in 2010–2011, many members of the Arab League as well as Turkey's traditional partners, like the United States, hardened their tone and demanded regime change in Syria. Ankara was reluctant but, in the light of the excessive violence of state repression against peaceful Syrian demonstrators, ended up siding with international opinion and in October 2011 broke off relations with Syria. However, it is very important to note here that unlike its Western allies, who were also members of the "Friends of Syria Group,"[2] Turkey severed ties in a more radical manner and, above all, it then provided open support for the opposition who had already taken refuge in Turkey in order to get organized. Thereafter, the Turkey-Syria border, desert land for over 900 kilometers, was very quickly breached by the massive flow of refugees and dissident groups from the Free Syrian Army who established their rear bases in Turkish provinces along the border from where they could lead the combat to liberate Syria (Daoudy 2016, 1074–1096).

The next events in the Turkish implication in the Syrian conflict are well known. Up until 2013, Turkey adopted the same lines as its Western allies and called out, loud and strong, for the fall of the Bashar regime as

---

[1] Interview with Lakhdhar Brahimi, in Paris, July 2014.

[2] The Friends of Syria Group is an international diplomatic collective of countries and bodies meeting periodically outside the UN Security Council to discuss the Syrian question. The collective was set up in response to the vetoes and blockages made by Russia and China who refused to condemn Syria. At the instigation of President Nicolas Sarkozy, the group tried to find a solution to the Syrian crisis after the Russian and Chinese vote on February 4, 2012. The group met at least four times in different capitals and then broke up following the worsening situation and the diverging opinions which appeared among members from 2013 onwards. See Lund, Aron. "Riyadh, Rumeilan, and Damascus: All You Need to Know About Syria's Opposition Conferences." *Carnegie*, December 9, 2015. https://carnegie-mec.org/diwan/62239?lang=en.

events unfolded, with the extreme violence and crimes committed by the state on its own unarmed and peaceful people. However, from 2013, the international alliance against the Syrian regime fell apart because of two fundamental disagreements.

Barack Obama had promised sanctions against Damascus the day when the "red line" of the use of chemical weapons was crossed. In August 2013, the Syrian regime gassed civilians, men, women, and children, in the Ghouta neighborhood near Damascus. The red line had been crossed but neither the United States nor their Western allies kept their promises and abandoned an entire population to civil war with a state where there were no limits and no scruples (Barkey 2016). Although Turkey was a member of the international alliance, it was bewildered by this attitude of the Western partners and was already deeply involved regarding both the millions of refugees to whom it had granted asylum and humanitarian aid and Syrian dissidents trying as far as possible to get structured and organized. As a neighbor, it could not, in all decency, close its eyes to the human catastrophe and thus found itself obliged to maintain a harsh position against the Syrian regime.

The second major split in the Turkey-Western alliance came with the rise of the jihadist threat in Syria which shaped the Western powers' strategy. In fact, from 2013 or 2014, Islamic State (IS) was growing stronger in the Syrian quagmire, already controlling a vast area it called the Caliphate and whose terrorists were striking in Europe, sowing death, fear, and terror, and the United States and Europe revised their main priority. From now on, the aim was transformed to eliminate the jihadist threat and not to topple Bashar al-Assad, who was nevertheless behind this barbarity and whose remaining in power reinforced jihadism. For Turkey, this shift was difficult to consider because it had adopted a hard-line view that the source of the jihadist problem was and remained the very violence of the Syrian regime. The problem was Bashar; the solution was the departure of Bashar. For the Turks, focusing on the elimination of the consequence, IS, did not remove the origin of this violence, Bashar.

In autumn 2015, this deep split between NATO founder members over the Middle Eastern theater began to interest Russia and Vladimir Putin, lacking in stature on the international scene. Men and weapons from Moscow arrived to give assistance to Bashar al-Assad's regime (Charap et al. 2019). The Syrian crisis had failed to follow the Arab Springs, which themselves had not succeeded. And the crisis was no longer a crisis; it had moved from its original dimension of popular, peaceful revolt against a despotic power and had degenerated into an appalling, lopsided civil war with state forces pitted against their own people. The democratic and social demands had been followed by dissent along religious, ethnic, and community lines to which were added the contradictory and opposing interferences of outside forces which have made the outcome of this conflict even more uncertain and distant. Not only is Turkey completely bogged down in the Syrian mire but its involvement in this war has become an issue in Turkish domestic politics in the sense that it is affecting the economy but also and above all the two major issues of the Alevi and Kurdish questions.

AGGRAVATION OF THE RELIGIOUS DIVIDE

Unlike the other countries affected by the Arab Springs, the population of Syria has a more diverse ethnic and religious composition, shot through with ancient divisions. In religious terms, most of the population is Sunni but power is in the hands of an Arab minority of Alawites, a kind of branch of Shia Islam. At the same time, Syria is also split between different ethnic groups. In effect, although most of the people are Sunni Arabs, almost 10% are Kurds, not forgetting the Christian and Druse minorities among other ethno-religious groups (Courbage 2012). In 2011, the driving force behind the Syrian protests was not ethnicity or religion but democracy. Like their Arab neighbors, the Syrian people rose up to demand political reforms and freedoms (Hinnebusch and Imady 2018). However, in Syria as well as in Turkey, the conflict took a religious turn or at least it was instrumentalized and interpreted as such. In order to better understand the "religious interactions" between Syria and Turkey during the war, the specific Turkish-Syrian case must be expanded by referring to the concept of "solidarity theology" employed by Nükhet Sandal (2019) who has based her research on studies by Christopher Browning and Pertti Joenniemi (Browning and Joenniemi, 2017, 31–47). What these three authors call "theological solidarity" describes how, when there is a threat to identity, real or fictional, a religious group can make defensive modifications to its own identity by incorporating or getting closer to another group where there are affinities, in order to better ensure its defense. This idea of "religious solidarity" is in fact a way of obtaining ontological security by adapting or mutating one's identity. Thus, as can be seen in the case between Turkey and Syria, the Syrian conflict, although it was not religious at the outset, crystallized around the antagonism between the Alevi minority in power and the vast Sunni majority in the Syrian national community. So, under the influence of the war, this antagonism has contaminated diverse Alevi groups which, divided in Turkey, have drawn together in the face of "danger" in order to better tackle the "Sunni" threat.

In fact, President Bashar al-Assad found himself in difficulties with this spontaneous popular movement which he systematically depicted as an insurrection by Sunni Islamist terrorists against the Alevi minority (Diehl 2012, 7–15). Although they are in power, the Alevi have historically been marginalized in Syria like the Alevis in Turkey with whom they share a similar conception of the worship of Ali, the central figure in Twelver Shi'ism and other branches of Shia Islam and to whom Bashar addresses his propaganda in order to gain their support. While the Alawites have been in power in Syria since 1970 because of the coup d'état headed by Hafez al-Assad, in Turkey, the Alevis might be Turkish-speaking or be ethnically Turkish, Kurdish, or Arab, but they are distinct from the Sunni majority and they feel the pressure (Jenkins et al. 2020; White and Jongerden 2003). They have not always had the same view of their Alevi identity and have little closeness to power (Zarcone 2018, 47–63; Massicard 2005, 361). Already, during the Ottoman Empire, they were often seen as the fifth column of the neighboring, rival Shi'ite Empire of the Safawids of Iran even though they were nevertheless quite different from Iranians. The Turkish republic, in principle secular and lay, but in reality in the hands of the Sunni, has made few efforts to integrate other religious groups, in the opinion of these groups who nevertheless represent between 10 and 20% of the population (Koçan and Öncü 2004, 464–489). Therefore, unlike the Sunni, they receive no state aid for the organization and financing of their religion for it is not officially recognized by the Turkish state. In fact, when Turkey was founded, the Christian and Jewish minorities were recognized but not the different religious groups in Islam, like the Alevi who say that they have a poor image in the eyes of the Sunni majority and are not properly respected in law regarding their basic rights.

However, and this crucial point must be stressed, as soon as it came to power, Erdoğan's AKP government started two "openings" or "processes" aimed at the Alevis and the Kurds, with a view to its project to join the European Union. For the Alevi question, this opening consisted in organizing, throughout the country, several meetings, round tables, and colloquiums to listen to and to gather the grievances and the propositions for reforms of their status and their community within the Turkish nation in order to pass legislation to satisfy them and improve their lot (Köse 2010, 143–164; Yılmaz 2020, 231–253; Lord 2017, 278–296). Erdoğan then sent several messages of sympathy and opening-up to the Alevis. One important initiative in particular deserves to be mentioned here.[3] In November 2011, President Erdoğan acknowledged the responsibility of the Turkish state in the massacre of Alevis at Dersim in 1937, something long demanded by the descendants of the victims. Of course, the move was symbolic and did not solve everything especially when it was received with circumspection and distrust, seen as a political and electoral calculation but it did at least have the merit of calming relations between the Sunni majority and the Alevi minority and reopening a dialogue that no one expected to be open or constructive. However, in 2011, the Syrian conflict degraded this trust and in the Alevi community most were skeptical and doubted the sincerity of the government to the point that, in the end, despite all Erdoğan's efforts (Phillips 2009), the Syrian crisis brought tension and solidarity to the different Alevi groups in Turkey (Mkrtich 2018, 24–40; Can 2017, 174–189). For them, whether they were Turkish-speaking or Kurdish-speaking, Erdoğan's fight with Bashar was aimed at all the Alawite community with whom the Alevis empathized. What is more, the rise to power of the jihadist elements, who had kidnapped the Syrian revolution, had a dramatic effect on the cohabitation in Turkey between the Sunni majority and the Alevi minority. Often in the vanguard of fights for freedom and democracy in Turkey, the different Alevi strands were worried by the rising Sunni jihadist threat in Syria and this time largely took the side of Bashar's regime, by organizing demonstrations in his support in the region of Hatay but also on social media (Mkrtich 2018, 24–40). Under the influence of religious solidarity, as presented above, the Alevi groups in Turkey drew more closely knitted together (Parlar Dal 2016, 1396–1420). It must be noted that in its turn, political power in Turkey had somewhat given in to the religious interpretation of the conflict. Thus, we note, in May 2013, for example, when a terrorist attack on the border town of Reyhanli cost the

---

[3] This initiative was not totally free from underlying political thoughts for Erdoğan's aim was also, if not above all, to discredit the main opposition party, the Republican Peoples' Party (CHP), heir to the party founded by Atatürk which had been in power at the time of the Alevi massacres.

lives of 53 Turks, President Erdoğan spoke of them as martyred "Sunni" brethren whereas he should have refrained from mentioning the Sunni identity of the victims. So, whereas before the Syrian crisis efforts had been made to satisfy the demands and democratic rights of Turkish citizens who were Alevi, Turkey's entanglement in Syria had not played out in favor of this democratic thrust which had difficulty in progressing. For example, the official recognition of *cemevi* as places of worship was no longer discussed, even though in daily life the *cemevi* functioned and were frequented as normal. Similarly, the struggle against discriminations, which Alevis say they suffer, is no longer a current topic. Thus, power in Turkey is refocused on the mainly Sunni identity and the demands for democratic equality by the Alevis are ignored. However, the devastating effect of the war in Syria on Turkish democracy has affected more deeply and more seriously the burning Kurdish question.

Aggravation of the Ethnic Division and the Breakdown of the Process to Resolve the Kurdish Question

The war in Syria has aggravated not just the religious question in Turkey between Sunnis and diverse Alevi groups. It has had an even more devastating effect on ethnic issues insofar as it has revived the war between the Turkish state and the Kurdish national movement and therefore added to the tension between Kurds and Turks in Turkey. To understand the aggravation of the Kurdish question in Turkey and the link to the war in Syria, there is no shortage of theoretical references and they are all linked to the concept of *spillover*. At this point, we can remind ourselves of the research carried out by Nicolas Sambanis (2002, 215–243), Kirstian Skrede Gleditsch and Idean Salehyan (2008, 58–76). These authors explain that, although bound by national frontiers, a civil war rarely has no consequences for neighboring countries since borders are permeable and activities and communities are interconnected. Extending this topic, works by Maarten Bosker and Joppe de Ree (2014, 206–221) highlight the near certain contagion of ethnic conflict from the moment when an ethnic group finds itself on either side of the demarcation line. In the same way, David Davis and Will H. Morre (1997, 171–184) state that a sectarian or religious conflict will spread in a neighboring country by a "demonstrative effect." And Erika Forsberg (2016, 75–90) details this idea when she considers that an ethno-religious conflict in a country acts as a catalyzer on the co-ethnics and co-religious in neighboring countries. The leaders of these minority groups, committed to the defense strategies of their community, take note and are inspired by the tactics used in order to mobilize their own troops and direct a more efficient combat. Finally, Kristian Skrede Gleditsch (2007, 293–309) states that when an insurrection raises a whole group in one country, the members of the same group in neighboring countries can imitate and/or join the movement but in an even more confrontational manner and less keen on compromise. This last element of analysis, as we shall see in the case that interests us, proved to be wrong on Turkish soil as the Kurds in Turkey did not raise the game relative to the positions and actions of the Syrian Kurds.

The Kurds account for about 15–20% of the population of Turkey and most of them reckon that their cultural and political rights are not recognized by the Turkish republic, despite a long struggle both peaceful and armed which has marked the history of the country. From 1984, when the PKK found refuge in neighboring countries and in Syria in particular, they began an armed guerrilla struggle and Turkey got caught up in a grisly routine of Kurdish terrorist attacks and reprisal punishments, which led to further attacks, and the country mourned the numerous victims on a regular basis. Since the beginning of the armed combat, the total number of casualties on both sides is around 40,000 dead.

From 1998, after a long period of tension between the two countries, when Turkey had even threatened military intervention in Syria, a new phase in Turkish-Syrian relations began, concerning the Kurdish question and support for the PKK. In 1998, the two countries signed an agreement in Adana about the fight against terrorism, and when the AKP came to power, its policy of "zero problems with neighbors" was aimed primarily at Syria who became an excellent Middle Eastern partner economically and even politically. As peaceful relations were established with Syria, which no longer supported the PKK, it was then easier for the AKP government to broach the Kurdish issue in Turkey. Unlike all preceding governments, the AKP showed political pragmatism and started a dialogue moving toward recognition of the Kurdish situation in Turkey (Gunter 2013, 101–111). There was an economic interest at stake but also a political issue because the Kurdish question was a blot on Turkey's bid to join the European Union and was slowing reforms which had become indispensable. In this field, Erdoğan's government took concrete initiatives to satisfy the cultural and political demands of the Kurds in Turkey particularly by opening fresh talks with the PKK, the central organization of the Kurdish nationalist movement but which had been classified as a terrorist movement by Turkey and also by its Western partners. Secret talks were held, first in Oslo in 2009, before being held openly. At the outset of the Syrian crisis, clashes still occurred between the Turkish army and the guerrillas in rural areas to the east, but violence eventually gave way to dialogue. The AKP party had the electoral support of the Kurds who appreciated the personality of its leader, Erdoğan. However, the aggravation of the situation in Syria, the militarization of the Syrian revolution, and the revival of the Kurdish question in Syria shattered the fragile foundations of this rapprochement and struck a fatal blow to the democratization that was unrolling in Turkey (Dag 2018, 1251–1270; Parlar Dal 2016, 1396–1420). How was it that the Syrian crisis damaged the Turkish-Kurdish dialogue in Turkey?

With war raging on the other side of its border, Turkey resumed the obsession with security, fearing a "spillover" effect or contagion. This tension and the return to security priorities above all, with the Syrian war in the background, would have a negative effect on the movement toward dialogue and agreement that had been set up between the Turkish state and the Kurdish national movement (Lawson 2016, 478–496; Zahra 2017, 27–39). While the Turkish authorities had succeeded in separating the Kurdish question in Turkey from the Kurdish question in Syria, the war had made demarcation lines hazy, it had brought mistrust and had again made it difficult for discussion between the Turkish government and the Kurdish nationalist movement. In Syria, about 10% of the population are Kurds and they belong to different political and social currents and groups, the most influential of which were already somewhat connected to other Kurdish movements outside Syria. Among them, the Kurdish Democratic Party of Syria (Partiya Demokrat a Kurdistanê, PDK) is an offshoot of the great Kurdish party in Iraq which has the same name and is headed by the Barzani family. Similarly, the other major Kurdish party in Syria is the PYD (Partiya Yekîtiya Demokrat, Democratic Union Party), which is an offshoot of the Turkish PKK, set up in 2003 (Tejel 2009, 108–133). Of all the Kurdish parties in Syria, it is this last one which has so far managed to limit the damage and take advantage of the war to build itself up. In fact, the PYD is the only armed and militarized group, thanks to its special links with the PKK on which it depends in fact, and it would quickly outstrip the other Kurdish movements which had been marginalized including by intimidation and violent means. In the war, the

PYD had bet that non-confrontation with Bashar's regime was the best option for the Kurds and chose alliance with Damascus (ICG, Middle East Report N°151 2014), whereas Turkey had fairly quickly opted to support the free Syrian army in the Syrian conflict, with a view to toppling Bashar. He found himself in difficulties with the rebellion and had undertaken reprisals against Turkey by playing the Kurdish card. So, from July 2012, the regime withdrew from some Kurdish zones on the border with Turkey and thereby granted autonomy to the Kurdish regions dominated by the PYD (Jongerden 2019, 61–75), knowing full well that this would antagonize Ankara. For the PYD, with the sustained support of the PKK, it was a historic chance to build a truly autonomous region for the Kurds in this territory with US support. And nothing threatened Ankara more than the idea of contagion and the potential implosion of present-day Turkey. In fact, the development of the situation in Syria has completely halted if not obliterated the efforts toward normalization of the Kurdish question in Turkey.

While in Syria the war continued, in Turkey, the government and the PKK, to which must be added the HDP party which served as a kind of legal front, found themselves in a dead-end situation, unable to build an acceptable compromise that suited their opposing positions. What the guerrilla struggle ceasefire and a more peaceful context had managed to obtain was henceforth impossible in the context of the Syrian war, where the Turkish government and the PKK found themselves allied against the two opposing camps and were vicarious rivals in an external conflict in order to shore up their own opposition position. This standoff, in which the Kurdish nationalist movement had the wind in its sails while the Ankara government was struggling, ended up crushing the fragile dialogue begun after difficult negotiations.

This break-up has first resulted from Kurdish electoral behavior which up until then had been mostly favorable to the AKP and which had had to switch its loyalty to provide more support for the pro-Kurdish HDP party, because of the political choices made by the AKP government in the war in Syria. Onetime allies in the negotiations to settle the Kurdish question, the diverging positions of the two parties, the AKP, and the HDP, in the Syrian conflict, sowed discord and worsened their relations on Turkish domestic policy issues. In electoral terms, the result was the Kurdish AKP vote slid toward the new HDP party, led by the young and charismatic Selahattin Demirtas. But the crumbling of the AKP vote was not just down to the Kurds. As the AKP party and its leader became more and more authoritarian, in particular since the Gezi protests were put down in 2013 and the war in Syria had reduced their popularity, not only the Kurds but a good number of liberal Turks, pro-democracy, pro-Western, and all those who had never accepted that an Islamist party was in power, expressed their discontent by voting massively for the HDP which had in fact become the party of all those who were anti-Erdoğan. Boosted by this popularity, the HDP party increased its criticism of the AKP's political management particularly of the Syrian crisis where Turkey and the Kurdish nationalist movement in Syria were on opposite sides. This might be viewed as a cynical electoral calculation but the fact is that during the Syrian crisis the HDP had become the hope of voters who wished to halt the rise of Erdoğan's authoritarianism, and from being an ally, the HDP became the AKP's main rival over the Kurdish question. This popular rush of support, motivated by its policy line and/or by the negative mistrust of the AKP allowed the HDP to achieve the unprecedented feat in modern Turkish history of entering parliament in 2015. Here, access was reserved to parties which obtained over 10% of the votes cast in the nationwide general election. To everyone's great surprise, the party, with a historic score of 13.2%, inflicted a serious blow on Erdoğan's overbearing party, which had to be content, for the first time in a while, with a "low" 41% of the votes, which meant it could not govern alone and was obliged to seek a coalition government. Erdoğan refused this, probably not wishing to share power, preferring to organize another election in November 2015. This second vote, five months after the first, handed him back the reins of power but in between times he had made the country pay a heavy price (ICG, Crisis Groupe Europe Briefing N°77 2015) over the end of the ceasefire and the renewal of guerrilla warfare by the PKK in Turkey (Yeğen 2015).

However, the HDP was not the only actor responsible for the electoral instrumentalization of the Kurdish question. First of all, the AKP had developed an electoral strategy specific to the Kurdish question. Its participation in talks about reforms in favor of the Kurds counted on a massive rallying of the Kurdish community whose votes it could rely on. And the AKP had in fact moved forward a little with each election as the peace process advanced. But with the Syrian crisis this tacit concordance failed and the Kurdish vote moved toward the HDP, meaning the AKP significantly lost the absolute majority in the general election of June 2015. But over and above the instrumentalization of the Kurdish electorate by the AKP or the HDP, it was the war in Syria and the attitude of the PKK, the real master of the Kurdish nationalist movement, which smashed up the peace process in Turkey and fostered Erdoğan's authoritarian rigidity.

In fact, the war in Syria changed the game for the protagonists engaged in the process of resolving the Kurdish question in Turkey. The Turkish state had changed, the Kurdish actors too, as well as the HDP but also and above all the PKK. This was nonetheless a terrorist organization but which because of the war in Syria had become a political discussion partner, a regional force, and even an international actor thanks to Western support in the war against IS. The PYD was strong because of the military power acquired in Syria thanks to its control over the YPG militia (Yekîneyên Parastina Gel, People's Protection Units) but was subject to the PKK, and this allowed this latter group to become more assertive in Turkey where it had opted in its long-term vision for a fresh direct confrontation with the Turkish state (Lawson 2016, 478–496). Although the PKK had agreed to peaceful negotiation and signed a ceasefire in March 2013 which obliged it to withdraw its forces from Turkish territory and, ultimately, to disarm and choose political action instead, the war in Syria halted this pacification movement. Its military prowess in Syria, encouraged by the international community and its control over the Kurdish region of Rojava, encouraged a 180° turn. Thus, disregarding the conditions imposed by the truce, the PKK did not withdraw its forces from Turkey. On the contrary, taking advantage of the slackening attitude and voluntary laxism of the Turkish security forces, it in fact set up its own rules in Kurdish space, sometimes with parallel tribunals and identity checks, flouting the law in force. But above all, taking advantage of the ceasefire, it concentrated new forces at certain strategic points in Kurdish towns in Turkey with the aim of shifting into a new phase of pressure and fighting, never before seen in guerrilla warfare against the Turkish state.

So, immediately after the elections held on June 7, 2015, which marked the end of the truce, the PKK took up arms again but changed its objective. Taking as its model the Kurdish towns in Syria which had become autonomous cantons run by PKK ideology and acting as a starting point for the constitution of an autonomous Kurdistan, the PKK restarted the armed struggle but this time not in the form of rural classic guerrilla warfare but with a new strategy of urban guerrilla in Kurdish towns in Turkey, like in Cizre or Nusaybin or Sur. The aim was to create mini autonomous zones like in Syria (Onat and Çubukçu 2019, 164–182). For weeks or even months, pockets of territory in Kurdish towns in Turkey were the theater of harsh fighting between the Turkish security forces and hundreds of young Kurds recruited there and led by experienced PKK guerrilleros, trained in Iraq or Syria. In line with the "spillover" theories, the aim was to extend into Turkey the experience of war and the political and territorial gains made in Syria, in order to earn a similar autonomy in Turkey. However, the limits of the "spillover" theory were shown when the PKK's strategy turned out to be very poor, both militarily and politically. Contrary to the PKK's calculations, the Kurdish towns did not rise up en masse to support the PKK's project for autonomy. The Turkish army is not the Syrian army, in difficulty because of a general, popular uprising, and the plan did not take into account the Turkish means deployed to this national security issue prioritized above all else. In the end, the PKK strategy was a disaster for the Kurdish question in Turkey and for Turkish democracy. It finished with crimes committed on both sides, by the PKK as much as by the Turkish army. And, on the rebound, it weakened the legal HDP pro-Kurd party which managed to remain above 10% of support but it nevertheless found itself marginalized after having lost some of its credibility with the electorate, both Kurds and Turks. At the same time, this PKK strategy had indirectly bolstered Erdoğan and, in the subsequent elections, he led his party to regain a majority in parliament with a score of 49.5% of the votes cast, which was clearly more than the 41% of the previous June. This electoral score was also due to his moving closer to the nationalist discourse of the Milliyetçi Hareket Partisi, MHP (Party of Nationalist Movement), which became his ally in parliament and on which he would also depend for all his domestic and foreign policies. This electoral victory concealed a whole series of fresh defeats for Turkish democracy. The Turkish government now in power had previously the support of pro-democracy groups like the HDP and also other liberal groups, but now is backed and dependent from the nationalist far-right in his combat against the Bashar regime, the PKK, and the so-called Islamic State. This armed trial of strength with the PKK was also and above all the starting point for the widespread repression of different Kurdish parties, organizations, and newspapers out of all proportion and which looked like revenge reprisals rather than the maintenance of law and order.

The Syrian crisis thus helped to break the pacification movement with the Kurds and set fire to the powder keg in the Kurdish regions and pushed Turkey into authoritarianism. Of course, the return to a more authoritarian political style was not just because of the Kurdish issue. Internal opposition forces also provoked it, especially by taking advantage of the failed coup on July 15, 2016. But here, once again, the influence of the war in Syria weighed on the factors aggravating the authoritarian reaction of the state.

We do not know all the details of the failed putsch and many shadowy areas still exist. But it seemed to have been the high point of a fratricidal duel between two men, Fethullah Gülen and Recep Tayyip Erdoğan, who had been allies in the past and had become implacable enemies (Azeri 2016, 465–478). But the reasons for the coup are not limited to this rivalry between the country's two strong men. The Syrian crisis and Turkey's delicate implication in the conflict had divided high-ranking officers in the Turkish army and some felt that Erdoğan's overthrow would be a good thing in order to put an end to what they called "the adventurism" of his policy in Syria (Barkey 2014, 113–134). For even today, Turkey's three military operations in Syria are not unanimously supported in Turkey including among the army. In fact, the Turkish army, at least during the early part of the conflict in Syria and before being taken in hand by Erdoğan, was still very much attached to the Kemalist principle of precautionary distancing regarding affairs in the Arab world and one of non-intervention abroad, with the sole exception of contexts that threatened Turkish minorities. Now, Erdoğan had not followed this principle of precaution and had dragged Turkey into the Syrian struggle which probably displeased certain generals who resorted to the putsch.

So, not only did the Syrian crisis act to both reveal and accelerate the weaknesses and shortcomings of Turkish democracy, but the conflict influenced different regional and international powers, obliging Turkey to make strategic choices which it would not have made outside the Syrian war. In fact, Ankara was obliged to review the links with traditional partners in the West but also with Russia, China, and others. This reconfiguring of Turkey's foreign policy would distance it from its democratic partners' favor of new, more authoritarian "allies."

THE SLIDE TOWARD A MORE AUTHORITARIAN LINE, THE RAPPROCHEMENT WITH RUSSIA

It must be remembered that before the Syrian crisis Turkey had been on excellent terms with the Syrian regime essentially for economic, security, and geopolitical reasons with a regional scope. In this view, it was vital for Ankara to maintain good relations with Damascus. After initial hesitations, when Ankara thought it might sway Bashar al-Assad and when the atrocities committed by the regime against unarmed, peaceful demonstrators became known, Ankara was influenced by its traditional Western alliances and was forced to break off relations with Syria, its neighbor, and friend.

Afterward, the complexification and the internationalization of the conflict in Syria made the country a handy new geopolitical chessboard for the regional powers, with Iran, Turkey, and the Gulf states in the lead, but also by proxy for the Western powers and Russia. This game put an end to the understandings between Turkey and its Western partners as Turkey's stance was for the fall of Bashar al-Assad, seen as conditional for the pacification of the region, while the Western powers changed strategy en route, abandoning the elimination of the root of the problem—Bashar—to focus instead on the elimination of the consequences—so-called Islamic State. It was this brutal shift and the way in which it was effected which shattered the agreement in Turkish-Western relations. The West's change of strategy in Syria, preferring their national security interests to eliminate terrorism there, did not take into account the same security interests in Turkey (who was nonetheless a member of NATO) under threat from another form of terrorism, the PKK, and from the policies of neighboring Syria with a common border 900 kilometers long. The first point of divergence or even of the breakdown between Turkey and the West was obviously the Kurdish element. The Kurds in Syria were ambiguous over the revolution and the Syrian regime, and this was reinforced by Bashar's strategic retreat from the Kurdish areas to concentrate his troops at the flash points where the regime was in difficulty, and they acquired a motivated military force encouraged by the PKK and structured under their guidance, along with the PYD and the YPG militias. These three formations which in reality were just one had undeniably been a determining force in the fight against IS. However, the YPG were keen to establish their own identity and to break free from the influence of the PKK and were incorporated into a large military force, the Syrian Democratic Forces (SDF). Except that the commanders remained Kurds, and behind it the PKK operated. Things got to the point where the West, caught in a dilemma, had to choose between Turkey and the SDF, dominated by the PKK, or to put it in other words, between an ally and member of NATO and a terrorist group on the blacklist in many states. Refusing to intervene directly and send in their troops, and betting on their proximity on the ground, they finally made their proxy fight against Islamic State (IS) with the Kurdish forces rather than with their Turkish ally. In fact, the military calculation proved to be right. By arming the Kurdish militias and turning a blind eye to the PKK's influence over them, the West certainly won the war over IS but imperiled the good political and geostrategic relations it had with Turkey. So, as the Turks never tire of repeating, the victory over IS, which in reality is incomplete, was won to the detriment of Turkey and in the assumption that this regional power would stay in the Western camp.

For the PKK and its Syrian structures, taking unexpected advantage of the sudden good relations with the West had effectively and efficiently fought the jihadists including beyond the zones of Kurdish settlements such as Raqqa and other regions, and this gave the PKK a strategic depth. However, at the same time, taking advantage of the arms supplied in particular by the United States, the PKK ramped up its guerrilla war against Turkey. And thus it was that, in the name of higher national interests, the West endorsed the weakening—and that is a euphemism, of a NATO member by NATO, thereby undermining the principle of equality in the alliance by establishing a hierarchy of importance among the members. For the Turks, the moral alliance was broken and this justified a self-defense distancing from the West which in fact would result in a closer relationship with Russia (Köstem 2020).

And this reversal was not obvious for, until November 2015, Turkey and Russia had supported completely opposite camps in the Syrian story, as Turkey backed the Syrian revolution while the Kremlin was for Bashar's regime. Turkish opposition to Russia was such that in November 2015 the Turks shot down a Russian plane which was bombing the anti-Bashar troops along the Turkish border and which had violated Turkish airspace. Despite this incident, Turkish foreign policy, pressed by the West's defection, had no other choice but to enter into a new phase by opting for a rapprochement as unannounced as it was spectacular with what the Turkish national subconscious perceived as the "hereditary Russian enemy."

In their tortuous shared history, each Turkish-Russian rapprochement has often been conditioned by their respective difficult relations with the West (Reynolds 2019). In the 1920s, the two young and vulnerable states, the Soviet Union and Kemalist Turkey, found common ground in their joint fight against Western imperialism (Tsvetkova 2018, 77–114; Gökay 1994, 41–57). The Cold War put a stop to this rapprochement but from the 2000s a Eurasianism current developed in both countries and voices were raised to demand that Turkey and Russia act together against the clearly Atlanticist West (Erşen 2011, 263–285; Svarin 2015). Though persistent, this current remained on the fringes and had little influence on the party and on Erdoğan's choices, but it should be noted that from a certain point on in the Syrian crisis, this opinion was echoed again in Ankara's halls of power. Therefore, if only to take one example, which is the highly prioritized security question of Kurdish irredentism and its regionalization thanks to the war in Syria, the Kurds had never received military support from Russia, as they had done from the West. Russia's support for the Kurdish cause in Syria was only ever political and never military, for apart from opening a PYD representation bureau in Moscow and the continued dialogue with the party, Russia had not cooperated militarily with the Kurds in Syria and had supplied no arms. On the contrary, the Western powers had armed the "offshoots" of the PKK in their own security interests. And, at the very time that Turkey was suffering the most negative effects of the Syrian crisis, the influx of refugees, economic losses, and the reinforcement of the Kurdish factor in Syria, it was Russia and not the West which opened a window of opportunity for Turkey's military intervention in Syria to reduce the military threat from the PKK. And despite their contrary objectives of the perpetuation or the fall of the Bashar regime, the security interest was paramount, in favor of a Turkey-Russia rapprochement.

Thus, it was that the Turkish army's purchase of S400 missiles in a Russian anti-aircraft defense system sealed the break with the Western alliance. The purchase of this equipment was incompatible with NATO's defense system, and Turkey as a member was severely condemned by its Western allies who saw this as an act of disloyalty. However, the Turks reversed this argument and accused the West of disloyalty for their reluctance to sell Turkey the Patriot system, which in any case was more expensive, and reluctance to aid a NATO member weakened by the Syrian war (Özel 2019).

Alongside this rapprochement with Russia, the human rights situation in Turkey has steadily deteriorated since 2013. Since the Gezi movement, which had drawn the West's condemnation, Turkey had grown ostensibly close to Russia who was totally uninterested in the human rights situation in Turkey. The vicious circle of all these factors caught Turkey in a trap where its security problems forced the insidious strengthening of an ever more authoritarian regime, this attitude pushing the West further away every day and encouraging the ideological and strategic rapprochement with the Russia of Vladimir Putin who was eager to exploit this clearly negative emulation and use Ankara to better settle the score with the West.

Conclusion

Thus, the Syrian crisis has been a turning point and a test for Turkey. A turning point, because history will remember a before and an after, seeing how deeply and fundamentally Turkey has been shaken to its core and transformed in all aspects. In domestic politics, in foreign policy, in the way it sees its position within the region and internationally, the war in Syria will have played a determining role for Turkey and within Turkey for years and maybe decades to come.

But the Syrian crisis has also been a test for Turkey on several points and first of all for Turkish democracy. In effect, while at first the Arab Springs seemed to confirm the special place that Turkey held in the Muslim world, the evolution of the Syrian crisis and the successive Turkish reactions showed that Turkish democracy was not so strong or solid or consistent as it would have liked to have seemed. Of course, misunderstandings, crises, and feelings of disloyalty between Turkey and its Western partners did not wait for the Syrian crisis to reveal themselves. The long relationship between Turkey and its partners since Turkey joined NATO has been marked by numerous crises, notably at the end of the Cold War when the Soviet rival disappeared. This common front revealed deep differences in the interests of all parties, and the Syrian crisis revealed these splits in dramatic fashion.

Thus, the Syrian crisis propelled Turkey toward another world, less liberal and less democratic, different or even opposed to its traditional Western allies. The ongoing security crisis in Turkey has thrown the country into a deep institutional and ideological crisis, whose outcome is obviously unpredictable at this point. The rapprochement with Russia gives a clue but it would be premature and counter-performative to place Turkey in a new bloc with clear contours and administered by Russia. In fact, there are many stumbling blocks with the Kremlin. The current dialogue between Moscow and Ankara, which is favored by the current situation and the immediate interests of both, should not hide the fact that on a number of issues, including the Syrian question, there are lines of divergence between the two countries, particularly on the delicate Kurdish question, which crystallize all of the Turkish political choices. However, it is exactly on the Kurdish obstacle that Turkish-Western relations mainly crumbled in Syria, and it is perhaps within the follow up to this analysis of the Kurdish question that the existential test lies regarding the solidity of the Turkish-Russian rapprochement and the maintaining of democracy in Turkey and the shape this takes.

REFERENCES

Aras, Bülent, and Hakan Fidan. 2009. "Turkey and Eurasia: Frontiers of a New Geographic Imagination." *New Perspectives on Turkey* 40: 193, 215.

Aras, Bülent, and Rabia Karakaya Polat. 2008. "From Conflict to Cooperation: Desecuritization of Turkey's Relations with Syria and Iran." *Security Dialogue* 39 (5): 495–515.

Azeri, Siyaves. 2016. "The July 15 Coup Attempt in Turkey: The Erdogan–Gülen Confrontation and the Fall of 'Moderate' Political Islam." *Critique* 44 (4): 465-478.

Barkey, Henry J. 2014. "Turkey's Syria Predicament." *Survival* 56 (6): 113–134.

Barkey, Henry J. 2016. "Syria's Dark Shadow Over US-Turkey Relations." *Turkish Policy Quarterly*, March 7. http://turkishpolicy.com/article/782/syrias-dark-shadow-over-us-turkey-relations. Accessed on April 23, 2021.

Bishku, Michael B. 2012. "Turkish-Syrian Relations: A Checkered History." *Middle East Policy* 19 (3, Fall): 36–53.

Bosker, Maarten, and Joppe de Ree. 2014. "Ethnicity and the Spread of Civil War." *Journal of Development Economics* 108: 206–221.

Bozarslan, Hamit. 2021. "Entretien avec Hamit Bozarslan – Le nouvel autoritarisme turc et ses répercussions sur la scène politique international." Interview by Nicolas Hautemanière. *Les clés du Moyen-Orient*, February 27, 2020, https://www.lesclesdumoyenorient.com/Entretien-avec-Hamit-Bozarslan-Le-nouvel-autoritarisme-turc-et-ses. Accessed on April 23, 2021.

Browning, Christopher S., and Pertti Joenniemi. 2017. "Ontological Security, Self-Articulation and Securitization of Identity." *Cooperation and Conflict* 52 (1, March): 31–47.

Can, Şule. 2017. "The Syrian Civil War, Sectarianism and Political Change at the Turkish-Syrian Border: The Syrian Civil War." *Social Anthropology/Anthropologie Sociale* 25 (2): 174–189.

Charap, Samuel, Elina Treyger, and Edward Geist. 2019. *Understanding Russia's Intervention in Syria*. Santa Monica, CA: RAND Corporation, https://www.rand.org/pubs/research_reports/RR3180.html. Accessed on April 23, 2021.

Courbage, Youssef. 2012. "Ce que la démographie nous dit du conflit syrien." *Slate*, October 15. http://www.slate.fr/story/62969/syrie-guerre-demographie-minorites. Accessed on April 23, 2021.

Çakmak, Cenap. 2016. "Turkish–Syrian Relations in the Wake of the Syrian Conflict: Back to Securitization?" *Cambridge Review of International Affairs* 29 (2): 695–717.

Çevik, Senem B. 2019. "Reassessing Turkey's Soft Power: The Rules of Attraction." *Alternatives: Global, Local, Political* 44 (1, February): 50–71.

Dag, Rahman. 2018. "The Spillover Effect of the Syrian Crisis on the Peace Process in Turkey." *Journal of Asian and African Studies* 53 (8): 1251–1270.

Daoudy, Marwa. 2016. "The Structure-Identity Nexus: Syria and Turkey's Collapse." *Cambridge Review of International Affairs* 29 (3): 1074–1096.

Davis, David R., and Will H. Moore. 1997. "Ethnicity Matters: Transnational Ethnic Alliances and Foreign Policy Behavior." *International Studies Quarterly* 41 (1): 171–184.

Diehl, Jackson. 2012. "Lines in the Sand, Assad Plays the Sectarian Card." *World Affairs* 175 (1): 7–15.

Duran, Burhanettin, and Nuh Yılmaz. 2011. "Whose Model? Which Turkey?" *Foreign Policy*, February 8. https://foreignpolicy.com/2011/02/08/whose-model-which-turkey/. Accessed on April 23, 2021.

Erşen, Emre. 2011. "Turkey and Russia: An Emerging 'Strategic Axis' in Eurasia?" *Eur-Orient* (35–36): 263–285.

Forsberg, Erika. 2016. "Transnational Dimensions of Civil Wars: Clustering, Contagion and Connectedness." In *What Do We Know About Civil Wars?* edited by T. David Mason, and Sara McLaughlin Mitchell, 75–90. Lanham, MD: Rowman & Littlefield.

Gleditsch, Kristian Skrede. 2007. "Transnational Dimensions of Civil War." *Journal of Peace Research* 44 (3): 293–309.

Gleditsch, Kristian Skrede, and Idean Salehyan. 2008. "Civil Wars and Interstate Disputes." In *Resources, Governance and Civil Conflict*, edited by Magnus Oberg, and Kaare Strom, 58–76. London: Routledge.

Gökay, Bülent. 1994. "The Turkish Independence War and Bolshevik Russia: Some New Aspects in the Light of Soviet Documents." *Turkish Studies Association Bulletin* 18 (2): 41–57.

Gunter, Michael M. 2013. "The Turkish-Kurdish Peace Process." *Georgetown Journal of International Affairs* 14 (1): 101–111.

Hinnebusch, Raymond, and Omar Imady, eds. 2018. *The Syrian Uprising, Domestic Origins and Early Trajectory*. London: Routledge.

Human Rights Watch. 2016. *Silencing Turkey's Media: The Government's Deepening Assault on Critical Journalism*. New York: Human Rights Watch. Accessed May 21, 2020. https://www.hrw.org/sites/default/files/report_pdf/turkey1216_web.pdf. Accessed on April 23, 2021.

International Crisis Group. 2014. "Flight of Icarus? The PYD's Precarious Rise in Syria." *Middle East Report* N°151, May 8. https://www.crisisgroup.org/middle-east-north-africa/eastern-mediterranean/syria/flight-icarus-pyd-s-precarious-rise-syria. Accessed on April 23, 2021.

International Crisis Group. 2015. "A Sisyphean Task? Resuming Turkey-PKK Peace Talks." *Crisis Group Europe Briefing* N°77, December 17. https://www.refworld.org/pdfid/5672b0ed4.pdf. Accessed on April 23, 2021.

Jenkins, Celia, Suavi Aydin, and Umit Cetin, eds. 2020. *Alevism as an Ethno-Religious Identity: Contested Boundaries*, London: Routledge.

Jongerden, Joost. 2019. "Governing Kurdistan: Self-Administration in the Kurdistan Regional Government in Iraq and the Democratic Federation of Northern Syria." *Ethnopolitics* 18 (1): 61–75.

Koçan, Gürcan, and Ahmet Öncü. 2004. "Citizen Alevi in Turkey: Beyond Confirmation and Denial." *Journal of Historical Sociology* 17 (4, December): 464–489.

Köse, Talha. 2010. "The AKP and the 'Alevi Opening': Understanding the Dynamics of the Rapprochement." *Insight Turkey* 12 (2): 143–164.

Köstem, Seçkin. 2020. "Russian-Turkish Cooperation in Syria: Geopolitical Alignment with Limits." *Cambridge Review of International Affairs*.

Lawson, Fred H. 2016. "Explaining the Spread of Ethnosectarian Conflict: Syria's Civil War and the Resurgence of Kurdish Militancy in Turkey." *Nationalism and Ethnic Politics* 22 (4): 478–496.

Lord, Ceren. 2017. "Rethinking the Justice and Development Party's 'Alevi Openings'." *Turkish Studies* 18 (2): 278–296.

Mango, Andrew. 1993. "The Turkish Model." *Middle Eastern Studies* 29 (4): 726–757.

Massicard, Élise. 2005. *L'Autre Turquie. Le mouvement aléviste et ses territoires.* Paris: PUF.

Mkrtich, Karapetyan. 2018. "The Alevi/Alawite Factor in Turkey—Syria Relations in the Light of the Syrian Crisis." *Journal of Liberty and International Affairs* 4 (3): 24–40. https://nbn-resolving.org/urn:nbn:de:0168-ssoar-617 56-8. Accessed on April 23, 2021.

Onat, İsmail, and Suat Çubukçu. 2019. "Unresolved Conflict, Urban Insurgency and Devastating Consequences in Turkey Between 2015 and 2016." *Journal of Policing, Intelligence and Counter Terrorism* 14 (2): 164–182.

Özel, Soli. 2019. "At the End of the Day, Where Will Turkey Stand?" Report *Istituto Affari Internazionali* (IAI).

Parlar Dal, Emel. 2016. "Impact of the Transnationalization of the Syrian Civil War on Turkey: Conflict Spillover Cases of ISIS and PYD-YPG/PKK." *Cambridge Review of International Affairs* 29 (4): 1396–1420.

Phillips, Chris. 2009. "Turkey, Syria's New Best Friend." *The Guardian*, October 1, https://www.theguardian.com/commentisfree/2009/oct/01/turkey-syria-friendship. Accessed on April 23, 2021.

Reynolds, Michael. 2019. "Turkey and Russia: A Remarkable Rapprochement." *War on the Rocks*, October 24, https://warontherocks.com/2019/10/turkey-and-russia-a-remarkable-rapprochement/. Accessed on April 23, 2021.

Sambanis, Nicholas. 2002. "A Review of Recent Advances and Future Directions in the Quantitative Literature on Civil War." *Defence and Peace Economics* 13 (3): 215–243.

Sandal, Nükhet A. 2019. "Solidarity Theologies and the (Re)definition of Ethnoreligious Identities: The Case of the Alevis of Turkey and Alawites of Syria." *British Journal of Middle Eastern Studies*.

Svarin, David. 2015. "Towards a Eurasian Axis? Russia and Turkey Between Cooperation and Competition." *Global Affairs* 1 (4–5).

Tejel, Jordi. 2009. *Syria's Kurds: History, Politics and Society*. New York: Routledge.

Tsvetkova, Tsvetelina. 2018. "Turkish National Movement and Soviet Russia in Caucasus (1919–1922)." *Journal of Balkan and Black Sea Studies* 1 (1): 77–114.

White, Paul J., and Joost Jongerden, eds. 2003. *Turkey's Alevi Enigma: A Comprehensive Overview*. Leiden: Brill.

Yeğen, Mesut. 2015. "The Kurdish Peace Process in Turkey: Genesis, Evolution and Prospects." *Istitutto Affari Internationali* Working Papers no. 11, May 2015, https://www.iai.it/sites/default/files/gte_wp_11.pdf. Accessed on April 23, 2021.

Yılmaz, İhsan. 2020. "The AKP's De-securitization and Re-securitization of a Minority Community: The Alevi Opening and Closing." *Turkish Studies* 21 (2): 231–253.

Zahra, Rahmouni Fatima. 2017. "Securitization and De-securitization: Turkey-Syria Relations Since the Syrian Crisis." *Asian Journal of Middle Eastern and Islamic Studies* 11 (2): 27–39.

Zarcone, Thierry. 2018. "La confrontation Sunnites-Alevis en Turquie: l'impossible reconnaissance." *Confluences Méditerranée* 2 (105): 47–63.

CHAPTER 4

Turkey and the Syrian Insurgency: From Facilitator to Overlord

Thomas Pierret

On October 26, 2020, Russian aircrafts attacked a training camp run by Syrian insurgent faction Faylaq al-Sham ("Sham Corps") in Kafr Takharim (Idlib), killing dozens. Faylaq al-Sham being the unofficial military wing of the Syrian Muslim Brotherhood (SMB) and Turkey's chief partner in Idlib, it was speculated that the airstrike was a warning from Moscow to Ankara regarding the latter's dispatch of a Syrian rebel contingent in support of Azerbaijan's offensive against the Armenian enclave of Nagorno-Karabakh (Saad and Gall 2020). The incident testified to the depth of Turkey's relationship with Syrian insurgents and to the latter's role in the recent militarization of Ankara's foreign policy.

Turkey has been the single most important influential sponsor of the Syrian insurgency. It was home to the birth of the Free Syrian Army and then served as the rebels' main back office. As the Gulf States and the United States gradually disengaged after 2015, Ankara became the sole

T. Pierret (✉)
CNRS, IREMAM, Aix Marseille Université, Aix-en-Provence, France
e-mail: pierret@mmsh.univ-aix.fr

© The Author(s), under exclusive license to Springer Nature Switzerland AG 2021
B. Balci and N. Monceau (eds.), *Turkey, Russia and Iran in the Middle East*, The Sciences Po Series in International Relations and Political Economy, https://doi.org/10.1007/978-3-030-80291-2_4

patron of Syria's armed opposition. The latter was subsequently turned into a support force for Turkish military interventions against the Islamic State (IS) and the PKK-affiliated People's Protection Units (YPG). In early 2020, Turkish soldiers and Syrian rebels jointly repelled a major loyalist offensive in Idlib. It was Ankara, too, that brought about the long-sought unification of northern rebel factions by engineering the creation of the Syrian National Army (SNA) in 2017.

Yet, Turkey only assumed this role gradually and reluctantly. It did not do so to pursue grandiose "neo-Ottoman" or "Islamist" ambitions, but in response to perceived threats that mainly pertained to domestic politics, namely Kurdish separatism and refugees. In this chapter, I analyze this process by identifying four main phases in the incremental deepening of Turkey's role as a sponsor of the Syrian insurgency: between 2011 and 2013, Ankara mainly acted as a facilitator; in 2014–2015, it emerged as a patron in its own right; 2016 and 2017 were marked by Turkey's direct military intervention and regimenting of Syrian rebels; since 2018, finally, the Turkish army has decisively stepped in as the protector of Idlib's rebel enclave.

Playing the Facilitator (2011–2013)

Turkey's stance toward the nascent Syrian insurgency was initially hesitant. In July 2011, defector officers announced the creation of the Free Syrian Army from the Kilis refugee camp. Yet, although increasing regime repression soon convinced Ankara to give up its attempted mediation between Assad and the opposition, Turkish authorities did not provide Syrian insurgents with any significant logistical support. Ankara's preferred option at that time was calling for a U.S.-led foreign military intervention that would swiftly topple the Assad regime, rather than supporting a still fledgling insurgency in a protracted civil war that, as eventually happened, would undermine Syria's territorial integrity and bolster Kurdish separatism. Moreover, Erdogan feared a backlash that would jeopardize the domestic stability and prosperity that characterized his first decade in power—proxy war comes with risks of retaliation, as was subsequently exemplified by the car bombs that killed seventy in the province of Kilis in early 2013 (Balci 2012; Stein 2015a).

It was in the spring of 2012, when Qatar and Saudi Arabia stepped in as the chief state sponsors of the rebellion that Turkey effectively became the main logistical hub of support for the Syrian rebels. Freighters and airlifters departing from Libya, Sudan, and later the Balkans brought in weapons that subsequently entered Syria through Kilis and Reyhanlı (Chivers and Schmitt 2013). In early 2014, the head of Turkish intelligence (MIT) Hakan Fidan would state in a closed meeting that his organization had supervised the passage across the border of two thousand trucks transporting military equipment (Uslu 2016, 787).

Back then, Ankara showed limited interest in the rebels' internal affairs. This was, in part, due to a lack of Arabic speakers within the Turkish military and MIT (Hokayem 2013, 118; interview with Turkish academic, Rome, June 30, 2013). This shortage was exposed when in August 2011, Arab Alawite MIT operatives from Hatay, who were in charge of linking up with Syrian army defectors in spite of their sectarian bonds with Syria's ruling minority, handed over runaway Syrian officer Hussein Harmush to the Assad regime (Aksalser 2015).

The AKP government's initial hands-off policy was also a function of its confidence in the appeal of its political model that, it was assumed, would inevitably bring pro-Turkish forces to power if Syria's regime was to fall. For sure, the AKP government identified the like-minded SMB as its foremost friend among the opposition. This was illustrated by Ankara's support for the July 2012 capture of eastern Aleppo by the then SMB-aligned Tawhid Brigade, an operation the MIT reportedly facilitated by turning the head of the city's Military Security Gen Muhammad al-Muflih (Zaman al-Wasl 2014).

Among rebel factions, however, the SMB's influence was dwarfed by that of wealthier Gulf-based "activist" (*haraki*) Salafi networks that, fortunately for Turkey, were also sympathetic to the AKP government. By late 2012, these networks were funding the two largest rebel coalitions, namely the Syrian Islamic Liberation Front and the Syrian Islamic Front, which later merged into a single Islamic Front. These coalitions recruited factions like the Tawhid Brigade and Faruq Battalions, which cooperated with Ankara over the control of the Bab al-Hawa and Tell Abiyad border crossings after their capture by the rebels in 2012; as the Faruq Battalions proved corrupt and inefficient, they were ousted by Ahrar al-Sham, another activist Salafi-funded faction that subsequently remained one of Ankara's preferred partners among the rebellion forces (Pierret 2017; interview with members of the Syrian National Coalition, Gaziantep, January 4, 2014).

Engaging cooperative Islamist militants did not prevent Turkey from helping with Western and Saudi-backed schemes designed to curtail the rise of the very same factions. It was in Antakya that state sponsors met in December 2012 to appoint Lt. Gen. Salim Idris as head of the Free Syrian Army's Supreme Military Council. Simultaneously, Turkey opened its military infrastructures to a vast CIA program (later known as Timber Sycamore) designed to funnel weapons toward "moderate" rebels. In 2014, Turkey became home to the Müşterek Operasyon Merkezi ("Joint Operations Center," MOM), a CIA-led, multinational operation room that vetted factions that were allowed to receive salaries and weapons such as U.S.-made TOW anti-tank guided missiles (Solomon 2017).

Tightening the Grip (2014–2015)

In the meantime, several developments paved the way for a more assertive Turkish policy. The first, in 2012, was the decision by a faltering Assad regime to entrust the YPG with the administration of the Kurdish-majority regions of Afrin, Kobane, and Qamishli. The resulting shift in Turkish policy first appeared during the battle of Ras al- 'Ayn (November 2012 to July 2013) that opposed Kurdish fighters and rebels backed by Ankara until the latter were expelled from the border town (Al-Shishani 2013). A second source of concern for Turkey was Assad's growing use of airpower, which entailed a steady rise in the number of Syrians seeking refuge in Turkey.

In mid-2013, Erdogan was still hoping that a U.S.-led foreign intervention could solve his problems in Syria. In August, accordingly, the sarin massacre perpetrated in Damascus was met with Turkish calls for a large-scale campaign of airstrikes (Stein 2015a). However, the Obama administration's eventual decision to eschew military action put Turkey in a bind. Now freed from the prospect of Western intervention, the Syrian regime stepped up barrel-bombings of opposition-held areas. Refugees, whose number was about to exceed one million, became a vexing domestic problem for the Turkish government that was already grappling with the Gezi Park movement and a major corruption scandal.

In the run-up to the local elections of March 2014, Turkish decision-makers were eager to hasten the fall of Assad or, at least, to divert attention away from domestic issues. The resulting change of policy was exposed by Gülenist elements within the state apparatus as part of their feud with the AKP. In January 2014, most famously, the Gendarmerie intercepted MIT trucks loaded with arms destined for Syrian rebels (Yildiz 2021). Two months later, other shipments that made it to Syria were put to use in the capture of Kassab, north of Latakia. Not only did rebels operate from across the nearby Turkish border, but they reportedly received support from the Turkish artillery, and a Syrian aircraft was shot down by a Turkish F-16 (Tastekin 2015). Fresh arms supplies also paved the way for another rebel onslaught against western Aleppo.

The spring 2014 rebel offensives also constituted a turning point regarding Turkey's readiness to partner with jihadi groups such as Jabhat al-Nusra. In his founding statement two years earlier, al-Nusra's leader Abu Muhammad al-Jolani had virulently attacked Turkey (Pierret 2017, 140). Throughout 2013, however, bilateral relations eased somewhat: first, because the divorce between al-Nusra and IS rid the former of its most uncompromising elements; second, because Turkey was looking for effective partners on the ground at a time when mainstream factions seemed increasingly inept. The rebels' northern push of 2014 also revealed Turkey's cooperation with Chechen commanders, some of whom had sought refuge in Turkey during the Chechen wars and were thus known to the MIT (Ali 2014).

While in need of the hardliners' effectiveness, Turkey was faced with growing U.S. emphasis on counter-terrorism in Syria. In May 2014, therefore, Ankara and Qatar co-sponsored the Revolutionary Covenant, a conciliatory document in which Islamist factions such as Ahrar al-Sham and Jaysh al-Islam asserted their rejection of the transnational jihadis' maximalist agenda (Lister 2016, 225–226). In June, the Turkish government finally bowed to long-standing U.S. demands to designate al-Nusra as a terrorist organization (Stein 2015a).

In the following months, however, similar circumstances produced similar outcomes. U.S. military intervention against IS in September 2014 was yet another disappointment for Ankara, which failed to convince Washington to seize the opportunity to enforce a no-fly zone in the north. At the domestic level, anti-Syrian riots erupted in the weeks preceding the August 2014 presidential elections, and CHP leader Kemal Kılıçdaroğlu promised to send Syrians back home if he won the June 2015 general elections (Hürriyet Daily News 2015).

This was the background to what would prove to be Turkey's last attempt at toppling Assad. In March 2015, a rebel commander recounted, "I could now get nearly all the weapons I wanted ... The Turks and their friends [i.e. Qatar] wanted this over with" (Chulov 2015). In the following weeks, Turkish-backed rebels made some advances in the western suburbs of Aleppo, while they captured the city of Idlib and headed for the regime's strongholds of Hama and Latakia.

The spring 2015 offensives marked yet another shift in Ankara's handling of its Syrian rebel partners. First, the scale and quasi-overt character of Turkish-Qatari support for a coalition including al-Nusra—namely, Idlib's Army of Conquest—was unprecedented. In parallel, as a means to make its Syrian partners more palatable to the United States, Turkey quietly supported Qatar's efforts to encourage al-Nusra to break from al-Qaeda, which came to fruition the following year (Stein 2015b).

In the months preceding the rebels' offensive in Idlib, the province had become a condominium of al-Nusra and Ahrar al-Sham after the former destroyed the main local U.S.-backed FSA factions, namely the Syria Revolutionaries Front and the Hazm Movement. In Aleppo, by contrast, the insurgency remained more mainstream and fragmented, a situation that granted Ankara greater clout over local rebel politics. In April 2015, Turkey had a Sham Corps member appointed as the commander of the Aleppo Conquest operation room that coordinated rebel operations in the area. In parallel, Ankara reportedly imposed the replacement of the founding leader of one of the most prominent local factions, namely the Nur al-Din Zenki Movement. He was reproached for the kidnapping of Italian humanitarian workers by one of his aides ('Anjarini 2015).

In September 2015, of course, Turkish hopes of a rebel victory were shattered by the Russian intervention. In response, Ankara initially escalated its efforts, a trend that culminated in November 2015 when the Turkish air force downed a Russian bomber over the Syrian border. As late as October 2016, brand new Turkish-made weapons were seen in rebel hands during the last attempt at breaking the siege of Aleppo (Ahrar al-Sham 2016). These were mere delaying tactics, however. After the November 2015 crisis, Ankara had found itself isolated and vulnerable to Moscow's economic sanctions and bombardments that drove refugees across the border into Turkey (Sly 2015). The Obama administration negotiated a partnership with Russia throughout 2016, and in June 2017, Donald Trump put an end to Timber Sycamore. Saudi Arabia prioritized its military effort in Yemen and, as of 2017, Qatar was to be almost entirely absorbed by its dispute with Saudi Arabia and the United Arab Emirates.

By the summer of 2016, already, it was clear that the AKP government had to seek a modus vivendi with Vladimir Putin, who showed himself to be supportive of Erdogan during the July coup attempt. The soon-to-be lone sponsor of the Syrian insurgency would now focus entirely on its two priorities in the conflict, namely rolling back the YPG and preventing further inflows of refugees into Turkey.

CARVING UP A BUFFER ZONE, "BUILDING AN ARMY DOWN THERE" (2016–2017)

Ankara's eagerness to put the rebel house in order in mid-2015 was driven by the need for credible partners if Assad were to fall, but also, more decisively, by the fact that Turkish decision-makers were planning to establish a buffer zone in the border areas then occupied by IS as a means to keep the YPG in check. As early as March 2014, Fidan had secretly proposed to wage a false-flag attack on the Turkish extra-territorial shrine of Sultan Suleiman Shah to justify the occupation of the surrounding areas controlled by IS, while "building an army [of Syrian rebels] down there" (Moore 2014). When the United States had extended the anti-IS Operation Inherent Resolve to Syria in September 2014, Turkish calls to rely on the rebels had gone unheeded. Instead, Washington chose to work with the YPG, which in 2015 started to expand southward and along the border. They captured Tell Abyad in June, thereby linking the Autonomous Administration's central and eastern cantons, while in Turkey the armed conflict between Ankara and the PKK resumed after a two-year ceasefire.

For its buffer zone plan to succeed, the AKP government needed the unwavering support of the Syrian rebels. Commanders who were deemed too close to the CIA (hence, potentially lukewarm toward Turkey's anti-YPG agenda) were sidelined or even arrested, while Ankara was reportedly pleased with al-Nusra's elimination of Idlib's U.S.-backed factions in early 2015 (Solomon 2017; interview with civilian member of Syrian opposition, Istanbul, April 15, 2015). Even Islamist hardliners had to show support or, at least, acceptance of Turkey's intentions: while Ahrar al-Sham dismissed a handful of recalcitrant hawkish clerics, al-Nusra quietly evacuated the northern countryside of Aleppo so as not to stand in the way of the Turkish army (Eldorar Alshamia 2015; Suwayd 2015).

Any discussion of Turkey's military intervention against IS inevitably raises the controversial question of Ankara's relationship to that organization in the preceding years. The first Turkish shells landed on IS positions in October 2013, when al-Baghdadi's men tried to seize border crossings from Turkish-backed rebel factions (Balci 2013). Internal records also show that early on, Turkish decision-makers feared that the Jihadi group might be "open to manipulation" (Moore 2014). Yet, IS's focus on northeastern Syria made it a stubborn enemy of the YPG; hence de facto it served Turkey's interests. Ankara's ambiguities, which provoked much discontent among its Western allies, found many illustrations: according to the newspaper *Cumhuriyet,* the Turkish police wiretapped, yet tolerated, armed deals between ISIS and Turkish citizens; in 2014–2015, the Turkish press abounded with reports of medical treatment granted to wounded ISIS fighters in border towns (Uslu 2016, 787–788); throughout 2014, Turkish authorities were slow to act upon (themselves belated) Western requests to seal its border to foreign volunteers trying to enter Syria, and to stop oil smuggling originating from IS-held territories (Stein 2015a).

There was more behind Turkish hesitations than a hope that IS would keep the YPG in check. Turkey feared IS retaliations in the form of terrorist attacks and hostage-taking—forty Turkish diplomats were kidnapped by IS in Mosul in June 2014 and then released in exchange for IS members detained in Turkey (Sly 2014). Oil smuggling was also beneficial to Turkish buyers whom the AKP government was loath to antagonize (Uslu 2016, 788). More fundamentally, Turkey's uncooperative attitude was a function of its disagreement with the United States' anti-IS strategy, which marginalized anti-Assad rebels to the benefit of the YPG. In order to bend Washington's approach to its own preferences, Ankara refused to put the Incirlik airbase at the disposal of Inherent Resolve until July 2015, after both parties finally agreed to include Syrian rebels in the anti-IS effort and to work for the establishment of a Turkish-held safe zone (De Young and Sly 2015).

Turkish pressures resulted in the creation of the Pentagon-run, overt Train and Equip program, whose first unit was disarmed by al-Nusra as soon as it crossed the border (Gutman 2015). The fiasco contributed to Washington's decision to sponsor the October 2015 establishment of the Syrian Democratic Forces (SDF), a multi-ethnic alliance placed under undisputed YPG leadership. For Turkey, another alarm bell rang in February 2016, when the YPG captured rebel-held Tell Rif 'at, north of Aleppo, and advanced toward the border town of A 'zaz. In the following months, Turkey's artillery and logistical support helped local rebels to deter the YPG while trying to move eastward against IS. This met with little success, hence the U.S. decision to support the SDF's capture of Manbij from IS in June in spite of Ankara's opposition to any Kurdish inroad west of the Euphrates. In the meantime, IS responded to Turkey's growing contribution to Inherent Resolve through deadly suicide attacks inside Turkey, notably killing 45 at Istanbul's Atatürk airport in June 2016, while firing rockets at the province of Kilis (Stein 2016).

Starting in August 2016, after the AKP government finally obtained the green light from the United States and Russia to enter Syria, the seven-month-long Operation Euphrates Shield cleared Jarablus and al-Bab of IS. This was the first instance of on-the-ground cooperation between the Turkish army and Syrian rebels, who were now receiving such heavy weapons systems as ACV-15 armored combat vehicles (Baladi, 2016). Euphrates Shield was followed in January-March 2018 by Olive Branch, which led to the capture of the YPG-held region of Afrin and the displacement of the majority of its Kurdish-majority population. In October 2019, finally, Peace Spring resulted in the capture of the mixed area of Tell Abyad and Ras al- 'Ayn. Apart from stifling YPG ambitions, the resulting buffer zone offered Turkey the opportunity to resettle displaced Arab communities originating from areas reconquered by the regime in the south, while promising to do the same later with Turkey-based refugees. This would help to address xenophobic sentiments at home and hinder future attempts at establishing Kurdish rule along the border (Al-Hilu 2021, 9–10).

During its operations in Syria, the Turkish army partnered with the Hawar Kilis operation room, that had been established in April 2016 by offshoots of the revived Train and Equip Program (e.g., Hamza Division and al-Mu 'tasim Division) and other northern Aleppo-based rebel units to coordinate anti-IS operations. This was the nucleus of the Syrian National Army (SNA) that was eventually established in December 2017, on the eve of operation Olive Branch. Although trained and funded, hence commanded, by Turkey, the SNA was theoretically subordinated to the Ministry of Defense of the Syrian National Coalition Interim Government (Yüksel 2019; Özkiklik 2019, 14; Al-Hilu 2021, 5). This (purely symbolic) assertion of Syrian sovereignty followed the same rationale as Turkey's refusal to formally annex the territories it administrates across the border. Indeed, formal partition would set a precedent that Ankara regards as highly perilous for its own territorial integrity vis-à-vis Kurdish separatist desires.

By 2020, the SNA's first three corps (*fayaliq*) claimed c. twenty-five thousand fighters grouped in 26 units of three main origins. A first category comprised local branches of factions such as the SMB-affiliated Sham

Corps, Levant Front, and Ahrar al-Sham. The second was made up of fighters that had sought refuge in the northern Aleppo countryside in previous years: Ahrar al-Sharqiyya and Jaysh al-Sharqiyya were formed by rebels expelled from Deir ez-Zor by IS in 2014, while Jaysh al-Islam and Faylaq al-Rahman had withdrawn from the suburbs of Damascus following the regime's recapture of the area in 2018 (Özkicilcik 2019, 10).

A third component of the SNA is Turkmen-led factions that are often recognizable by names that refer to Ottoman Sultans (Sultan Murad Bloc, Sultan Mehmet Fatih, the notoriously unruly Sultan Suleiman Shah Brigade) or to Turkic civilization (Samarkand Brigade). Comprising ten percent of the first three corps' manpower, Turkmens are largely overrepresented within the SNA considering that they accounted for less than three percent of Syria's prewar population (Özkicilcik 2020, 24). This is due to the concentration of Turkmen communities in Northern Syria but also, of course, to Turkey's policies. From the onset of the war, Ankara valued Turkmen rebel factions for reasons of language, considering its aforementioned lack of Arabists. During the Kassab offensive, Turkmen intermediaries were reportedly tasked to send the coordinates of regime positions to the Turkish artillery. Partnering with Turkmen rebels was also a matter of legitimacy, the AKP government's support for ethnic brethren in Syria being spared the bitter criticisms formulated by the opposition against other aspects of Erdogan's strategy. In the MIT trucks affair, for instance, the authorities insisted that arms shipments were destined for Turkmens (Tastekin 2015).

Ankara convinced the Pentagon to make Turkmen commanders the mainstay of the Train and Equip program by highlighting their non-Islamist orientation (Erkuş 2015). After the establishment of the SNA, likewise, Turkmen-led factions enjoyed preferential treatment from Turkey, which enabled them to hire non-Turkmen fighters (Hage Ali 2017). Accordingly, such factions formed the backbone of the Syrian mercenary contingent deployed by Turkey in Libya and Nagorno-Karabakh in 2020 (Tsurkov 2020).

Ankara initially conceived of its Syrian rebel partners as a force that could undermine YPG dominance beyond the narrow limits of Turkish-occupied areas. In 2016–2017, in particular, Turkey tried, and failed, to foster the emergence of Arab and Kurdish insurgent groups within SDF-held territories (Enab Baladi 2016). The Ahfad Salah al-Din Brigade, the Kurdish component of the Hawar Kilis operation room, could have played a critical role in that endeavor, but it was disbanded by Turkey in 2017 because of its opposition to the planned operation against the Kurdish-majority region of Afrin (Ibrahim 2017). As for the SNA factions from Deir ez-Zor, that have been regarded by Turkey as a potential asset if SNA operations ever were to extend to eastern Syria, they have become the epitome of the SNA's rogue behavior, which has materialized in looting and ransoming (particularly of Kurdish residents of Afrin), and infighting over spoils and other economic resources (Heller 2017; WhatsApp interview with Syrian analyst, March 3, 2018; Al-Hilu 2021, 8).

Ironically, although Turkey initially opposed U.S. insistence that Train and Equip units should not fight the regime, the same restraint was imposed on the SNA. It was in Idlib instead that Turkey's military deployment would eventually lead to genuine military cooperation with the rebels against the regime.

Idlib: Drawing a Line in the Sand (2018–2020)

Following the fall of eastern Aleppo to regime forces in December 2016, Turkey, Russia, and Iran launched a series of meetings held in Astana, Kazakhstan (Heller 2017). Discussions initially focused on the establishment of a ceasefire, which Ankara sought for two main reasons. First, it needed to prevent regime advances that would provoke new population movements toward the border. Second, Moscow's acquiescence was required to prepare the offensive against Afrin. The Astana talks thus paved the way for Turkey's first military deployment in Idlib in October 2017. A dozen observation posts were established west of the Damascus-Aleppo railway in order not to stand in the way of the pro-regime forces that recaptured Idlib's eastern edges in the following months. Turkish positions also sealed Afrin from the south, thereby preparing the ensuing pincer move against the Kurdish enclave.

While Idlib's rebels had hitherto enjoyed greater independence from Turkey than their counterparts in Aleppo, they were now summoned by Ankara to comply with what they perceived as unholy bargains. The SMB's Sham Corps, whose representatives led the rebel delegation in Astana, emerged as the pillar of Ankara's influence among local insurgents. Yet, precisely because of Turkey's protection, the Sham Corps was spared aggressive moves by Jabhat al-Nusra (now renamed Hay'a Tahrir al-Sham, "Syria's Liberation Committee," henceforth HTS) against what the jihadi group branded as the "Astana factions." Between 2017 and 2019, indeed, three main rounds of infighting brought c. ninety percent of the greater Idlib area under HTS's control (Khatib 2018). Several factions consequently sought protection by merging with the Sham Corps (WhatsApp interview with Syrian analyst, February 19, 2019).

In the face of al-Jolani's hegemonic ambitions, Turkey had few options. Mainstream rebel factions were too weak to contain the jihadi group's power grab. A direct military confrontation with HTS would have been costly for the Turkish military, while bringing more refugees and terrorism onto Turkish soil. At the same time, it rapidly appeared that HTS's bombastic statements against the Astana Process accompanied a pragmatic posture regarding Turkish interests. While HTS fighters escorted the Turkish military convoys that entered Idlib, the group's clerics legitimized cooperation with Ankara on the basis that a dozen outposts did not give the latter effective control over the region (Farghali 2017). In January 2019, while his men were dealing a decisive blow to their rivals from Ahrar al-Sham, al-Jolani even expressed support for further Turkish military operations against the YPG east of the Euphrates (Enab Baladi 2019). In parallel, HTS entrusted Idlib's governance to a nominally independent civilian administration, the Syrian Salvation Government, which met with low-level Turkish officials over technical issues such as health (Shaam 2017). Al-Jolani's embrace of realpolitik convinced al-Qaeda loyalists to split from HTS and, in early 2018, establish Hurras al-Din ("Guardians of Religion").

Turkey's cautious engagement did not preclude measures aimed at containing HTS. MIT was probably behind significant defections that befell the group on the eve of Turkey's 2017 military deployment (Erkoyun and Perry 2017). In parallel, Ankara pushed for the unification of Idlib's mainstream faction, which in May 2018 formed the National Front for Liberation (FNL) headed by Sham Corps' Col Fadlallah al-Hajji. In October 2019, the NFL officially joined the SNA, a move designed to deter further aggression from HTS while bolstering the position of the Interim Government (officially the SNA's supreme authority) within the Turkish-Russian sponsored committee in charge of drafting a new Syrian constitution. Although the merger brought the number of SNA corps from three to seven, and its manpower from c. twenty-five thousand men to an alleged eighty thousand, it had limited practical implications because what was required in Idlib was cooperation with HTS in the face of advancing pro-regime forces (Özkicilcik 2019, 9–10).

Assad and his allies had only agreed to recognize Idlib as a "de-escalation zone" in order to focus their energies on the reconquest of southern rebel-held areas. As soon as this goal was achieved in the summer of 2018, loyalist forces prepared for a large-scale offensive against Idlib. Turkey's countervailing military build-up along the border convinced Russia to sign the Sochi agreement in September. This provided for the withdrawal of heavy weapons and HTS fighters from the rebel-held areas extending from the frontline to the M4 (Latakia-Aleppo) and M5 (Damascus-Aleppo) highways, and for the reopening of the latter to civilian traffic. Although HTS accepted the broad lines of the agreement, it undermined this in late 2018 by further expanding its own domain to the detriment of rival factions, while Russia subsequently added a demand to hold joint patrols with the Turkish military along the contentious highways. Consequently, pro-regime forces resumed their operations in the spring of 2019 and, by February 2020, had retaken most of the M5 (International Crisis Group 2020).

Loyalist advances resulted in the displacement of hundreds of thousands toward the border, and in the encirclement of several Turkish outposts that were eventually evacuated in early 2021. In the meantime, however, Turkey had drawn a line in the sand through unprecedented military support for the rebels. Liberal provisions of artillery ammunitions were handed over to the NFL that, conveniently (considering that Turkey officially considers HTS as a terrorist organization), was given the command of HTS's heavy-weapons regiments within the Fath Mubin ("Great Conquest") operation room (Hamawi 2019).

Indirect support proved insufficient, however, and by mid-February 2020, loyalists were only a dozen kilometers away from the city of Idlib. Turkish artillery and commandos equipped with anti-aircraft missiles assisted the rebels' successful pushback, which in turn prompted loyalist attacks against Turkish troops. After an airstrike killed dozens of Turkish soldiers in Balyun on February 27, Ankara launched operation Spring Shield: while its ground force in Idlib was brought to twenty thousand, its F-16 shot down three Syrian aircraft, and armed drones destroyed dozens of loyalist vehicles. On March 5, Turkey and Russia agreed to a ceasefire that provided for joint Turkish-Russian patrols on the M4, while the M5 was definitively lost to the regime (International Crisis Group 2020).

Ankara's growing military footprint provided it with greater leverage over HTS, forcing it to display its goodwill by acceding to Turkey's demand to join a tripartite military council headed by representatives of

HTS and the NFL's Sham Corps and Ahrar al-Sham (Barish 2020). Deepening Turkish involvement in Idlib also brought about new perils. From September 2020 onward, Turkish soldiers were the targets of several attacks by previously unknown militant groups such as the Abu Bakr al-Siddiq Company (Modon 2021). These groups were possibly front organizations for parties that, like Hurras al-Din, were attempting to sabotage the March 5 ceasefire and punish Ankara for prompting HTS to crack down on Jihadi hardliners.

Conclusion

Until 2013, Turkey acted as the facilitator of a proxy-war strategy that was primarily designed by the Gulf States and the United States. While it granted Syrian rebels and their sponsors access to its territory, it barely interfered in the rebellion's internal politics. However, as the rapidly growing number of Syrian refugees compounded popular discontent with the AKP government, the latter's policy shifted due to impatience with Obama's pusillanimity during the August 2013 chemical weapons attack crisis, and with the poor military performance of the moderate rebels. The battle of Kassab in 2014 marked a turning point as the Turkish army provided near-direct support for an offensive led by hardline Islamist factions. One year later, it was once again dissatisfaction with the United States (for its refusal to include an anti-Assad dimension in Operation Inherent Resolve against IS), and the Turkish opposition's escalation of its anti-refugee rhetoric as elections drew nearer, that convinced Ankara to fully back the northwestern rebel push that ultimately contributed to Russia's decision to enter the war on Assad's side in September 2015.

In parallel, Turkey's hold over northern Syrian rebels tightened in response to the rise of the YPG. Starting with the battle of Ras al-'Ayn in late 2012, Ankara used Assad's armed opponents as a proxy force against the PKK-affiliated group. From 2016 onward, as the Turkish army carved up a buffer zone in IS- and YPG-held territories, and as other state sponsors disengaged, northern rebel factions were dealt with as an auxiliary force owing full obedience to its lone Turkish patron. This process culminated in the establishment of the Syrian National Army in 2017.

In HTS-dominated Idlib, Turkey has been chiefly concerned with the risk of a massive influx of refugees resulting from loyalist offensives. Because its light military deployment of 2017 proved insufficient to deter aggression, Turkish armed forces engaged pro-regime forces in 2020.

Once again, direct military intervention turned from what had originally been designed as a cautious, arm's length management of the rebels' internal affairs into a more hands-on strategy. In the aftermath of Operation Spring Shield, indeed, Ankara pressured HTS into forming a joint military council with Turkish-backed factions.

Turkey initially proved willing to engage with whatever rebel faction showed itself to be pragmatic enough to work with, from FSA-banner moderates to Islamist hardliners. Ankara's more selective policy in subsequent years was not based on ideology but on the criteria of military effectiveness and loyalty. Likewise, Turkish preference for select factions should not be interpreted as part of a project to turn them into a hegemonic force within the rebellion but rather as a quest for—sometimes, literal—interpreters to help it navigate an alien, exceedingly complex factional environment. Such privileged intermediaries were chosen on the basis of ideological sympathies, as were the SMB and a broad range of other Islamist factions, but also for ethnic reasons, a pattern most clearly illustrated by the prominent role of Turkmen commanders within the SNA. Maintaining such special relationships without undermining its ties to other political and military forces among the Syrian opposition will undoubtedly constitute one of Turkey's main challenges in the future.

Bibliography

Ahrar al-Sham. 2016. "Mujahidin Storm Positions of Assad's Militias in Western Aleppo." YouTube video. Posted by "Ahrar al-Sham" (channel closed).

Aksalser. 2015. "Haraba min sijinihi ila Suriya wa-asbaha 'unsuran fi milishiat al-Assad [He Fled from Prison to Syria and Became a Member in Assad's Militias]." hhttp://3ksalser.com/?page=view_articles&id=390be021b6aea7cfef398c995fe64a59. Accessed on April 7, 2021.

Ali, A. 2014. "Al-shishaniyyun wal-istikhbarat al-turkiyya [Chechens and the Turkish Intelligence]." *Al-Safir* http://www.assafir.com/Article/1/343375. Accessed on April 7, 2021.

Al-Hilu, Khayrallah. 2021. "The Turkish Intervention in Northern Syria." Technical Report, Middle East Directions (MED), Wartime and Post-Conflict Syria. *European University Institute*, January. https://cadmus.eui.eu/handle/1814/69657. Accessed on April 7, 2021.

Al-Shishani, Murad Batal. 2013. "Turkey and Syria's Jihadis: More than Free Passage?" *The Turkey Analyst*, May 22. https://www.turkeyanalyst.org/publications/turkey-analyst-articles/item/13-turkey-and-syria's-jihadis-more-than-free-passage?.html. Accessed on April 7, 2021.

'Anjarini,   S.   2015.   "Al-asabi'   al-turkiyya   hadira
da'iman   [Turkish   Fingers   Everywhere]."   *Al-Akhbar*.
https://al-akhbar.com/Syria/22764/ة-التركي-الأصابع-ة-الحلبي-الشطرنج-رقعة-على-عات
المجمو-قادة-دائما-ةحاضر. Accessed on April 7, 2021.

Baladi News. 2016. "Picture of Levant Front Fighters (page deleted)".

Balci, Bayram. 2012. "Turkey's Relations with the Syrian Opposition." *Carnegie Endowment for International Peace*, April 13. https://carnegieendowment. org/2012/04/13/turkey-s-relations-with-syrian-opposition-pub-47841. Accessed on April 7, 2021.

Balci, Bayram. 2013. "Turkey's Flirtation with Syrian Jihadism." *Carnegie Middle East Center*, November 7. https://carnegie-mec.org/diwan/53532. Accessed on April 7, 2021.

Barish, M. 2020. "Ikhraj Ahrar al-Sham min al-majlis al-'askari maslaha mushtaraka bayn al-Julani wa-l-Ikhwan al-Muslimin [Excluding Ahrar al-Sham from the Military Council is in the Common Interest of Jolani and the Muslim Brotherhood]." *Modon*. https://www.alquds.co.uk/أحرار-الشام-من-المجلس-العسوريا-إخراج/. Accessed on April 7, 2021.

Chivers, C.J., and Eric Schmitt. 2013. "Arms Airlift to Syria Rebels Expands, With Aid From C.I.A." *New York Times*, March 24. https://www.nytimes. com/2013/03/25/world/middleeast/arms-airlift-to-syrian-rebels-expands-with-cia-aid.html. Accessed on April 7, 2021.

Chulov, Martin. 2015. "Amid the Ruins of Syria, Is Bashar Al-Assad Now Finally Facing The End?" *The Guardian*, May 24. https://www.theguardian.com/world/2015/may/24/syria-iran-isis-battle-arab-world. Accessed on April 7, 2021.

De Young, Karen, and Liz Sly. 2015. "U.S.-Turkey Deal Aims to Create De Facto 'Safe Zone' in Northwest Syria." *Washington Post*, July 26.

Eldorar Alshamia. 2015. "Ahrar al-Sham tufsilu ahad a'da' al-maktab al-shar'i li-'adam indibatihi [Ahrar al-Sham Dismisses a Member of Its Legal-Religious Council for Indiscipline]." https://eldorar.com/node/84520. Accessed on April 7, 2021.

Enab Baladi. 2016. "Ajnad al-Hassake. 'Awdat al-jaysh al-hurr ila al-Jazira [Ajnad al-Hassake: Free Army Returns to the Jazira]." https://www.enabbaladi.net/archives/102660. Accessed on April 7, 2021.

Enab Baladi. 2019. "Jolani: nahnu ma'a tawajjuh Turkiya li-l-saytara 'ala sharq al-Furat [Jolani: We Support Turkey's Move to Capture the Eastern Bank of the Euphrates]." https://www.enabbaladi.net/archives/276416. Accessed on April 7, 2021.

Erkoyun, Ezgi, and Tom Perry. 2017. "Turkey Seeks to Isolate Syria Idlib jihadists Opposing Truce." *Reuters*, October 3. https://mobile.reuters.com/article/amp/idUSKCN1C81UN. Accessed on April 7, 2021.

Erkuş, Sevil. 2015. "Turkey to Train, Equip Syrian Rebels in Border Province, Too." *Hürriyet Daily News*, March 24. https://www.hurriyetdailynews.com/turkey-to-train-equip-syrian-rebels-in-border-province-too-80135. Accessed on April 7, 2021.

Farghali, A. 2017. Telegram Post, October 12.

Gutman, Roy. 2015. "What Really Happened to the U.S. Train-and-Equip Program in Syria?" *McClatchy*, December 21. https://www.mcclatchydc.com/news/nation-world/world/article50919765.html. Accessed on April 7, 2021.

Hage Ali, Mohanad. 2017. "Turkey's Men." *Carnegie Middle East Center*, November 15. https://carnegie-mec.org/diwan/74726?lang=en. Accessed on April 7, 2021.

Hamawi, O. 2019. "Ma ba'd Kafr Nabuda? [What After Kafr Nabuda?]." *Modon*, May 28. https://www.almodon.com/arabworld/2019/5/28/ما-بعد-كفر-نبودة. Accessed on April 7, 2021.

Heller, Sam. 2017. "Turkey's "Turkey First" Syria Policy." *The Century Foundation*, April 12. https://tcf.org/content/report/turkeys-turkey-first-syria-policy/. Accessed on April 7, 2021.

Hokayem, Emile. 2013. *Syria's Uprising and the Fracturing of the Levant*. Oxon: Routledge.

Hürriyet Daily News. 2015. "President Praises Disaster aid Agency." February 18. https://www.hurriyetdailynews.com/president-praises-disaster-aid-ageny--78549. Accessed on April 7, 2021.

Ibrahim, M. 2017. "Kurdish FSA Commander Loses His Faction After Refusing to Fight." *Syria Direct*. https://syriadirect.org/news/'afrin-is-a-red-line'-kurdish-fsa-commander-loses-his-faction-after-refusing-to-fight/ (this page is no longer available).

International Crisis Group. 2020. "Silencing the Guns in Idlib." Middle East Report, no. 213. May 15. https://d2071andvip0wj.cloudfront.net/213-silencing-the-guns-idlib.pdf. Accessed on April 7, 2021.

Khatib, K. 2018. "Faylaq al-Sham: al-hiyad al-sa'b ka-khiyar istratiji [Sham Corps: Delicate Neutrality as a Strategic Choice ?]." *Modon*, March 31. https://www.almodon.com/arabworld/2018/3/31/فيلق-الشام-الحياد-الصعب-كخيار-استراتيجي. Accessed on April 7, 2021.

Lister, Charles. 2016. *The Syrian Jihad: Al-Qaeda, the Islamic State and the Evolution of an Insurgency*. London: Hurst.

Modon. 2021. "Majmu'a majhula tatabanna istihdaf junud atrak fi rif Halab [Unknown Group Claims Responsibility for Targetting Turkish Soldiers in Aleppo Countryside]." *Modon*, January 18. https://www.almodon.com/arabworld/2021/1/17/ريف-حلب-في-أتراك-جنودا-تستهدف-جديدة-مجموعة-مجهو. Accessed on April 7, 2021.

Moore, Jack. 2014. "Full Transcript of Leaked Syria 'War' Conversation Between Erdogan Officials." *International Business Times*, March 28. https://www.ibtimes.co.uk/turkey-youtube-ban-full-transcript-leaked-syria-war-conversation-between-erdogan-officials-1442161. Accessed on April 7, 2021.

Özkizilcik, Ömer. 2019. "The Components of The National Army and The Implications of The Unification." SETA, October 11. https://www.setav.org/en/analysis-uniting-the-syrian-opposition-the-components-of-the-national-army-and-the-implications-of-the-unification/ (this page is no longer available).

Özkizilcik, Ömer. 2020. *The Syrian National Army.* Seta, 2020 (withdrawn).

Pierret, Thomas. 2017. "Syrian Salafis at War." In *Salafism After the Arab Awakening: Contending with People's Power,* edited by Franceso Cavatorta and Fabio Merone, 137–153. London: Hurst.

Saad, Hwaida, and Carlotta Gall. 2020. "Russian Airstrikes Kill Dozens of Turkish-Backed Rebels in Syria." *The New York Times*, October 26.

Shaam News Network. 2017. "Mu'awin wali Hatay yazuru Idlib [Assistant of Hatay Governor Visits Idlib]." http://www.shaam.org/news/syria-news/-تزامناً-مع-حراك-حكومة-الإنقاذ-في-تركيا-معاون-والي-هاطاي-يزور-إدلب.html. Accessed on April 7, 2021.

Sly, Liz. 2014. "Turkish Parliament Authorizes Potential Military Action in Syria and Iraq." *Washington Post*, October 2. https://www.washingtonpost.com/world/middle_east/turkish-parliament-authorizes-military-action-in-syria-iraq/2014/10/02/cca5dba8-7d0c-4e70-88bb-c84abbdca6d2_story.html. Accessed on April 7, 2021.

Sly, Liz. 2015. "Russian Airstrikes Force a Halt to Aid in Syria." *The Washington Post*, December 14. https://www.washingtonpost.com/gdpr-consent/?next_url=https%3a%2f%2fwww.washingtonpost.com%2fworld%2fmiddle_east%2frussian-airstrikes-force-a-halt-to-aid-in-syria-triggering-a-new-crisis%2f2015%2f12%2f14%2fcebc4b66-9f87-11e5-9ad2-568d814bbf3b_story.html. Accessed on April 7, 2021.

Solomon, Erika. 2017. "The Rise and Fall of a US-Backed Rebel Commander in Syria." *The Financial Times*, February 9. https://www.ft.com/content/791ad3bc-ecfc-11e6-930f-061b01e23655. Accessed on April 7, 2021.

Stein, Aaron. 2015a. "Turkey's Evolving Syria Strategy." *Foreign Affairs*, February 9. https://www.foreignaffairs.com/articles/turkey/2015-02-09/turkeys-evolving-syria-strategy. Accessed on April 7, 2021.

Stein, Aaron. 2015b. "What Idlib Takeover Means for Turkey." *Al Jazeera*, April 5. https://www.aljazeera.com/opinions/2015/4/5/what-idlib-takeover-means-for-turkey. Accessed on April 7, 2021.

Stein, Aaron. 2016. "ISIS and Turkey: The Rocket Threat to Kilis." *Atlantic Council*, April 26. https://www.atlanticcouncil.org/blogs/menasource/isis-and-turkey-the-rocket-threat-to-kilis/. Accessed on April 7, 2021.

Suwayd, R. 2015. "Al-Nusra tabda' bi-l-insihab mi rif Halab [Al-Nusra Starts Evacuating Aleppo's Countryside]." *Al-Araby al-Jadeed.* https://www.alaraby.co.uk/%22-تبدأ-بالانسحاب-من-ريف-النصرة22% حلب-تحضير أللمنطقة-الآمنة. Accessed on April 7, 2021.

Tastekin, Fehim. 2015. "Wiretaps Reveal Turkey's Attacks on Syrian Regime Positions." *Al-Monitor*, February 18. https://www.al-monitor.com/pulse/originals/2015/02/turkey-syria-weapons-civil-war-kessab-armenian.html#ixz z6mXEoXR3s. Accessed on April 7, 2021.

Tsurkov, Elizabeth. 2020. "The Syrian Mercenaries Fighting Foreign Wars for Russia and Turkey." *New York Review of Books*, October 16. https://bit.ly/34njjvc. Accessed on April 7, 2021.

Uslu, Emrullah. 2016. "Jihadist Highway to Jihadist Haven: Turkey's Jihadi Policies and Western Security." *Studies in Conflict & Terrorism* 39 (9): 781–802.

Yildiz, Ayse. 2021. "Ex-officer Arrested in Turkey's MIT Trucks Case." *Anadolu Agency*, January 8. https://www.aa.com.tr/en/turkey/ex-officer-arrested-in-turkeys-mit-trucks-case/2103498. Accessed on April 7, 2021.

Yüksel, Engin. 2019. "Strategies of Turkish Proxy Warfare in Northern Syria." CRU Report November 2019. *Clingendael.* https://www.clingendael.org/pub/2019/strategies-of-turkish-proxy-warfare-in-northern-syria/. Accessed on April 7, 2021.

Zaman al-Wasl. 2014. "Al-'amid al-Muflih yatawassat li-l-'awda ila hadn al-watan [Gen al-Muflih Seeks Mediation to Come Back to the Homeland]." https://www.zamanalwsl.net/news/article/50904. Accessed on April 7, 2021.

CHAPTER 5

Moscow and the Challenge of Rebuilding Syria

Igor Delanoë

Almost a decade after the beginning of Syria's civil war, the United Nations have assessed the damage caused by the war to Syria's economy at $443 billion, with 12 million involuntary internally displaced persons (IDPs) and refugees (United Nations Economic and Social Commission for Western Asia, Centre for Syrian Studies 2020, 13). After having won the military campaign and saved Bashar Al-Assad from being toppled, Moscow has sought to win peace and consolidate its influence in the Levant. The end of the active phase of the military operations in early 2017 shortly after east Aleppo fell into the regime's hands has marked the transformation of the war, which morphed from a high-intensity conflict into a low-intensity one, with local and temporary violent fighting, as demonstrated in February–March 2020 in Idlib. Russian forces had demonstrated their ability to handle this level of conflict and after the regime had retaken, one after the other, the so-called de-escalation zones

I. Delanoë (✉)
French-Russian Analytical Center Observo, Moscow, Russia
e-mail: igor.delanoe@ccifr.ru

© The Author(s), under exclusive license to Springer Nature
Switzerland AG 2021
B. Balci and N. Monceau (eds.), *Turkey, Russia and Iran in the Middle East*, The Sciences Po Series in International Relations and Political Economy, https://doi.org/10.1007/978-3-030-80291-2_5

79

defined in the framework of the Astana Process,[1] in 2018 Moscow decided to undertake the process of Syria's reconstruction in the area held by the loyalist forces. This new phase was launched while the Russia-sponsored political process was taking shape following the Syrian's People Congress held in late January 2018 in Sochi. Contrary to the USA, which brokered the peace in 1979 between Israel and Egypt, Russia cannot afford to pay for the reconciliation of the various antagonistic actors in the Syrian crisis. Neither can the Kremlin bankroll the Syrian state and finance the reconstruction of Syria on its own, nor does it want to. Furthermore, Moscow can hardly draw on experiences of State Building, let alone Nation Building, and therefore it has promoted the idea of a collective and international effort to rebuild the country. The Russians have explored various and sometime contradictory options to create a dynamic aimed at attracting foreign investors while regularly calling for sanctions on Syria to be lifted to ease the economic burden on Damascus. So far, these efforts have delivered few results compelling the Kremlin to finally focus on the limited but nevertheless existing possibilities offered by bilateral cooperation. This chapter focuses on Moscow's approach regarding Syria's reconstruction. Facing considerable obstacles in attracting foreign financial support, in the meantime Russia has developed a bilateral agenda with the Arab Republic. In the first part, this chapter deals with the vectors, the actors, and the contradictions inherent to the bilateral approach. The second part examines the Kremlin's 2018 attempt to create an international momentum on the issue of the return of the refugees, and through this agenda, to trigger international economic assistance to Syria.

Russia's Business in Syria: A Preferred Government-To-Government Approach

Syria's Attempted Initiatives at Reconstruction

Despite deep structural domestic challenges, the Syrian government has pushed several initiatives to try to present the local context as promising,

---

[1] The Astana Forum was created in late December 2016 by Turkey, Russia, and Iran. In May 2017, it established four "de-escalation zones" in Deraa, Homs, Eastern Ghouta and Idlib, designed to be safe havens for civilians. Today, only the Idlib zone remains. See Jaecke and Labude (2020, 1).

as well as the wide range of business opportunities offered by Syria's reconstruction. In mid-2015, the first edition of the international fair "Rebuilding Syria"—a yearly business expo forum gathering companies from the infrastructure and building sectors—took place. According to the organizers, since then, this business event has gained traction, attracting mostly Syrian companies, but also foreign actors from EU countries, from Asia and the Middle East.[2] In 2016, a new law enabling public–private partnership (PPP) came into force, and a PPP Council was established under the auspices of the prime minister of Syria (International Labor Organization 2016).[3] In April 2017, Damascus formulated the main orientations of its strategy to rebuild the territories under its control, and officially shifted from an "economy of war" to an "economy of peace" (Matveev 2019a). The major business rendezvous remains the Damascus International Fair, usually held in September. During the 60th edition in 2018, China pledged to invest $2 billion in Syria's economy, while Damascus was to benefit from the $23 billion in loans and aid that Beijing earmarked for the Arab region in July 2018 (*Diplomat* 2018). In spite of US pressure and the risk of sanctions, many countries and foreign entrepreneurs have participated in these business events.[4]

The Syrian business environment may be described as difficult not only because of the war and the international sanctions but also because of the structural corruption and heavy bureaucracy, which may deter foreign investors from venturing into the country (Matveev 2019b). The Caesar Act, signed by President Trump in December 2019 which entered into force in June 2020,[5] further complicates the attraction of potential international investors. Yet, these new US sanctions were probably not aimed at deterring European, let alone American investors from working in Syria

[2] For instance, according to the organizers, 270 companies from 29 countries including France, Switzerland, Spain, Germany, India, and China participated in the 2018 edition of this business forum. Browse the official website of the exposition: http://www.re-buildsyria.com/.

[3] See the webpage of the International Labor Organization for the details of the law: http://www.ilo.org/dyn/natlex/natlex4.detail?p_lang=en&p_isn=104777&p_count=3&p_classification=01.02.

[4] For instance, during the Damascus International Fair in September 2018, the German company Siemens had one of the biggest stands. Interview carried out by the author with a representative of a Western NGO operating in Syria, Moscow, October 2018.

[5] The Caesar Act establishes additional sanctions and financial restrictions on institutions and individuals related to the conflict in Syria. See the details on the webpage of the US Congress: https://www.congress.gov/bill/116th-congress/house-bill/31.

but rather they sought to deter Gulf entrepreneurs. Indeed, in 2019, the Emiratis and, to a lesser extent, the Saudis, displayed a renewed interest in stabilizing their relations with Syria. In late December 2018, the United Arab Emirates (UAE) and Bahrain reopened their embassies in Damascus, seven years after having closed their diplomatic representation (*Reuters* 2018a). This move was seen as the potential prelude to diplomatic normalization between the Syrians and Gulf Cooperation Council countries, on the one hand, and to incoming Emirati investments in Syria, on the other. Before the war, the UAE had some $20 billion invested in Syria's economy, mainly in luxury real estate, transport infrastructures, and trade (Daher 2019). The normalization of the Emirati-Syrian relations was all the more welcomed by Moscow as it may also be seen as a counterweight to growing Turkish and Iranian influence in Syria. Expansionism by Ankara and Tehran plays into Russia's hands in the sense that for Riyadh and Abu Dhabi, they have become greater challenges than Bashar Al-Assad remaining in power. Yet, the reply to Moscow could be that Turkey's presence and activity in Syria today is a direct product of Moscow's cooperation with Ankara, starting in 2016.

Russia's Preferred Top-Down Approach to Frame Syria's Reconstruction

Russia has regularly complained about the international sanctions and asked for them to be lifted in order to alleviate the economic situation in Syria, vainly seizing in fall 2020 the opportunity of the COVID-19 context to request this. The Kremlin has also harshly criticized the US military presence—presented as an "occupation"—on the oil-rich region east of the Euphrates. From Moscow's perspective, the American military footprint in eastern Syria not only spoils the political process sponsored by Russia through its military partnership with the Kurds, but is also seen as economic predation. Indeed, in June 2020, local authorities in eastern Syria signed a deal with the US oil company Delta Crescent LLC, headquartered in Delaware, to exploit the Syrian oilfield located east of the Euphrates and then trade the oil (*Politico* 2020). The various layers of obstacles and economic restrictions on Damascus have not deterred major Russian conglomerates from starting to do business or expand their already existing affairs in the Arab Republic, under the auspices of the Kremlin. Moscow's reach into Syria's market has been traditionally strong on the government-to-government level (G2G) and, to a lesser extent, at the business-to-government level (B2G). The footprint of Russian small and medium size companies is rather weak on Russia's economy as they represent only a fraction of the GDP (around 20%). This explains why the business-to-business (B2B) contacts between Russia and Syria are structurally weak, if not to say almost non-existent. Moscow has not outlined any comprehensive strategy regarding its approach to rebuilding Syria. To some extent, there are even signs that the Kremlin has outsourced this task to Russian conglomerates, which can do business in the framework defined by the Kremlin. This is especially the case for the oil and gas sectors. In January 2018, Russia and Syria signed an agreement which gives exclusive rights to Russian energy companies to extract oil in the areas under the direct control of Damascus. A statement by the then Minister of Energy, Alexandre Novak, who mentioned a "roadmap" for restoring and developing oil fields and deposits, shortly followed this deal (Ramani 2019). In May 2020, Vladimir Putin upgraded the rank of Aleksandr Efimov, Russia's Ambassador to Syria, who was appointed Special Envoy of the President for Developing Ties with Syria (*Kommersant* 2020b). Behind this title lies a clear agenda regarding the promotion of bilateral commerce and investments. Nearly three years after the end of the active phase of Russia's military campaign, this also indicates that the Kremlin may be disappointed by the post-war business opportunities and intends to boost its economic footprint through the diplomatic channel. However, it remains to be seen to what extent the role of the Russian Ministry of Foreign Affairs is taken seriously in Damascus where other Russian actors interact with Syrian business.

In that regard, Deputy Prime Minister Yury Borisov plays a key role. Yury Borisov, who has direct access to Vladimir Putin, supervises a wide range of industrial sectors in Russia, spanning from the agro-industry to military-technical cooperation, the military-industrial complex, and energy. He is also co-chair of the Permanent Russian-Syrian Intergovernmental Commission for Economy, Commerce, Science, and Technology Cooperation. He visited Damascus in April and December 2019, and again in September 2020, with Russia's Minister of Foreign Affairs, Sergei Lavrov. His military connections and his direct access to the Kremlin provide him with a stronger influence in the discussion with his counterparts in Syria. During his December 2019 visit, he announced that Russia would invest $500 million to develop the commercial port of Tartus, where in 2017 Russia secured its military base for 49 years. He also stated that the sole Syrian fertilizer plant in Homs had been reconstructed and that $200 million were aimed at its reactivation (*RIA Novosti* 2019b). In December 2019, two unknown Russian energy companies—Velada and Merkury—signed an agreement with the Syrian government regarding the offshore oil exploitation of blocks n° 23 (Velada), 7, and 19 (Merkury). According to various sources, these entities are linked to the businessperson Evgeniy Prigozhin, who allegedly has direct ties with the Kremlin, and is the owner of Wagner security company (*Novaya Gazeta* 2020). The Syrian Ministry of Economy eventually registered them in Damascus in November 2020. For its part, the Russian oil company SoyuzNeftGaz started the offshore exploration phase on block n° 2 in late 2019, following an agreement signed with Syria back in December 2013 (*RIA Novosti* 2019a). Although under US sanctions, in June 2019 one of Russia's largest construction companies, StroyTransGaz, which has operated in Syria since 2005, received the lease of the Tartus commercial port for 49 years, and plans to widen and modernize its infrastructures. This may be linked to the phosphate business since StroyTransGaz obtained the exploitation of two mines near Palmyra in March 2018 and needs to access wider export capacities (*Financial Times* 2019). Reconstruction projects linked to the transport sector are also reportedly underway under Russia's supervision and may involve companies like UralWagonZavod which may handle the project for a rail connection between Damascus international airport and Damascus downtown, and Almaz-Antey, which may be in charge of re-equipping Damascus airport.

To date, the Russia-Syria B2B connection remains poor. Russian small and medium size companies may display a certain interest in doing business in Syria, especially in the PPP framework. However, they are anxious and deterred by legal issues mainly relating to the safety of their financial and technology investments, and the opacity of the tenders (Matveev 2019b). Road shows have been organized by Russian authorities for Russian small business companies in Syria as well as B2B meetings with Syrian entrepreneurs since the end of the 2010s. The acquisition of Tartus port by StroyTransGaz may reassure some Russian small entities interested in Syria's business potential in various sectors, including agriculture, industrial manufacturing, construction, oil and gas exploitation, mining, railways, information technology and cybersecurity. Russian small business nevertheless still appears deterred by the lack of transparency of the Syrian market and the sanctions (Matveev 2019d). In that regard, the discrete visit paid to Damascus by Chief Military Prosecutor of Russia

Valery Petrov in early September, and later by the Head of the Investigative Committee of Russia Alexander Bastrykin on October 1, 2020, may be seen as a signal sent to the domestic business audience that Moscow is committed to securing economic spheres in Syria. Other factors such as security play a negative role in attracting small Russian entrepreneurs. Contrary to Russian conglomerates, small business cannot afford armed guards and enhanced security to protect their employees and offices.

Black Sea Connections: The Politicization of Limited Economic Opportunities

Russian-Syrian bilateral commerce has collapsed during the last decade, being slashed from nearly $2 billion in 2008, to a little bit more than $174 million in 2019, including $4 million of imports from Syria (see Table 5.1—Statistics of Russia Federal Border Service). Russia has explored the development of direct economic relations between Crimea and the Arab Republic to support bilateral commerce. A Syrian delegation of 80 people was invited to the 2018 edition of the Yalta International Economic Forum—the fourth of its kind. The Crimea Republic had dispatched a business delegation to Syria in October 2018 to prepare the documents to be signed during the business forum in Yalta, with the idea of contributing to the reconstruction of the country (*Izvestia* 2018). Crimean ports are much closer to Syria than Russia's Baltic ports—respectively 4 to 5 days away, compared to 24 days sea voyage. At some point, Crimea may be able to meet Syria's demand in the sector of rail equipment and agriculture. Companies based in Kerch, like Fiolent or Selma, manufacture rails and electro-technical equipment that could be exported to the Arab Republic (*Rossiskaya Gazeta* 2019). A Syrian-Crimean Chamber of Commerce was established in December 2018, and both partners worked out the creation of maritime companies for their trade. The recognition by Damascus of the independence of South Ossetia and Abkhazia

Table 5.1 Russia-Syria bilateral trade (2008–2019), $US million

2008	*2009*	*2010*	*2011*	*2012*	*2013*	*2014*	*2015*	*2016*	*2017*	*2018*	*2019*
1979	1173	1158	1991	657	338	594	312	194	282.7	401.1	173.8

Source Author elaboration on the basis of the Russian Federal Customs Database

in May 2018 was above all a political gesture toward Moscow and had a secondary economic meaning. Some time later, in April 2019, the tax-free agreement signed in 2018 by Sukhumi and Damascus for their bilateral trade was ratified (*RIA Novosti* 2019c). In 2020, Syria eventually struck its first deal to purchase Russian wheat (200,000 tons) (*Zerno on Line* 2020). For the country which has struggled with dramatic fires and poor harvests, this seems to be a thin lifeline.

These Black Sea connections reflect Moscow's willingness to build another politico-economic reality, outside the framework of traditional international standards. However, by building fragile economic bridges with these sanctioned republics, the Kremlin further deters potential foreign actors from investing in Syria, since they would work in a business environment near "toxic" entities. On the other hand, with regard to their experience, Russian and Iranian companies are more comfortable with the idea of working in a sanctioned environment. However, the fact that this initiative to connect Syria, Crimea and Abkhazia occurred in 2018–2019, at a time when Moscow submitted its roadmap for Syrian reconstruction to the USA, confirms that there is little coordination, or even no strategy, in Russia as to how to attract foreign economic actors to rebuild the Arab Republic. Moscow's initiatives might also reflect the Kremlin's disillusion with regard to the involvement of Western countries in the reconstruction in Syria, while Eastern actors from Asia and the Gulf—which do not really care about Crimea, may still inject money into the Arab Republic.

Russia's Refugee Initiative to the Rescue of the Reconstruction of Syria

Facing difficulties in attracting economic aid and investments to Syria due to the international sanctions, Russia built on the idea of the return of the refugees as a way to support domestic reconciliation and the country's reconstruction. However, Moscow's initiative for the refugees faced the political resistance of Western countries and the skepticism of Damascus.

Moscow's Roadmap for the Return of the Syrian Refugees

Russia seized the opportunity of the meeting between presidents Putin and Trump in Helsinki on July 16, 2018, to hand the USA, via a military channel, a roadmap for the reconstruction of Syria and the return of 1.7 million of the 5.5 million Syrian refugees in a first ambitious stage

(*Reuters* 2018c). Planned under the auspices of the Joint Coordination Centre of the Russian Defence Ministry and the Russian Foreign Ministry for refugees, this initiative also aimed at giving an impetus to the stalling political process supervised in Geneva by then UN Special Envoy for Syria, Staffan De Mistura. It was also designed to foster the formation of the Constitutional Committee formally created during the Congress of Sochi in January 2018.[6] With this roadmap, Russia tried to link the question of the return of the Syrian refugees directly to the issues of the political settlement of the crisis and the challenge of the construction. However, contrary to the Europeans and the Americans who had demanded concrete commitments regarding the political transition and the strict enforcement of UN Resolution N° 2254 (December 18, 2015) before committing any financial assistance, Russia's initiative first put forward the issue of the return of the refugees. However, in the absence of any agenda regarding political transition in Syria, Moscow's plan was doomed to fail from the very beginning, at least in the Western countries' eyes. Despite the fact that Moscow planned that 200,000 people could return to Syria from Europe, and deep intra-EU tensions regarding the question of the migrants, the Europeans suspected Moscow of maneuvering in order to circumvent the delicate question of the political fate of Bashar Al-Assad.

On the other hand, two other countries were more successfully targeted by Russia's proposal: Lebanon and Jordan, home to refugees numbering, respectively, 976,000 (almost a quarter of the population of Lebanon) and 670,000, according to the United Nations High Commissioner for Refugees. Moscow's plan was rather ambitious since it envisioned the progressive return of no fewer than respectively 890,000 and 150,000 of the Syrian refugees to Syria (*News24* 2018). The Kremlin bet in particular on its relatively good and expanding ties with Amman and Beirut to promote this roadmap, and ease the burden of the refugees on these two countries, which displayed a genuine interest in Moscow's plan. Shortly after the roadmap was presented to the USA in late July 2018 Russia and Lebanon established a joint committee for the return of

---

[6] On January 30, 2018, this congress gathered 1500 Syrians presented by Moscow as representatives of the Syrian people to create an umbrella platform that would bring together those who were already part of existing negotiating tracks such as Astana and Geneva. However, the outcomes of the Sochi Congress were disappointing, even from Moscow's perspective. See Barmin (2018).

the refugees (The National News July 26, 2018). Russian and Lebanese convergences on the issue of the refugees were taking shape against a background of a relative rapprochement between Moscow and Beirut. A few months earlier, in February 2018, a robust bilateral defense agreement[7] had been prepared, before the Lebanese Parliament eventually rejected it in late March-early April due to US political pressure (Kuznetsov 2018). Moreover, beyond the question of the refugees, the Kremlin also sees its relationship with Lebanon through the lens of Syria's economic reconstruction. Developing ties with Beirut may, in Moscow's eyes, boost Russia-Syria business relations, as there are deep personal connections between Lebanese and Syrian citizens, some of the latter having obtained Lebanese citizenship (Matveev 2019c). However, considering the scale of the Lebanese domestic crisis, it remains to be seen to what extent the country can act as a "bridge" for Russia's business in Syria and Syria's reconstruction. The catastrophic explosion in the port of Beirut that occurred on August 4, 2020, deprived Syria of the main entry point for freight coming from the Gulf (Matveev 2020). The capacities of the port of Tripoli cannot match the demand, and international maritime operators are reluctant to use Tartus and Latakia in Syria because of the sanctions. Jordan also displayed strong interest in Russia's plan, and on October 15, 2018, the Nassib checkpoint at the Syrian-Jordanian border was reopened three years after it closed (*Reuters* 2018b). For Amman, the issue was not only the departure of the refugees, but also the revival of the economic ties with Syrian and the progressive reactivation of political relations with its neighbor (Haddad Kreidie, Marks 2018). As early as November 2018, a Jordanian parliamentary delegation was visiting Damascus (*Roya News* 2018). Egypt was also part of the plan with 100,000 refugees supposed to return to Syria.

With more than 3.5 million persons on its soil Turkey hosts by far the largest number of Syrian refugees. According to Moscow's initiative,

---

[7] This bilateral defense agreement contained five main points. First, Russian warships were granted the right to visit Lebanese ports and the possibilities of undergoing repair in Beirut. The Russian air force would have gained access to Lebanese airspace. Secondly, the deal mentioned the joint use of three bases (Ryak, near the Bekaa region, another near Saida and the third in the governorate of Akkar in the north) for the purpose of antiterrorist missions. Thirdly, the parties agreed to share information and to cooperate on antiterrorist questions. Fourth, the Russian anti-air systems based in Syria would have defended Lebanese airspace. Lastly, Russia committed to the supply of military hardware in the framework of a renewed military-technical cooperation. See Kuznetsov (2018),

300,000 refugees could return home from Turkey. In October 2019 in Sochi, Russia and Turkey struck a deal regarding northeast Syria. Article 8 of the document emphasizes that they will make "joint efforts […] to facilitate the return of refugees in a safe and voluntary manner" (President of Russia 2019) and to resettle them in a 120-km long strip of land between the towns of Ras al-Ayn and Tal Abyad controlled by Turkish troops and proxies. However, the exact number of refugees is not stated in the text. A few weeks before, President Erdogan had stated during a speech he delivered at the UN General Assembly that Turkey had drawn up a plan that was supposed to resettle around one million Syrian refugees in a safe zone 480 km long (*Reuters* 2019). In short, the Turks promoted their own plan to relocate the Syrian refugees to Syria, in the so-called safe zones they intended to create in northern Syria, after having cleared these areas from any Kurdish-linked combat activities.

Linking the Issue of the Refugees to the Political Process

While Russia's plan could also be seen as part of a broader diplomatic effort to develop its ties with Lebanon and Jordan, its concrete results were nevertheless quite limited regarding the goal to favor the return home of the Syrian refugees. As of 2018, only 56,000 persons—or nearly 1% of the overall refugees outside Syria—had returned home (United Nations Economic and Social Commission for Western Asia, Centre for Syrian Studies 2020, 28). According to the UN, the overall number of people who had returned home in 2020, including IDPs should have been 260,000 whereas Russia's figures are much higher, with 850,000 people (*Kommersant* 2020a). While it may not have effectively delivered its plan, Russia's strategy however sent a signal to regional players that Moscow was ready to play a humanitarian role. However, the fact that it took place while the Kremlin was experiencing difficulties establishing the Constitutional Committee created by the Syrian People Congress held in Sochi on January 30, 2018, fueled suspicion regarding its real goal. The Kremlin's proposal regarding the refugees was indeed largely seen in the EU and the USA as an attempt to bolster Russian sponsored political talks more than a genuine roadmap to resettle the refugees. The question was also raised regarding Damascus's interest in seeing the Sunni population it perceived as disloyal returning to Syria. Russia has criticized Western attitudes, saying that "the politicization" of the issue of the refugees was counterproductive (*TASS* 2020), and was later joined in its criticisms by

Lebanon which deplored the West's attempt to prevent the return of the refugees (*RIA Novosti* 2020).

In 2018 Russia raised the idea of holding an international conference for the return of the refugees. As part of the package presented to the Americans in summer 2018, this project gained traction with great difficulty and the conference was eventually held in Damascus on November 11–12, 2020. The event gathered 37 countries (including Iran, India, China, Brazil...), while Western actors, deterred by US pressure or just feeling uncomfortable with the idea of doing business in Syria, boycotted it.[8] During the conference, Moscow pledged $1 billion to rebuild Syria (*Kommersant* 2020a), a sum that could be added to the $850 million committed by Moscow back in April 2016 (*Kommersant* 2016).[9] Other fora have figured out financial assistance to Syria. The last Brussels Conference on "Supporting the Future of Syria and the Region" co-sponsored by the UN and the EU—the fourth of its kind—was held in late June 2020. During this conference, participants pledged 6.9 billion euros, of which two-thirds came from the EU (Aksenyonok 2020). For their part, the "Friends of Syria" members, a group of countries including the USA, Great Britain and France, pledged a $9.6 billion assistance package provided that a political process toward a post-Assad Syria takes shape (*Arab Weekly* 2020).

The Limited Impact of the Syrian Factor on Russia's Domestic Context

According to official statistics, since 2010 Russia has granted temporary asylum to 8307 persons coming from Syria.[10] If in 2011 only two Syrians were granted this status, the maximum was reached in 2015 after Moscow's military intervention with 1924 requests receiving a positive answer. Formally, this means that people getting this status can stay in Russia for a year and have the possibility to work. However, they do not receive any kind of financial or material assistance (Glazunova 2019).

---

[8] The biggest delegation was the Russian one while other countries were represented at the level of their respective ambassador. See *Kommersant* (2020a).

[9] This money was set to be injected for the reconstruction of oil and gas facilities, and electrification.

[10] See the database of Rosstat (in Russian): http://gks.ru/free_doc/new_site/population/demo/tab-migr4.htm. In comparison, Russia has granted temporary asylum to more than a million Ukrainians since 2014.

Most of the Syrians living in Russia under this status are based in Moscow or in the region of Moscow. Considering the Russian policy relating to asylum seekers, Syrian refugees do not represent an economic burden for the Federal budget. Therefore, and contrary to what happens in Western Europe and in Turkey where the question of the social cost of the migrants has been polarizing, this issue is not really raised in Russia regarding people coming from the Middle East and North Africa. In Turkey, the question of the Syrian refugees has even become a domestic issue, conducting to inter-community tensions (Turkey's Syrian Refugees: Defusing Metropolitan Tensions 2018).

In Russia, the Syrian factor tends to be perceived by the Russians through the lens of security and relations with the West. Surveys carried out by Russian polling institutes after Moscow's military campaign show an eroding interest by the population for the Syrian story. If only 8% of the respondents declared that they followed the Syrian crisis with attention in June 2013, this figure jumped to 25% in October 2015, soon after Russia's military intervention in Syria. In April 2018, in the context of tensions between the Euro-Atlantic community and Russia regarding the alleged use of chemical weapons by the loyalist forces in Douma, 31% of the Russians polled declared they were following the events in Syria attentively (86% with those who declared they were just paying attention to the situation in the Arab Republic). Yet, the prism remains the relations with the West since 55% declared simultaneously that they feared the Syrian dossier might trigger a "Third World War".[11] According to a survey carried out by another center, the VTsIOM, in February 2018, 34% of the people polled supported Russia's involvement in the Syrian conflict, while 24% would prefer to see a more cautious involvement.[12] In April 2019, Levada released a new survey whose results highlighted the Russians' clear disinterest for Syria. Only 61% declared they had an interest in the Syrian conflict (respectively 13% having a strong interest—the lowest rate since 2013—and 48% just paying some attention, the lowest rate ever). Those answering that they knew absolutely nothing about Syria were 39%, which

[11] See the results of the survey (in Russian) on the Levada Center website: https://www.levada.ru/2018/05/16/siriya/.

[12] See the results of the survey on the VTsIOM website (in Russian): https://wciom.ru/analytical-reviews/analiticheskii-obzor/novaya-vspyshka-vojny-v-sirii-mnenie-rossiyan.

is the highest rate ever since Levada began this survey.[13] While 51% of the people polled supported Russia's policy in Syria, 55% called to put an end to the military operation in the Arab Republic. The social orientations of Vladimir Putin's new mandate (since March 2018)—pension reforms, increase in VAT, national projects to boost Russia's GDP…—on the one hand, and the nature of the conflict in Syria that has morphed into a low-intensity war, on the other, can explain the relative disinterest of the Russians. Therefore, the Kremlin cannot count on the Syrian dossier to boost its popularity. Patriotism relating to the military campaign has exhausted its potential for domestic political support with most of the people being much more worried by the socioeconomic context, especially since the COVID crisis has erupted. And the question of the Syrian migrants does not really fit into this picture. Neither does the issue of Syria's reconstruction, which remains far from the Russian reality.

CONCLUSION

Russia has not drafted any comprehensive strategy regarding Syria's reconstruction and cannot support the reconstruction of the country on its own, and has never intended to do so. The reconstruction process has more to do with cementing the Kremlin military victory into a political success through the attraction of financial aid supporting Syria's reconstruction, in the frameworks outlined by Moscow. However, considering the context of persisting confrontation between Russia and the Euro-Atlantic community, this approach does not appear realistic. Since 2018, the Kremlin has tried to push the reconstruction agenda through initiatives that highlight the fact that, in its eyes, rebuilding the country should be part of the national reconciliation process. In the meantime, the Kremlin has helped major Russian conglomerates to secure key deals in the Arab Republic in the infrastructure, telecommunications, electronics, energy, and construction sectors. Mostly relying on government-to-government level contacts through the Permanent Russian-Syrian Intergovernmental Commission, Russia has sponsored conglomerates robust enough to run the financial and security risks of investing in Syria and has facilitated their access to the Syrian government. Besides this business-to-government approach, Moscow still promotes

---

[13] See the results of the survey (in Russian) on the Levada Center website: https://www.levada.ru/2019/05/06/sobytiya-v-sirii/.

the idea of involving small and medium Russian business in the reconstruction of the Arab Republic. Yet, poor records of fruitful connections between Russian and Syrian small businesses, and a not very conducive business environment in Syria, have so far prevented the B2B level from gaining traction. Tomorrow, should Western companies decide to work in Syria, Russian small and medium business will have even more difficulty accessing market shares. Therefore, the Kremlin has sent the signal that it considers a more centralized approach where the Permanent Russian-Syrian Intergovernmental Commission could play a greater role in the future.

References

Abu Ismail, Khalid, Bilal Al-Kiswan, Salim Araji, Omar Dahi, Raymond Hinnebusch, Omar Imady, Manuella Ehme, and Ahmad Shikh Ebid. 2020. "Syria at War: Eight Years On." Report. *UN-ESCWA*, September 24. https://reliefweb.int/sites/reliefweb.int/files/resources/Syria-at-War-8-years-on-Report-Final.pdf.

Aksenyonok, Alexander. 2020. "Rebuilding Syria: Is 'Selective Cooperation' Between Russia and the EU Possible?" *Valdai Discussion Club*, August 20. https://valdaiclub.com/a/highlights/rebuilding-syria-is-selective-cooper ation-between/.

Arab Weekly. 2020. "China's 'Rebuilding' Role in Iraq Could Serve as a Template for Syria After Years of Conflict." March 1.

Barmin, Yuri. 2018. "The Syrian Congress in Sochi: Too Much Too Soon." *Russian International Affairs Council*, February 2. https://russiancouncil. ru/en/analytics-and-comments/analytics/the-syrian-congress-in-sochi-too-much-too-soon/.

Daher, Joseph. 2019. "The Dynamics and Evolution of UAE-Syria Relations: Between Expectations and Obstacles." Technical Report, EUI RSCAS; Middle East Directions (MED); Wartime and Post-Conflict in Syria; 2019/14. European University Institute. doi: https://doi.org/10.2870/40366.

Diplomat. 2018. "China and the Reconstruction of Syria." July 28.

Financial Times. 2019. "Moscow Collects Its Spoils of War in Assad's Syria." September 1.

Glazunova, Lyubov. 2019. "Problemy sirijskih bežencev v Rossii." *Riddle.*

Haddad Kreidie, Lina, and Jesse Marks. 2018. "Jordan's Interest in a Stable Syria." *Carnegie Sada*, August 23. https://carnegie-mec.org/sada/77094.

International Crisis Group. 2018. "Turkey's Syrian Refugees: Defusing Metropolitan Tensions." Europe Report N°248, January 29. https://www.

crisisgroup.org/europe-central-asia/western-europemediterranean/turkey/248-turkeys-syrian-refugees-defusing-metropolitan-tensions.

Izvestia. 2018. "Ålta rasširået gorizonty." April 20.

Jaecke, Gregor, and David Labude. 2020. "De-escalation zones in Syria." Country Report. *Konrad Adenauer Stiftung*, June 3. https://www.kas.de/en/country-reports/detail/-/content/de-escalation-zones-in-syria.

Kommersant. 2016. "Rossiâ potratit €850 mln na vosstanovlenie Sirii." April 25.

Kommersant. 2020a. "Spasti râdovogo beženca." November 12.

Kommersant. 2020b. "Putin vvel dolžnost' specpredstavitelâ po Sirii i naznačil im posla v Damaske." May 25.

Kuznetsov, A. 2018. *O vozmožnom voennom sotrudničestve meždu Rossiej i Livanom.* Institut bližnego vostoka.

Matveev, Igor. 2020. "Rossii pora opredelit'sâ s èkonomičeskoj strategiej v Sirii." *Ekspert.*

Matveev, Igor. 2019a. "Russian-Syrian Business Cooperation: Challenges and Prospects." Discussion Paper. *Geneva Center for Security and Peace.*

Matveev, Igor. 2019b. "Russian Businesses Wary of Syria Reconstruction Investments." *Al-Monitor.*

Matveev, Igor. 2019c. "Russia, Lebanon Seek Synergy in Projects to Rebuild Syria." *Al-Monitor*, August 7. https://www.al-monitor.com/originals/2019/08/russia-seek-embrace-lebanon-syria-reconstruction-plan.html.

Matveev, Igor. 2019d. "Syrian Reconstruction Expo Draws Russian Businesses." *Al-Monitor*, September 30. https://www.al-monitor.com/originals/2019/09/russia-syria-iran-investments-challenges.html.

News24. 2018. "Hundreds of Syrian Refugees Return Home from Lebanon." July 28.

Novaya Gazeta. 2020. "Vagner. Pervaâ neft'" January 19.

President of Russia. 2019. "Memorandum of Understanding Between the Russian Federation and the Republic of Turkey." October 22, 2019. http://en.kremlin.ru/supplement/5452.

Politico. 2020. "Little-Known U.S. Firm Secures Deal for Syrian Oil." August 3.

Ramani, Samuel. 2019. "Russia's Eye on Syrian Reconstruction." *Carnegie Sada*, January 31. https://carnegieendowment.org/sada/78261.

Reuters. 2018a. "UAE Reopens Syria Embassy in Boost for Assad." December 27.

Reuters. 2018b. "Jordan and Syria Reopen Nassib Border Crossing." October 15.

Reuters. 2018c. "Exclusive: Despite Tensions, Russia Seeks U.S. Help to Rebuild Syria." August 3.

Reuters. 2019. "Turkey Plans $27 Billion Housing Project in Northeast Syria." September 27.

RIA Novosti. 2019a. "V Sirii soobŝili o načale geologorazvedki nefti sovmestno s Rossiej." December 25.

RIA Novosti. 2019b. "Rossiâ vosstanovila rabotu edinstvennogo v Sirii zavoda udobrenij." December 17.

RIA Novosti. 2019c. "Siriâ ratificirovala soglašenie o bespošlinnoj torgovle s Abhaziej." April 19.

RIA Novosti. 2020. "Prezident Livana: Zapad mešaet iniciative po vozvraŝeniû bežencev v Siriû." May 4.

Rossiskaya Gazeta. 2019. "Ot porta k portu." January 22.

Roya News. 2018. "Jordanian Parliamentary Delegation Visits Damascus." November 19.

TASS. 2020. "Posol RF zaâvil, čto Zapad sil′no politiziruet process vozvraŝeniâ bežencev v Siriû." November 11.

The National News. 2018. "Lebanon and Russia form committee on Syrian refugee repatriation." July 26.

Zerno On Line. 2020. "Siriâ vpervye v 2020g. smogla zaklûčit′ kontrakt na zakupku rossijskoj pšenicy." July 10.

CHAPTER 6

The Role of Iran in the Syrian Conflict

Bayram Sinkaya

Soon after the Arab Spring shattered Arab politics in early 2011, Bashar Assad, who had earlier replaced his father as the President of the Ba'ath regime in Syria, faced a number of domestic, regional and international challenges that aimed at forcing him to leave power. The ensuing crisis turned into a severe challenge for the ongoing alliance between the Islamic Republic in Iran and Ba'athist Syria for over three decades. Ayatollah Ali Khamenei, the Supreme Leader of the Islamic Republic, clarified Iran's position with regard to the Syria crisis in a speech he gave in June 2011 and proclaimed its resolve to stand behind Assad's rule (Abdo 2011). Accordingly, Iran has remained one of the few international actors that have stood alongside the Assad administration.

Above all else, the support for Assad was not a novel idea in Iran, instead it was based on the maintenance of the longstanding alliance between Damascus and Tehran (Goodarzi 2006; Ehteshami and Hinnebusch 1997). Moreover, that alliance had overcome the most severe

B. Sinkaya (✉)
Department of International Relations, Ankara Yıldırım Beyazıt University, Ankara, Turkey
e-mail: bsinkaya@ybu.edu.tr

B. Balci and N. Monceau (eds.), *Turkey, Russia and Iran in the Middle East*, The Sciences Po Series in International Relations and Political Economy, https://doi.org/10.1007/978-3-030-80291-2_6

challenge since its inception. Various implications of the Iranian involve-ment in the Syria crisis, and Iran's motivations for standing behind Assad have been questioned by many analysts (Phillips 2016). This chapter aims to review Iranian foreign policy toward the Syria conflict and to analyze the potential reasons that led Iranian decision-makers to lend their support to the Assad regime. It asserts that there have been several complementary narratives in circulation among the Iranian political elite that justify its involvement in the Syrian conflict and maintenance of the alliance. Accordingly, it discusses the importance of Syria under Assad through the prism of various narratives that circulated among the Iranian elite. And then, it examines the ways in which Iran has supported Assad throughout the conflict.

The Syria Conflict from the Perspective of the Iranian Elite

There are several narratives that circulate among the Iranian elite that justify Iranian involvement in the Syria conflict in support of Assad (Sadeghi-Boroujerdi 2014; Al-Smadi 2017). Those narratives are closely interlinked and complementary to each other. The first narrative is the requirement for the axis of resistance to be protected. As is well known, one of the constant themes/principles in the Islamic Republic's foreign policy, as an extension of its anti-imperialist rhetoric, has been its positioning against Israel and the USA, the so-called arrogant powers. Conversely, both Israel and the USA have designated the Islamic Republic a "hostile regime"—allegedly for its support for "terrorist organizations" and its threat to regional security and stability—and have pursued various strategies that aimed to contain, weaken, and even change the regime in Iran. Besides geopolitical and strategic considerations, inspired by the Iranian conviction of the perennial fight between good and evil, the elite of the Islamic Republic have talked of an eternal confrontation between the camps of "world imperialism" and "oppressed nations." This ideolog-ical view became dominant in Iranian foreign policy-making particularly after the growing influence of the Islamic Revolutionary Guard Corps (IRGC) in politics over the past two decades. According to that view, the USA and Israel, the primary exemplars of the imperialist camp, would never cease their plots and conspiracies against the camp of the oppressed people, arguably led by the Islamic Republic regime (Sinkaya 2016a, 67). Therefore, Iranian leaders have viewed the whole Middle East region, like most parts of the world, as a theater of confrontation between the two camps. Likewise, they are inclined to assess every single event in the neighboring areas through the prism of that eternal cosmic struggle. The American attempts to revise security arrangements and the political architecture of the Middle East after September 11, 2001, while designating Iran and Syria as part of the "axis of evil"—to be contained, defeated and transformed—led Iran to assume the mantle of "resistance" across the region (Ezadi and Akbari 2010, 37–38; Niakoee et al. 2013). Hence, the outbreak of the crisis in Syria and the ensuing developments were primarily assessed by the Iranian leadership as an extension of the perennial fight between imperialism and resistance.

Syrian rejection of peace with Israel arguably because of the latter's ongoing occupation of parts of the Golan Heights, its harboring of a number of Palestinian resistance organizations, and its bordering Lebanon made Syria an invaluable partner for Iran in the conflict between imperialism and resistance. In the words of Ali Akbar Velayati, former minister of foreign affairs and senior adviser to the Supreme Leader, Syria under Assad was regarded by Iranians as the "golden string of the resistance" (*Mehr News Agency* 2011). According to the Iranian view, regional and global powers aiming to destroy the resistance front fomented the plot in Syria while ostensibly supporting the freedoms of the Syrian people. In this respect, the then Secretary of Supreme National Security of Iran, Saeed Jalili, stated in mid-2012, "Syria is paying the price for supporting the resistance against the Zionist occupation" and reiterated Iranian firmness in standing with the Assad regime (*IRNA* 2012). Likewise, the then IRGC Commander Mohammad Alia Jafaari stated in April 2014 that Iran was "proud of supporting the resistance of the Syrian people [...] against the United States and Israel" (Donya-e Eqtesad 2014).

The second narrative that vindicated Iranian support for Assad's rule is the discourse of "strategic loneliness" (Juneau 2014). While the discourse of resistance had been built on an ideological and anti-imperialist perspective, it had also intricately intertwined with the Iranian national security culture that determined the nature and the content of its approach to the conflict in Syria. Besides some geopolitical and historical considerations, Iran is considered by the ruling elite as "strategically alone" in the region in terms of ethnicity, religion, culture and political perspectives. As a result of its "strategic loneliness," Iran is considered to be isolated and encircled by rival powers or enemies on all sides, which has amplified "security paranoia among the political elite" (Vakil 2018, 109).

The strategic loneliness led the Iranian leadership to embark on building strategic depths in its environs, and to employ the doctrine of "forward defense" (Yossef 2019) or "comprehensive deterrence" (Ahmadian and Mohseni 2019). That is, in order to compensate for its isolation, "Tehran has sought to build an asymmetric and unconventional support structure by cultivating like-minded "non-state" actors in the wider region" (Behravesh 2017). In this respect, preserving the alliance with Syria that links Iran to the "resistance organizations" has become crucial for the Iranian establishment.

There is an intricate relationship between the Iranian national security culture highlighting its loneliness and Iranian regional ambitions to project power beyond its borders. The edges of the so-called Iranian activities for defensive purposes—i.e., "comprehensive deterrence" or "forward defense"—in the near neighborhood meshes with its search for regional power status and domination (Yaari 2017). Its search for regional status is also built on a national security culture narrative emphasizing Iran's exceptional and unique status in the Middle East and the Islamic world. Accordingly, Iran has a unique geo-strategic location bridging the old continents. It is unique and exceptional in relation to its neighbors in terms of being the inheritor of one of the earliest civilizations in world history and the heir to a high culture (Zibakalam 2009). It is exceptional, also, because it realized the first "Islamic revolution" in the Muslim world. Moreover, the Islamic Republic regime has not succumbed to many challenges and pressures, and has preserved its revolution and regime over the last four decades. The Iranian perseverance in preserving its revolution has culminated in a kind of "arrogance of non-submission" among the Iranian elite (Ehteshami 2002, 285). Relying on its so-called exceptional position in the region and non-submission, many Iranians support the Iranian search for regional power status. The Iranian quest for regional power status requires it to pursue active policies in the near neighborhood for building strategic depth, cultivating pro-Iran groups, and maintaining and empowering existing allies. Then, the maintenance of an alliance with Assad's Syria, the only ally of Tehran, is singled out as invaluable in the Iranian strategic mind. Hence, the third narrative, the discourse of the Iranian quest for power has also resulted in the Iranian defense of Assad.

The former famous Commander of the *Quds Force*, in charge of operating most Iranian activities in the Middle East, Qasem Soleimani, acknowledged in September 2013 that "the resistance serves the interests of Iran" and backing the resistance has been important for the protection of its interests (*Young Journalists Club* 2013a). The building of an alliance with Syria and Hezbollah in Lebanon provided Iran with a strategic depth extending into the Mediterranean, which allowed it to overcome the challenge of being contained by hostile powers and regional rivals (Sajidi 2014). It also provided Iran with an opportunity to project power beyond its borders. Indeed, in his meetings with Assad in October 2010, and eight years later, in February 2019, Khamenei defined Iran and Syria as "strategic depths" for each other (*Tehran Times* 2019a, b). Likewise, Mahdi Ta'eb, chair of Ammar Headquarters, a think-tank operating under the auspices of Khamanei, called Syria "the 35th province of Iran" and stressed that "if Iran loses Syria, it cannot protect Tehran" (*Radiofarda* 2013).

What made Syria the "golden ring of the resistance" or the "strategic depth" of Iran is its functioning as a bridge connecting Iran to the Levant. Syria has played a special role in transmitting Iranian logistic support to the "resistance" organizations led by Hezbollah. Hence, Iran's strategic interest in Syria and the Levant lay in the preservation of a pro-Tehran regime in that country. It was very critical for Iran considering the then regional rivalry among Iran, Saudi Arabia and Turkey, and growing international pressure on Iran orchestrated by Israel and the USA (Goodarzi 2013).

Another narrative that justifies Iranian involvement in the Syria conflict is the discourse of fighting against terrorism. From the very beginning, Iran endorsed Assad's claim that the protestors were extremist groups. Iranian statesmen continuously asserted that the challenge in Syria mainly stemmed from the presence—and "implantation" of—extremist, and terrorist groups in the country (*Young Journalists Club* 2013b). The emergence of al-Nusra Front and ISIS as formidable extremist actors in the Syrian theater in early 2013 provided some validity to the Iranian arguments. In his first address to the UN General Assembly in September 2013, President Hassan Rouhani called for a "World Against Violence and Extremism." Former Deputy Foreign Minister Amir-Abdollahian, penned an article for *al-Monitor* in March 2014, and claimed that the Assad government in Syria was essentially fighting against extremist terrorists (Amir-Abdollahian 2014). Thus, terrorist groups in Syria did not only attack the Assad government but also threatened regional stability and Iranian security. Indeed, ISIS claimed responsibility for the attacks on the Iranian parliament and the mausoleum of Ayatollah Khomeini in

Tehran, in June 2017. Besides mobilizing Iranian society to support Iran's struggle in the region, the discourse of fighting terrorism invoked by the Iranian elite aimed to provide legitimacy for Assad's use of violence against the rebels and opponents, and to attract international sympathy for Iran's regional activities.

Complementary to the previous discourses, the Iranian elite circulated a sectarian narrative in order to mobilize religious sentiments and Shi'ite fighters in the service of the Iranian strategy of defending Assad. The same "terrorist" groups fighting against Assad, and the resistance axis, were presented as lackeys of the enemies of Islam: the USA and Zionism, and their regional clients. They were also called anti-Shi'ite fanatics, committed to destroying the authentic line of Islam (represented by the Shi'ite movement) and the holy shrines in Syria and Iraq (Aarabi 2020, 47). In particular, the idea of defending the shrine of Sayyidah Zaynab, daughter of Imam Ali ibn Abi Talib, located in the southern outskirts of Damascus, turned into a symbol of Shi'ite mobilization (Mathiesen 2013; Symth 2015).

Considering the aforementioned narratives validating the Iranian role in the conflict, it is almost impossible to distinguish between Iran's ideological motivations, national security interests and regional ambitions. Various narratives circulating among the elite justifying its involvement in the conflict in support of Assad culminated in wide-scale approval of Iranian regional policies by Iranian public opinion. Moreover, notwithstanding the persistence of "marginalized" critiques, the various narratives ensured the continuity of Iranian policies with regard to the conflict.

The maintenance of the alliance between the Islamic Republic and the Assad regime, however, turned the Syrian opposition into an opponent of Iranian policies in the region. Moreover, a large part of the Syrian opposition qualified Iran as an "occupying power" and a "sectarian enemy (*Naame Sham* 2014; Hassan 2016). Additionally, the opposition ensured the backing of Iran's regional rivals and Western countries, which heightened Iranian anxiety regarding a regime change in Syria. A prospective collapse of the Ba'ath regime in Syria would not only remove the special partner of Iran in the region, but would also threaten Iran's acquisitions and influence in the region. A regime change in Syria would cut its access to Lebanon, eventually lead to the weakening of Hezbollah, and be alarming for the pro-Iran and Shi'ite-dominated government in Iraq. Indeed, the ensuing developments in the region proved the destabilizing effects of the Syria conflict on Iraqi politics. It emboldened the opponents of the Iraqi government and unleashed a series of anti-government protests that became entangled in a struggle against the Iranian influence in that country.

Against this background, Iran pursued two simultaneous strategies toward the conflict in Syria. The first is the fully fledged defense of the Assad regime by providing it with the necessary military and economic support. Iran's second strategy relied on the diplomacy track to save Assad and keep Iranian influence in Syria.

IRAN'S DEFENSE OF THE ASSAD REGIME

Aside from rhetorical nuances uttered by Iranian statesmen, keeping Assad in power remained the most preferable scenario for Iran. Velayati acknowledged that the removal of Assad was considered "a red line" for Tehran, which was resolved to keep him in power (*Press TV* 2016). In the early stages of the conflict, Iranian support for Assad was limited to providing him with technical equipment for chasing opposition activists, and advising Syrian officials on the suppression of mass demonstrations. Once the anti-regime protests had turned into a protracted armed conflict beginning in 2012, and severely threatened the rule of Assad, Iran mobilized extensive military means and economic resources in order to back his "resistance."

Iranian military support for Assad could be examined under three headings: provision of military supplies, deployment of Iranian forces, and mobilization of fellow Shi'ite fighters. Since the eruption of the conflict, Iran has become the primary supplier of arms for the Assad regime. Iranian supplies included missiles, rockets, drones, etc. In order to transfer arms to Syria, Iran initially utilized highways, railways and airways extending from Tehran to Damascus via Turkey. However, Turkish prohibition of such Iranian shipments in early 2011 forced Iran to build an air corridor between Iran and Syria through Iraqi airspace. Iranian exploitation of Iraqi air space led to some friction between the USA and Iraq. Additionally, the USA sanctioned leading Iranian air companies for carrying military equipment and personnel to Syria. Finally, Israel started to hit alleged Iranian deliveries of weapons and warriors. Then, Iran engaged in building a land corridor extending from Tehran to Beirut, which was helped by instability in Iraq and the Iranian involvement in there.

Iran's military support for Assad included the deployment of officers from IRGC, the Army, and the Iranian Police, first as advisors, later as combatants. The Quds Force of IRGC was active in the Syrian theater from the very beginning of the opposition demonstrations. Then Deputy Commander of the Quds Force, Ismael Kaani, and IRGC Commander Mohammad Ali Jafari separately confirmed the presence of Quds members in Syria (*Radiofarda* 2012). However, the number of troops deployed by Iran was always controversial and changed depending on the intensity of the conflict. A conservative estimate, as of early 2014, stated that nearly 60–70 senior officers accompanied by many commissioners and volunteers were present in Syria (Saul and Hafezi 2014). By mid-2015, it was estimated that there were approximately two thousand Iranian warriors in Syria, which was reinforced in the following year (McInnis 2015). Another report claimed that, as of 2016, the total number of IRGC personnel and Iranian paramilitary forces deployed in Syria was between 6500 to 9200 (Ansari and Tabrizi 2016, 5).

In addition to advising, training and supporting established security institutions in Syria, the Quds Force reportedly organized, trained and equipped the National Defense Force (NDF), resembling the Basij organization of Iran. Referring to the NDF as a volunteer mobilization force numbering around seventy thousand members, Hossein Hamedani, then IRGC Commander in charge of Iranian operations in Syria, called it the formation of "a second Hezbollah" (Sadeghi-Boroujerdi 2014, 55, 63). Besides the NDF, Iran recruited local people from the zones of armed conflict as local defense forces and mobilized local Shi'ite and Alawite militias.

Iranian support for Assad was also marked by its mobilization of Shi'ite militias from different countries. First, Lebanese Hezbollah joined the war immediately after the Syrian regime forces lost control over the al-Qusayr district adjacent to the Lebanese border, in 2012. After that, reportedly more than six thousand Hezbollah members fought on different fronts along with the regime forces (De Luce 2015). Likewise, hundreds of Iraqi Shi'ite militias, who were later organized under the *Abo'l Fadl Abbas* Brigade, flocked to the Syrian theater as of 2012 in the name of protecting the shrine of Sayyida Zaynab (Sadeghi-Boroujerdi 2014, 59). In the same vein, Iran mobilized Shi'ites from Afghanistan and Pakistan that fought under the *Fatemiyoun* and *Zainabiyoun* brigades along with the regime forces.

The mission of Iranian forces and their allies in Syria was not limited to defending holy shrines or positions of the Syrian government led by Assad, but also included fighting against the rebels and "terrorists" in different parts of the country. When al-Nusra and ISIS seized considerable areas, Iranian generals refocused their efforts and turned to fight against terrorism. After Assad's allies took control of Abu Kamal, the last stronghold of ISIS in Syria in November 2017, Soleimani sent a letter to Khamenei, informing him of the "termination of the rule of [… the] U.S./Zionist-made terrorist group" (*Khameneiir* 2017).

Iran also provided an economic lifeline to the Assad regime. In addition to paying salaries to the Shi'ite militias and equipping them, Iran provided Syria with low-interest credits and discounted or free oil products (Philips and Lee 2015). Iran granted over 5.6 billion dollars credit in order to finance Syria's imports of oil and food stuffs. Additionally, Iran provided some aid in order to meet basic consumer needs. Iranian companies were engaged in recovering and operating some power plants in Syria in order to supply electricity. In order to prop up the ailing Syrian economy, the Iranian government signed a free trade agreement with the Assad government in December 2011, with the aim of increasing the amount of bilateral trade from 500 million US dollars to two billion. In order to boost trade with Syria, the two governments promoted mutual trade fairs. Stefan de Mistura, then Special Envoy of the UN and the Arab League for Syria, estimated in 2016 that annually it cost Iran six billion dollars to support Assad. According to Western intelligence, Tehran was estimated to spend an annual average of 15–20 billion dollars on Syria, including its payments to the Shi'ite militants (Lake 2015).

Iranian Diplomacy to Save Assad

Underestimating the extent of the Assad regime's use of extreme force against the opposition and Iranian assistance to it, in the rising spiral of violence, Iranian diplomats protested against the militarization of the conflict and called for a political solution. Former Minister of Foreign Affairs, Ali Akbar Salehi reiterated his government's view of the developments in Syria in a meeting with his Syrian counterpart Walid Moallem in March 2013, at the height of the armed clashes between the rebels and the regime forces (*Young Journalists Club* 2013c). There were four points highlighted by Saleh, and continuously repeated by Iranian diplomats. First of all, according to the Iranian view, Bashar Assad was considered to be the elected and legal president of Syria. Moreover, he enjoyed the support of the Syrian people, which helped him to withstand many pressures. Second, no one has the right to dictate their will to the Syrian people and decide on government in Syria. Any external call for Assad to leave power is regarded by Iranians as interference in domestic affairs. Third, the main reasons for the deepening of conflict in Syria were the implantation of foreign fighters and the arming of the Syrian opposition by external powers. The Assad government was primarily fighting against extremists and terrorists. Fourth, the only solution to the conflict was political negotiation between the opposition and the government. Syrian people have citizenship rights and legitimate demands in seeking freedoms, and the government should answer the demands of the people. However, the role of external powers in solving the conflict should be limited to stopping the flow of arms and foreign fighters to Syria and helping the Syrian government to stabilize the country.

Against its rhetoric of finding a political solution for the conflict, it was beyond the capacity of Tehran to ensure such an answer. Above all else, the Islamic Republic's access to the Syrian opposition and rebels was very limited because of the maintenance of a long-lasting alliance between the Assad regime and the Islamic Republic. Moreover, the Islamic Republic's active military support for Damascus from the outset of the conflict curtailed Iranian capacity to cultivate effective ties with the opponents of Assad.

Additionally, the conflict was rapidly internationalized in a short space of time. The USA and the EU imposed some sanctions against Syria as early as May 2011 "for human rights abuses" and "unacceptable violence against peaceful protestors" (*BBC News* 2011). Many countries including Turkey and the Gulf kingdoms withdrew their ambassadors from Damascus in August, arguably in protest against Assad's resistance to reform demands. The Arab League suspended Syria's membership in November 2011. An international initiative called the Group of Friends of the Syrian People consisting of representatives from over 60 countries and observers from international and regional organizations including the Arab League, the Organization of Islamic Cooperation (OIC) and the Gulf Cooperation Council (GCC) held consecutive meetings in the spring of 2012. In order to establish an inclusive front organization bringing together diverse groups, foreign supporters of the opposition arranged the National Coalition for Syrian Revolutionary and Opposition Forces in Doha, in November 2012. The National Coalition was soon recognized by many states including the USA, France, the UK, Qatar, Saudi Arabia, and Turkey as "the legitimate representative of the Syrian people."

Iran was excluded from most of the international and regional forums addressing the conflict in Syria. In reaction to the internationalization of the conflict and its exclusion from those platforms, Tehran organized an international conference, which envoys from nearly thirty non-Western countries attended in August 2012. The final communique of the conference reflected Iranian concerns and diplomatic perspectives (*Iran Primer* 2012). A week after the formation of the Syrian National Coalition in Doha, Tehran hosted a "national dialogue" conference with the participation of over two hundred representatives from various political parties, communities and regions in Syria, with the purpose of ending the violence in the country (Rezaian 2012). Iranian initiatives, however, did not yield considerable results.

Under those conditions, Iranian diplomacy primarily aimed at preventing any military intervention, particularly American, that would lead to a regime change in Damascus. Hence, it supported any proposal that did not envisage an immediate regime change. In this regard, while denouncing the Friends of Syrian People meetings and the Arab League initiative that asked for Assad's elimination from power, Tehran supported the Annan Plan of March 2012 (*Al Jazeera* 2012). However, Iran was left out of the Action Group for Syria, which was established within the framework of the Annan Plan.[1] Moreover, the Action Group held a conference in Geneva in June 2012, and called for "the establishment of an inclusive transitional governing body with full executive powers" (*UN News Center* 2012) that hinted at the removal of Assad from power. For that reason, Tehran did not approve the Geneva communique, however, it showed its willingness to be part of the process.

In the meantime, Iran strived to obtain a place for itself in various proposals for the solution of the conflict. Thereby, it aimed at both providing a diplomatic shield for Assad, and ensuring a secure role for Iran in order to perpetuate its lasting interests in Syria. Iran welcomed the then Egyptian President Mohammad Morsi's call for the establishment of a quartet—comprising Egypt, Turkey, Saudi Arabia and Iran—in

---

[1] The Action Group consisted of the five permanent members of the UN Security Council, plus the EU, and four regional countries (Turkey, Iraq, Qatar, Kuwait). Kofi Annan advocated Iranian participation in the negotiations and visited Tehran in July 2012.

August 2012 in order to address the Syria conflict within the framework of OIC. After several rounds of meetings between Egypt, Iran, and Turkey—boycotted by Saudi Arabia—this initiative remained inconclusive as well.

An opportunity emerged for Iran to join the UN-sponsored Geneva meetings (Geneva II) in early 2014, when Ban Ki-moon, Secretary General of the United Nations, sent an invitation to the Iranian government. However, because of the reactions of the USA and the Syrian National Coalition, and because Iran did not approve the Geneva I communique, he was forced to withdraw that invitation (Charbonneou and Nichols 2014). Following a series of failed peace initiatives, and the Russian military involvement in the conflict, the foreign ministers of the USA and Russia co-chaired a new attempt to prepare international talks for solving the Syria conflict. Then, for the first time, Iran was invited to join the International Syria Support Group and peace negotiations to be held in Vienna in late October 2015. Iran played a minor role in the Vienna talks that endorsed the Geneva Communique of 2012 and called for negotiations between representatives of the Syrian government and the opposition. But it did not mean a change in Iran's policy of support for Assad, and Tehran repeated that "only the Syrian people enjoy the right to decide" his fate and future role in the country (*Iran Primer* 2015).

Iran was not alone in its bid to prevent military intervention in Syria and to stave off pressure over Assad. Since the outset of the conflict, Russia had adopted a position similar to the Iranian one in terms of rejecting foreign interference in Syria and providing justifications for Assad's battering of his opponents. Russia also continued its provision of arms and military equipment to the Assad regime and, exploiting its status on the UN Security Council, did not allow extraordinary measures to be taken against Assad. When the prospect of American military intervention escalated to an alarming level because of the Assad forces' alleged use of chemical weapons in the summer of 2013, Iran and Russia increased their coordination in the Syrian theater. Russia also continuously supported the Iranian bid to gain a seat in international negotiations over the future of Syria that eventually became successful in the Vienna talks. In return, Iran welcomed the Russian military involvement in the theater in September 2015, ostensibly for helping the Syrian government to fight against ISIS and "takfiri terrorists." Tehran opened its air space and the airbase in Hamadan for use by Russian warplanes. Iran and Russia, along with Syria and Iraq, set up a joint "information center" in Baghdad in order to coordinate their activities against ISIS.

Ironically, the discourse of fighting terrorism, particularly ISIS, in Syria—along with Iraq—drew and provided justification for American troop deployment on the ground after 2014. Moreover, successive US administrations nurtured and maintained a partnership with the People's Protection Units (YPG)—an offshoot of the Kurdistan Workers' Party (PKK)—seeking Kurdish autonomy in the north of Syria. Then, Iranian leaders started to emphasize the importance of preserving the territorial integrity of Syria. The American partnership with the YPG was also worrying for Turkey, which was one of the factors that led Ankara to revise its Syria policy.

The common grounds between Iran and Russia, along with Turkey's changing strategic considerations relating to Syria, helped to set up a trilateral meeting among the foreign ministers of the respective countries in December 2016, in Moscow. The declaration issued at the end of the meeting reiterated the parties' "full respect for the sovereignty, independence, unity and territorial integrity of the Syrian Arab Republic as a multi-ethnic, multi-religious, non-sectarian, democratic and secular state." The parties also reiterated their commitment to a peaceful solution to the conflict in Syria, and to fight jointly against ISIS and al-Nusra. They also declared "their readiness to facilitate and become the guarantors of the prospective agreement, being negotiated, between the Syrian government and the opposition" (Sinkaya 2016b) Thus, the Moscow declaration paved the way for the Astana Process for the solution to the protracted conflict in Syria. The Astana Process led by Iran, Russia and Turkey has proved to be the most enduring cooperation platform to expand local cease-fires and provide a temporary stability in the country, and to promote Syrian-led negotiations within the framework of UN Security Council Resolution 2254. The Astana Process, however, has yet to achieve a lasting resolution of the conflict.

CONCLUSION

Virtually a decade after the outset of the conflict, Bashar Al-Assad, underpinned by his allies led by Iran and Russia, has preserved his power in Damascus and recovered his authority in most of the country. Assad paid a visit to Tehran in February 2019, where he expressed his gratitude to Iran. In his meeting with the Supreme Leader Khamanei, Assad said,

"The Islamic Republic of Iran stood on our side in a sacrificing way and it is imperative to congratulate Your Excellency and all Iranians on this victory and to thank them." (*Tehran Times* 2019a). Commenting on the visit, Ayatollah Mohammad Ali Movahedi Kermani, Tehran Friday prayer leader, stated that it "sent a clear message to the Israeli regime and the USA. that the Islamic Republic would stay in Syria" (*Tehran Times* 2019b).

In parallel to Assad's claimed victory, Iranian activities in Syria have been directed with two purposes. The first is the strengthening of military cooperation between the two countries. Defense ministers of the two countries, Amir Hatami and Abdollah Ayub signed a military cooperation agreement in August 2018 (*RFE/RL* 2018). Subsequently, General Bagheri, Joint Chief of Staff of the Iranian Armed Forces, visited Damascus in July 2020, where he signed an agreement with his Syrian counterpart in order to enhance military and security cooperation between the two countries. The agreement reportedly envisaged the deployment of Iranian aerial defense systems in Syria that aimed at strengthening Syria's air defense. Besides validating the Iranian military presence in the country, the agreement is also regarded as an attempt to deter and prevent Israeli air attacks inside Syria, also to reduce Syrian dependency on a Russian air defense system commanded by Russian advisers, and to replace an older system unable to detect and neutralize Israeli air strikes (Dekel 2020).

The second direction of Iranian activities after the victory declared by Assad turned on reaping some economic dividends. Counting on its constant support for Assad's rule, Iran expected a greater role in the reconstruction of the country (Azizi 2019). In this regard, the Syrian government reportedly rewarded IRGC affiliated companies with lucrative contracts that were mostly "related to the reconstruction of electricity equipment, power plants and transmission lines" (Majidyar 2017). One of those contracts granted Telecommunications Company of Iran (TCI) the right to build a mobile phone network in Syria. Tehran is also projecting to build a railroad to connect Iran via Iraq to the Syrian port of Latakia. Likewise, Iran has been attempting to build a gas pipeline extending from the Iranian South Pars gas-field to Syria.

Aside from the expected economic interests, Iranian military and political influence in Syria is regarded by the Iranian elite as a foreign policy achievement. In a speech delivered on the occasion of the 40th anniversary of the "Islamic revolution" in February 2019, Khamenei counted "the expansion of the powerful political presence of the Islamic Republic of Iran in West Asia" and "Iran's strong presence near the borders of the Zionist regime" among the achievements of the revolution (*Khamenei.ir* 2019).

Consequently, Iran's motivation, role, strategy and means employed in the Syrian conflict have evolved in due course depending on changing conditions on the ground. Initially, arguably, it was defensive and committed to keeping the Assad regime in power, to keep the "resistance axis" intact, and to prevent regional rivals from gaining a strong foothold in Syria. Later on, it engaged in establishing clients in Syria that would help Iran to deepen its influence in the country. The Russian military involvement in the crisis in favor of Assad in September 2015, released pressure on Assad. After that, the Iranian strategy in Syria embarked on preserving Iranian influence in that country. It went as far as entrenching Iranian military power as well as strengthening economic and socio-cultural ties between the two countries. Meanwhile, Iranian authorities deemed their presence in Syria valuable as leverage against Israel, as well as being a strategic position that would counterbalance potential US attempts in the region. Thus, the Iran-Syria alliance that was initially based on an ideological-geopolitical positioning of the two states, has been activated to stave off vital threats against the Assad regime and has finally ended up being an instrument for greater Iranian influence over the Middle East, particularly in the Levant.

REFERENCES

Aarabi, Kasra. 2020. *Beyond Borders: The Expansionist Ideology of Iran's Islamic Revolutionary Guards Corps.* Tony Blair Institute for Global Change.

Abdo, Geneive. 2011. "How Iran Keeps Assad in Power in Syria." *Foreign Affairs*, August 25.

Ahmadian, Hassan, and Payam Mohseni. 2019. "Iran's Syria Strategy: The Evolution of Deterrence." *International Affairs*, 93 (2).

Al Jazeera. 2012. "Kofi Annan's Six-Point Plan for Syria." March 27.

Al-Smadi, Fatima. 2017. *Iran and the Arab Revolutions: Narratives Establishing Iran's Monopolism.* Al Jazeera Centre for Studies.

Amir-Abdollahian, Hossein. 2014. "Iran's Four-Part Plan for A Political Solution in Syria." *Al-Monitor*, March 5.

Ansari, Ali, and Aniseh Bassiri Tabrizi. 2016. "The View from Tehran." In *Understanding Iran's Role in the Syrian Conflict*, edited by Aniseh Bassiri Tabrizi and Raffaello Pantucci, 3–10. London: RUSI.

Azizi, Hamidreza. 2019. "Iran Seeks Economic Benefits from Syria." *Atlantic Council*, February 22.

BBC News. 2011. "EU Imposes Sanctions on President Assad." May 23.

Behravesh, Maysam. 2017. "But Really, Why Is Iran Still Backing Assad? A Psychological Analysis." *Middle East Eye*, February 15.

Charbonneou, Louis, and Michelle Nichols. 2014. "The U.N. Invitation That Nearly Undid Syria Peace Talks". *Reuters*, January 22.

De Luce, Dan. 2015. "Syrian War Takes Rising Toll on Hezbollah." *Foreign Policy*, July 9.

Dekel, Udi. 2020. ""Alliance of Survivors": Iran and Syria and their Military-Technology Agreement." *INSS Insight*, 1349. https://www.inss.org.il/pub lication/syria-iran-agreement/. Accessed on 7 April 2021.

Donya-e Eqtesad. 2014. Sarlashkar Jaafari: Ba Eftekhar az Suriye hemayet mekoneem. April 30.

Ehteshami, Anoushiravan. 2002. "The Foreign Policy of Iran." In *The Foreign Policies of Middle Eastern States,* edited by Raymond Hinnesbusch and Anoushiravan Ehteshami. Boulder, CO: Lynne Rienner.

Ehteshami, Anoushiravan, and Raymond Hinnebusch. 1997. *Syria and Iran: Middle Powers in a Penetrated Regional System.* London: Routledge.

Ezadi, J., and H. Akbari. (2010). "Baraavarde Dahayi Savvome Monasabate Rakhbordeye Jomhouri Eslami-ye Iran ve Suriye: Hamgeraayi ya Gesist?" *Rohnameye Seyasetgozareye Seyasi, Defa'i ve Amniyati* 1 (2).

Goodarzi, Jubin M. 2006. *Syria and Iran: Diplomatic Alliance and Power Politics in the Middle East.* New York: I.B. Tauris.

Goodarzi, Jubin M. 2013. "Iran: Syria as the First Line of Defence." In *The Regional Struggle for Syria*, edited by J. Barnes-Decay and D. Levy, 25–32. London: European Council of Foreign Relations.

Hassan, Hassan. (2016). "Rebel Groups' Involvement in Syria." In *Understanding Iran's Role in the Syrian Conflict*, edited by A. Bassiri Tabrizi and R. Pantucci, 33–38. Occasional Paper. London: RUSI.

Iran Primer. 2012. "Tehran Conference Statement on Syria." *USIP – The Iran Primer*, August 10.

Iran Primer. 2015. "Iran Attends Syria Peace Talks in Vienna." *USIP – The Iran Primer*, November 17.

IRNA. 2012. "Syria Is Paying Price of Support for Resistance to Zionist Occupation: Jalili." July 3.

Juneau, Thomas. 2014. "Iran Under Rouhani: Still Alone in the World." *Middle East Policy* 21, no. 4.

Khamenei.ir. 2017. "Gen. Soleimani Congratulates Ayatollah Khamanei and Muslims on ISIS Termination." November 21. https://english.khamenei.ir/ news/5283/Gen-Soleimani-congratulates-Ayatollah-Khamanei-and-Muslim s-on. Accessed on 7 April 2021.

Khamenei.ir. 2019. "The 'Second Phase of the Revolution' Statement Addressed to the Iranian nation." February 11. https://english.khamenei.ir/news/6415/The-Second-Phase-of-the-Revolution-Statement-addressed-to-the. Accessed on 7 April 2021.

Lake, Eli. 2015. "Iran Spends Billions to Prop Up Assad." *Bloombergview*, June 9. http://www.bloombergview.com/articles/2015-06-09/iran-spends-billions-to-prop-up-assad. Accessed on 7 April 2021.

Majidyar, Ahmad. 2017. "Iran Expands Its Economic Sphere of Influence in Syria." *Middle East Institute*, September 13.

Mathiesen, Toby. 2013. "Syria: Inventing a Religious War." *NYR Daily*, June 12. http://www.nybooks.com/blogs/nyrblog/2013/jun/12/syria-inventing-religious-war/. Accessed on 7 April 2021.

McInnis, J. Matthew. 2015. "How Many Iranian Fighters are Fighting and Dying in Syria?" *Newsweek*, October 28.

Mehr News Agency. 2011. "Selselayi moqavamat aleyhe Esrael az Shahrahi Suriye Anjam Megirad." *Mehr News*, December 30.

Naame Sham. 2014. *Iran in Syria: From an Ally of the Regime to an Occupying Force*. http://www.naameshaam.org/wp-content/uploads/2014/10/report_iran_in_syria_201411.pdf. Accessed on 7 April 2021.

Niakoee, S. A., A. Esmaeli, and A. Setude. 2013. "Tabyîne Rakhbordî Amniyati Iran der Ghebâle Bohrane Suriye (2011–2013)." *Pajoohashaye Seyasi Jahane Eslam* 3 (1).

Phillips, Christopher. 2016. *The Battle For Syria: International Rivalry in the New Middle East*. New Haven: Yale University Press.

Philips, Matthew, and Julian Lee. 2015. "How Iran Oil Tankers Keep Syria's War Machine Alive." *Bloomberg Business*, June 24. http://www.bloomberg.com/news/articles/2015-06-24/how-iranian-oil-tankers-keep-syria-s-war-machine-alive. Accessed on 7 April 2021.

Press TV. 2016. "Ouster of Assad Iran's redline: Leaders Adviser." April 10.

Radiofarda. 2012. "Farmandehi Sepah Hozoure A'zaye nirouye Qods dar Suriyeh ra tekid kard." September 16. http://www.radiofarda.com/content/f4_iran_revolutionary_guards_iran_syria_admitt/24709851.html. Accessed on 7 April 2021.

Radiofarda. 2013. "Mahdi Taeb: Avlaviyate Suriye beraye İran bîsh az Khuzestan est." April 14 http://www.radiofarda.com/content/f11-mahdi-taeb-says-Syria-is-more-important-than-oilrich-khouzestan/24902500.html. Accessed on 7 April 2021.

Rezaian, Jason. 2012. "Iran Hosts Syrian Peace Conference." *The Washington Post*, November 18.

RFE/RL. 2018. "Iran, Syria Sign Deal on Military Cooperation." August 27. https://www.rferl.org/a/iran-syria-sign-deal-on-military-cooperation/29455495.html. Accessed on 7 April 2021.

Sadeghi-Boroujerdi, Eskandar. 2014. ""Salvaging the "Axis of Resistance," Preserving Strategic Depth." *Dirasat: King Faisal Center for Research and Islamic Studies* 1.

Sajidi, Amir. 2014. "Bohrane Suriyeh ve Dekhalathaayi Ghodrathaayi Bigâneh." *Pajoohashnameye Revabete Baynalmelal* 6 (24). http://fa.journals.sid.ir/JournalListPaper.aspx?ID=49055. Accessed on 7 April 2021.

Saul, Jonathan, and Parisa Hafezi. 2014. "Iran Boosts Military Support in Syria to Bolster Assad." *Reuters*, February 21.

Sinkaya, Bayram. 2016a. *The Revolutionary Guards in Iranian Politics: Elites and Shifting Relations*. London: Routledge.

Sinkaya, Bayram. 2016b. "Trilateral Meeting Between Turkey, Iran, and Russia, and the Moscow Declaration." *ORSAM*, December 22. https://www.orsam.org.tr/en/trilateral-meeting-between-turkey-iran-and-russia-and-the-moscow-declaration/. Accessed on 7 April 2021.

Symth, Phillip. 2015. "The Shiite Jihad in Syria, and its Regional Effects." WINEP, *Policy Focus* 138.

Tehran Times. 2019a. "Syrian President Meets Ayatollah Khamenei in Tehran." February 25.

Tehran Times. 2019b. "Assad Trip Communicates Iran's Plan to Stay in Syria: Cleric." March 1.

UN News Center. 2012. "UN-Backed Action Group Agrees on Measures for Peaceful Transition in Syria." June 30. http://www.un.org/apps/news/story.asp?NewsID=42367#.Vc8KcIt_1Vg. Accessed on 7 April 2021.

Vakil, Sanam. 2018. "Understanding Tehran's Long Game in the Levant." *Uluslararası İlişkiler* 15 (60).

Yaari, Ehud. 2017. "Iran's Ambitions in the Levant." *Foreign Affairs*, May 1.

Yossef, Amr. 2019. "Upgrading Iran's Military Doctrine: An Offensive 'Forward Defense'." *Middle East Institute*, December 10.

Young Journalists Club. 2013a. "Soleimani: Establishment of Democracy in Islamic World to Benefit Iran, Harm West." September 14. https://www.yjc.ir/en/news/2125/soleimani-establishment-of-democracy-in-islamic-world-to-benefit-iran-harm-west. Accessed on 7 April 2021.

Young Journalists Club. 2013b. "Rouhani Says US Lacks Legitimacy to Attack Syria." September 4. http://www.yjc.ir/en/news/2058/rouhani-says-us-lacks-legitimacy-to-attack-syria. Accessed on 7 April 2021.

Young Journalists Club. 2013c. "Bohraane Suriye Raahe Halle Nezami Nedared; Avvalen Khaste Iran Tovkefe Khoshounet der Suriyeh ast." March 2. http://www.yjc.ir/fa/news/4293643/حران سوریه هب راه-%80%E2%8Cحل-ظامی-ند داردنب اول. است سوریه همدرخ شوذتدّ وق فاي ران-خوا سته. Accessed on 7 April 2021.

Zibakalam, Sadegh. 2009. "Iranian 'Exceptionalism'." *Middle East Institute*, June 29.

CHAPTER 7

The Changing Dynamics in the UAE–Syria Relationship

Khalid Almezaini

The United Arab Emirates (UAE) external behavior toward Syria since 1971 reflects a fluctuating and changing relationship determined by regional dynamics. Syria was trapped between siding with the Gulf states or Iran, where both provided significant economic assistance to attract the Syrian government. In 1978, the Gulf states pledged a yearly stipend of $1.8 billion to Syria, but Iranian aid was also significant—providing as much as $1 billion in some years in different forms (Morris 1993). This economic dimension and other political factors influenced the relationship not only with the UAE, but also with other Gulf states. Assistance to Syria was reduced or almost frozen in 1986, making Syria's relations with Iran stronger. During the Iraqi invasion of Kuwait in 1990/1991, Syria showed great support for Kuwait. This position toward Kuwait brought Syria back to the Gulf, where diplomatic ties improved, and foreign aid again began to flow. Therefore, since 1991 and until 2011, the UAE has

K. Almezaini (✉)
Zayed University, Abu Dhabi, UAE
e-mail: khaled.almezaini@zu.ac.ae

© The Author(s), under exclusive license to Springer Nature Switzerland AG 2021
B. Balci and N. Monceau (eds.), *Turkey, Russia and Iran in the Middle East*, The Sciences Po Series in International Relations and Political Economy, https://doi.org/10.1007/978-3-030-80291-2_7

almost been consistent but cautious depending on regional dynamics and Syria's position toward various conflicts and states in the region.

Syria's complex regional and international relations contributed to the survival of al-Assad's regime over the past years. It was expected that the dramatic events that began with the popular uprising in 2011 would lead to vital changes in Syria. However, due to the diverse interests of regional and international actors, the Syrian regime has survived the conflicts after ten years since the start of the uprising. Regional and international actors, such as Qatar, Saudi Arabia, the UAE, Iran, Turkey, Russia, the United States, and some European countries, have engaged in this crisis, supporting some non-state actors as well as the Syrian regime. In particular, the United Arab Emirates started in the conflict by supporting some groups such as the Free Syrian Army, but later sided with Russia and re-established relations with al-Assad's government. This was seen as a surprising move by the UAE, yet this converges with its overall objectives in the Middle East. It has been clear since the start of the uprising in Syria that the UAE's support for different groups has been limited and cautious. Unlike Saudi Arabia and Qatar, the UAE has not been strongly supporting the opposition. It has kept its role limited due to the involvement of Russia, the United States, and some other Western allies. It has found itself in a position where some of its allies are in diverging positions, mainly Russia and the United States. While siding with the Syrian people, the Emirates kept some indirect ties with Damascus during the first few years after the uprising.

This chapter seeks to examine three main questions: First, how do we explain UAE–Syria relations since the start of the uprising in 2011; second, how does the UAE maintain relations with Syria while working at the regional level to confront the rise of Hezbollah and Iran; and third, how did the UAE manage to re-establish diplomatic relations with Syria again? The paper argues that the new realities in the Middle East have been among the main reasons for the Emirates' fluctuating relationship with Damascus. Its role in Yemen, Libya, the Horn of Africa, and other areas has influenced the UAE to change its behavior toward Syria. The UAE is a small power, but it has some elements that allow it to engage in the region. Yet, this small power cannot engage fully, using military or financial capabilities, in all conflicts in the region. It is definitely an aspiring small power with regional middle-power capabilities. The strategic hedging policy adopted by the Emirates has contributed to its changing relationship with Syria. Therefore, the chapter will consist

of five main sections: First, it provides a brief analysis of UAE–Syria relations before 2011, second it examines UAE–Syria relations since 2011;
third, it explains the changing dynamics between 2015 and 2018; fourth,
it analyzes the rapprochement with Syria in 2018, and finally it assesses
UAE foreign aid toward Syria and Syrian refugees.

UAE–Syria Relations: Brief Background Before 2011

Over the years, the United Arab Emirates' relations with Syria have
been driven by three main dimensions: ideologies, regional interests, and
regional allies. During the early years of its establishment, specifically in
the 1970s, the UAE was greatly influenced by Arab Nationalism, where
the former President Shaikh Zayed Bin Sultan was a strong supporter of
regional cooperation and unity. This behavior strengthened the relationship between the two countries, particularly after the rise of the UAE as an
important foreign aid donor to Syria. During the 1970s and 1980s, Syria
was among the largest UAE aid recipients. This was due to Syria's support
for the Arab cause, mainly when Syria was part of the "Confrontation
States" (which also included Jordan and Egypt) during the 1967 war and
1973–1974. It was evident that most donors at that time prioritized Arab
states because of the clear influence of this regional ideology. However,
despite the shared regional ideology, Syria's interest has changed significantly, and during the Iraq-Iran war it decided to side with Iran. Morris
(1993) argues that Syrian support of Iran during the Iran-Iraq War
influenced Syrian-Gulf relations and cost Syria much-needed economic
support. Despite the fact that Syria was the "beating heart of the Arab
nation" which played a pivotal role in regional politics (Belcastro 2020),
its regional relations began to change significantly. Since the early 1980s,
Syria began to make significant changes in its regional behavior. Regional
dynamics and changes influenced Syria's orientations in the aftermath of
the Iraq-Iran war. Syria felt betrayed by Egypt, its relationship with Iraq
was faced with many challenges, and later this relationship failed. Due to
these and other regional changes, Syria allied itself with Iran. Belcastro
(2020, 55–56) points out that "left isolated and feeling threatened
by both Israel and Iraq, the Syrian leader found an ally in the Islamic
Republic of Iran." Therefore, Syria's re-alignment toward Iran and siding
against Iraq during the 1980s had great implications for its relations with
the UAE and other Gulf Cooperation Council (GCC) states. Since 1990,

UAE–Syria relations have fluctuated but these also have depended on the intentions and regional orientations of both states. Al-Qasemi (2020) demonstrates that "a fluctuating relationship continued between the UAE and Syria from the 1990s, only to turn sour from 2011 as Syria's uprising morphed into a civil conflict involving external actors." She also adds that "the relationship between the UAE and Syria has not been linear. Multiple players and political factors have influenced the nature and direction of the relationship since the 1980s" (Al-Qasemi 2020). It is important to note that despite the fluctuating relationship, the UAE's foreign policy has been consistent and has continued to work under the umbrella of the GCC and particularly Saudi Arabia.

Despite regional changes and particularly Iran's continued perceived threat toward the UAE, the latter continued providing foreign aid to Syria and improved diplomatic relationship throughout the 1990s and the 2000s. This has created a relatively healthy relationship. The number of investments on both sides has increased, and particularly the number of Syrians residing in the UAE is nearly 250,000 (Embassy of the United Arab Emirates in Washington DC). Nonetheless, between 2000 and 2011, the UAE relation with Syria was influenced again by Syria's position toward the Gulf states vis-a-vis Iran. The Gulf states tried to steer Damascus away from Tehran due to its support for Hezbollah in Lebanon. This attempt, however, failed, but pressure on Syria led it to reduce its presence in Lebanon after Hariri's assassination. Before 2011 Syria had significant investments in the UAE due to Syrian businessmen's close contact with the regime. Between 2000 and 2011 this allowed the two countries to focus on economic relations while at the same time the UAE tried to influence the Syrian regime through the Gulf Cooperation Council (GCC).

THE UAE AND SYRIA SINCE 2011

Syria is probably one of the most complex cases that have experienced the popular uprising, and this was clearly reflected in how regional states reacted. While there are states in the region that opposed the uprising in Syria, there are others which maintained some links with al-Assad's government. This division in the Arab Middle East created ambiguity around the Syrian case, on whether to side with the people or the government. Therefore, the UAE acted cautiously toward Syria; it has neither fully supported the popular uprising, nor fully sided with the government.

This was seen as a balanced approach where the UAE, as a small power, sought maximum gains from either side. Other scholars argued that the UAE was very clear and straightforward about its change in policy toward Syria until 2015, since when it has fully supported the Syrian people (Ghadban 2020). In fact, there were some links with the Syrian government before 2015. This was due to the fear it might allow for extreme groups to establish control over a wide territory in Syria. Todman (2016) clearly points out that "the other GCC members (referring to the UAE, Kuwait, and Oman) are much more cautious about regime change, and they are especially wary of any steps that would allow Salafi-jihadi groups to establish a permanent foothold in Syria."

It is, therefore, important to look at the UAE–Syria relationship during the first 4–5 years. The Emirates was extremely cautious about how events unfolded in the Syrian conflict. It observed what the uprising would lead to during the first few years. However, the UAE knew that Syria is not at all similar to other Arab cases because of the nature of Syrian society, where different religions and sects exist, and the number of Syria's allies, both at the regional and international levels, which matter for the survival of the state. Therefore, the UAE realized the large number of actors involved in the conflict. There were, and still are, actors who are both allies and friends of the UAE, and there are actors who are considered to have differences with the Emirates. As a consequence of this, the Emirates found itself in a difficult position on how to react toward instability in Syria. It has, on various occasions, supported the various forums where the Syrian opposition met, such as Friends of Syria.

Following in the steps of other regional allies, the UAE decided to support some opposition groups that are mainly less religious and oppose the rise of the Muslim Brotherhood (MB), such as the Free Syrian Army. Most of the groups that were established, both secular and religious, had established some kind of links in Qatar, Turkey, and other Arab states but not in the UAE. This shows the fact that UAE was not interested in deepening relations with many of the groups that have emerged, for example, the Free Syrian Army (FSA) which is a loose conglomeration of armed brigades formed in 2011 by defectors from the Syrian army and civilians backed by the United States, Turkey, and several Gulf countries (Aljazeera 2018). The nature of the UAE support for the Free Syria Army has not been straightforward. There have been some challenges in the relationship with this group due to the fact that the UAE was not the only one providing assistance to the FSA. According to Daher (2019),

Emirati support for the groups was provided through programs run by the US Central Intelligence Agency, notably in southern Syria through the Military Operations Centre based in Jordan. However, Katzman (2014) points out that in contrast to other GCC allies, the UAE was not reported to have supplied Syrian rebels with weapons. Therefore, financial assistance was the only kind of support the UAE has provided for rebels in Syria. Yet it has contributed, using military air force, in the fight against Islamic State (ISIS).

In addition, the UAE has been accused of funding further groups (other than the Free Syrian Army). Surprisingly, this included religious groups which are opposing or fighting against Iranian forces in Syria. Benedetta Berti and Yoel Guzansky (2014, 25–34) argue that Saudi Arabia, alongside the United Arab Emirates and Qatar (which has since cut back on its involvement), has been aiding all the rebel forces it regards as suitable for the anti-Iranian cause within the Syrian rebel camp. Berti and Guzansky (2014, 25–34) also point out that there have been private donations coming from the UAE for radical Sunni rebels, "at the same time, this policy has not prevented private donations from the Gulf states, notably Kuwait and the UAE, reaching the more radical Sunni rebel groups. This has caused further radicalization and fragmentation within the rebel ranks in a rampant competition for funds and influence that has strengthened the more radical elements among the anti-Assad supporters." There is, however, no evidence to prove that private donations have gone out of the UAE to support radical Sunni groups. Line Khatib (2019, 385–403) demonstrates that "this hesitation about intervening and potentially ending up contributing to the polarization and escalation of the crisis at least partly explains the initial reluctance of Saudi Arabia and the UAE to support Syria's Islamist groups and militias." She further adds that "indeed, for the first two years of the conflict, Saudi Arabia and the UAE opted to support the most secular segments of the opposition: former Ba 'thists such as Riad Hijab and Mustafa al-Assad, secular intellectuals such as Michel Kilo (rooted in the Christian community) and secular-leaning representatives of the Free Syrian Army such as Lu'ay Miqdad." Furthermore, in July 2013 the Emirates backed the newly elected president of the Syrian National Coalition, Ahmad Jarba, a tribal leader from the Shammar clan in the north-eastern Syrian province of Hasakah, well-known for its close links with Saudi Arabia (Daher 2019). In fact, after 2013, the UAE's position toward the Syrian crisis moved from being moderate and supporting some opposition groups to clearly showing signs of a shift toward the regime.

The UAE has also contributed to or been part of some of the international coalition groups that have opposed the Syrian regime since 2012 such as "Friends of Syria" also known as the "London 11." According to Daher (2019), "the UAE became a member of the international coalition of states opposed to the Damascus regime known as the 'Friends of Syria' at its first meeting in Tunis in February 2012. In 2013, the UAE was one of the 'London 11' states which met the opposition's Syrian National Coalition in the British capital." It has also contributed to various events to support Syrian refugees during the crisis such as the Brussels V Conference in 2021. In fact, it was one of the first countries that responded to the growing humanitarian crisis in Syria. Between 2012 and 2015, the UAE provided up to $600 million of aid to Syrian refugees. In 2013, about 65% of UAE humanitarian aid went to Syria (Financial Tracking Service 2013a). However, since 2014 humanitarian aid to Syria from the UAE began to decrease.

Therefore, between 2011 and 2015, the UAE was active in engaging with Syrian opposition, in providing assistance to Syrian refugees and had limited links with the Syrian government. Links with Damascus have probably been through various business circles in both countries. Daher (2019) highlights that.

> Several internationally sanctioned pro-regime businessmen have also continued to do business through local companies with relative freedom in the UAE, including Bashar al-Assad's first cousin, Rami Makhlouf, and Samer Foz. Many other Emirati businessmen known to be close to the UAE government also maintained relations with Damascus long after the eruption of Syria's protest movement. Some established new companies in Syria and/or opened branches of their UAE-based companies in the country. For example, Abdul Jalil al-Blooki, a businessman close to the ruling family in Abu Dhabi, established a development and investment company in Syria in 2013. (Financial Tracking Service 2013a)

Toward the end of 2015, the UAE began clearly to shift its policy toward Syria due to the fact that after almost five years of conflict there were no signs of any kind of stability, as well as this change being influenced by the involvement of Russia.

Regional Dynamics and UAE's Change of Policy Toward Syria: 2015–2018

During the first few years of the uprising in Syria, the UAE learned significant lessons on how to act in a conflict where many actors are involved. The desire of the UAE as a small state with some characteristics of a middle power to engage in a complex region with multiple conflicts required a consistent foreign policy. The ability to influence and exert power despite the small state size shows the evolvement of the Emirates over the past ten years as a main player in the Middle East. It is not a middle power but has some characteristics of regional and international middle powers. Therefore, the UAE began to shape its foreign policy toward all issues in the region with clear objectives. Since the early months of 2011 the UAE has been clear on its opposition to the role of the Muslim Brotherhood across different countries in the region, countering all types of violent non-state actors, supporting secular-oriented governments in the region, and following a strategic hedging policy to maintain good relations with all powers outside and inside the region. El-Dessouki and Mansour (2020) define strategic hedging as a "mixed strategy of cooperation and conflict, relying on both soft and hard power tools. It is a combination of policies that, on one hand, stress engagement and integration mechanisms and, on the other, emphasize realist-style balancing. A hedging state cooperates with the powerful threatening state (PTS) to avoid threats or/and getting involved in unequal conflicts (soft balance)."

As the implications of the first few years of the uprising in Syria began to be clearer, the UAE slowly shifted away from all types of Syrian opposition by 2015. This is confirmed by Daher (2019) who points out that this shift in UAE foreign policy regarding the Syrian conflict has its roots in regional developments in 2014 and 2015. In addition, the arrival of international powers, mainly Russia and the United States, was a clear sign for the Emirates to reconsider its position in the conflict. The Emirates found that alignment with one major power might not fully be rewarding, such as dependency on the United States, and therefore the fear of having disproportionate political, economic, and military losses pushed the UAE to improve relations with all international powers. Aldardari (2020) clearly argues that during the initial years of the conflict, the UAE was clear in its opposition to the Syrian government, that was evident in the inister of Foreign Affairs' statement in 2013. She adds that this "began to change in 2015, when the UAE's minister of state supported

Russia's military intervention. With time, the UAE's calculations changed as Turkey's role in Syria increased, 'radical Islamist' groups emerged, and Russia solidified Assad's hold on power (Aldardari 2020)." It is important to note that members of the Syrian Muslim Brotherhood were hosted in Turkey in 2011, and in Istanbul, together with other opposition groups, signed a declaration about protecting human rights in Syria, including the freedom of expression and freedom of religion (Szymanski 2017, 63–84). According to Fulya Doğruel "while Turkey's support for the rebels has increased over time, the logistic support it has provided, along with the support from Saudi Arabia, to those opposing the Assad regime has made no distinction between the opposition groups, which has resulted in radical Islamists groups gaining more dominance in Syria (Karakoç and Doğruel 2015, 351–366)." The UAE and Turkey are locked in a regional struggle to influence and exert power to increase the number of their allies.

Therefore, there are five main reasons for the UAE's change in behavior toward Syria. First, as explained earlier, the intervention of Russia and the United States in Syria did put the UAE in a difficult position on whether to side with Russia which has good relations with Syria, or the United States that it is siding against al-Assad. The UAE is on good terms with both powers, and as a result it had to act cautiously in regard to this conflict. Second, the increasing role of Turkey and its support for different groups opposing al-Assad. From the UAE's perspective, this might lead to the establishment of a Syrian government siding with Turkey but not with the UAE. This conflict between the UAE and Turkey in regard to supporting or opposing the Muslim Brotherhood extends to other parts of the region, but in Syria it has led to some kind of a proxy war. This tense relationship between the two countries has existed since the start of the uprising in 2011. Third, despite the continuous support of various regional and international actors for different opposition groups in Syria, al-Assad's government remains intact. The inability of opposition groups to further weaken al-Assad is a clear sign that Russia has great influence over the dynamics in Syria. Consequently, the UAE realized that maintaining or improving relations with Damascus has better outcomes for UAE–Syria relations. Al-Assad's government is perceived as less affiliated with any religious ideologies and, therefore, the UAE sees this as an alignment with its regional objectives, such as opposing the Muslim Brotherhood. Fourth, the UAE's regional activism had put pressure on its military and financial expenditures. As tension escalates in Yemen and Libya, the small state was unable to continue providing military support or even financial aid to three or more platforms simultaneously. Therefore, it is to the benefit of the UAE to engage with the Syrian government rather than opposition groups. Fifth, due to US changes in its foreign policy toward the Middle East and the Gulf in particular, the UAE has increased the diversification of its security partners. As a result, improving relations with Russia will improve the UAE's chances of influencing Syria, at the same time strengthening the growing Emirates-Russia relationship. Over the past couple of years, the diplomatic, economic, and military spheres have improved significantly. Due to this and shared interests in different parts of the region, the two countries (Russia and the UAE) have probably more commonality and agreement regarding Syria than for any other area in the region. Ramani (2019) explains that "on Syria, however, the UAE's current position shares more common ground with Russia than any other Gulf Arab country, except Oman, which—in keeping with its policy of neutrality and engagement with all regional parties—maintained an embassy in Damascus throughout the Syrian civil war." He adds that "although the UAE officially opposed Syrian President Bashar al-Assad's retention of power, Abu Dhabi distinguished itself from Saudi Arabia and Qatar by refusing to support armed Islamist opposition groups in Syria."

Therefore, these factors and reasons paved the way for the UAE to reconsider its relations with Syria. It has moved from being inclined toward opposition but maintaining very limited links with the government, to disconnecting itself from opposition and slowly supporting Damascus. This behavior reflects the dynamics in Syria as well as in the Middle East in general, in particular, confronting Iran and the Muslim Brotherhood allies across different parts of the region in order to continue its influence and exert power across the region.

2018 AND THE UAE'S SHIFT TOWARD SYRIA

The aspiration of the UAE to influence opposition groups has been extremely limited and has not ended in the way the Emirates wanted. In fact, it adopted a less adamant intention to support the removal of al-Assad from power, particularly after Russia's rising role in Syria. Therefore, the UAE's behavior toward Syria was perceived as a double standards policy. Consequently, by December 2018, the Emirates ended its vague approach toward Syria and restored its diplomatic relations with Damascus. This rapprochement with Syria was due to three main factors.

First, Russia's heavy involvement in Syria by supporting al-Assad was a clear sign for the UAE that it should balance its role in this conflict. The relationship between these two countries is getting stronger at all levels, specifically after the changing US policies toward the Gulf states and the region in general. Russia and the UAE found common ground in reducing tension in Syria, but most importantly they have shared interests. According to Santucci (2020), the position of the UAE has been placed on a more common footing with Russia—the latter having emerged as a player in 2015—as both recognized that al-Assad could be included in Syria's future. The Emirates continue to improve its relations with Moscow, and in particular it has an ambitious objective to influence Russia's policies in the future regarding this conflict and other issues in the region. According to Nada Ahmed (2020) "Russia and the UAE have been working on strengthening their economic relations in the past six years, with non-oil trade between the two states reaching $15 billion." Moreover, Ahmed (2020) explains that in 2017, the UAE also partnered with Russia's defense giant, Rostec, to develop fifth-generation light combat fighter aircraft.

This cooperation between the two countries led to both contributing to fighting Islamist groups in Syria. More importantly for the UAE is the fact that along with Russia they can oppose Turkey's attacks on Syria and its involvement there. Ramani (2019) points out that Russia and the UAE are united in their opposition to potential Turkish attacks on Kurdish militias in north-eastern Syria. He adds that since Turkey launched Operation Olive Branch in January 2018 and carried out an offensive against the Kurdish-majority city of Afrin, the UAE has claimed that Ankara's conduct constitutes a collective security threat and has criticized its attempts to create a buffer zone in north-eastern Syria (Ramani 2019). However, the UAE's opposition to Turkey is not only due to its operation in Syria, but also due to Turkey's support for the Muslim Brotherhood across the region. Aydıntaşbaş and Bianco (2021) argue that:

> Both Turkey and the UAE are eager to develop competing narratives on the supposedly ideological character of the conflict, and to find various platforms on which to present their competing visions for the region. But these efforts mask the true nature of the struggle. While the two countries

have been on the opposite sides of nearly every regional conflict since 2011, it is debatable to what extent ideology—'moderate versus Islamist' for Abu Dhabi, and 'competitive democracy versus authoritarian monarchy' for Ankara—shapes their rivalry. The dispute is complicated but, at its core, primarily involves a struggle for internal regime consolidation and regional influence.

Conflict in Syria was an opportunity for the UAE to engage with Russia to influence the latter's behavior toward Turkey. Across the Middle East, the two countries (Turkey and the UAE) are engaging in proxy wars that have contributed to the instabilities in the region. However, the UAE's cooperation with Russia in Syria has, relatively, reduced the number of non-state actors fighting in Syria. Turkey was also blamed for supporting some jihadists entering Syria through its territory. Uslu (2016, 771–802) demonstrates that.

> Turkish support to jihadists is not merely a tactic aimed at removing Assad from power. It stems from a strategic decision on the part of Turkish authorities to influence Middle East affairs through non-state actors, much as Iran has been doing for some time. Turkey's support of jihadists transiting into Syria and its establishment of close ties with Hamas and the Muslim Brotherhood are joint aspects of this strategy.

Therefore, the UAE and Russia dimension in Syria brought benefits for the two countries due to their shared interests. While the UAE does support the aspirations of the Syrian people, it understands that this case is very complex and unlike other Arab states it requires a careful approach. It is important to note that despite the UAE-Russia partnership in Syria, the former is careful about Turkey-Russia relations in other aspects.

The second reason as to why the UAE reopened its embassy in Damascus was to support a secular government. It was clear that the UAE's role in Syria is to confront the rise of any religious movements. However, due to the increasing role of some regional states that support Islamist movements, the UAE opted to stand with al-Assad because of his ideological position against extreme Islamist movements. This also goes in line with Russia, whose foreign policy in the region is secular in nature. Ramani (2020, 125–140) also argues that "although Emirati officials did not reiterate Russia's contentions on Islamism during the early stages of the war, former Syrian diplomat Bassam Barabandi notes that Abu Dhabi's chief priority was to ensure that Syria had a secular government." He adds that "the pursuit of this goal caused the UAE to host pro-Assad business people even as it sought to diplomatically isolate Damascus" (Ramani 2020, 125–140). This has been a consistent foreign policy objective of the UAE in the past ten years. Most of its activism in the region reflects more of a secular approach than one that is religious or ideologically oriented. Since early 2011, the UAE government has promoted a moderate Islam that is not politicized.

Third, the economic dimension played a significant role in pushing the UAE for rapprochement with Syria. It can be interpreted by two main points. First, during the first few years of the uprising in Syria, the UAE financed some groups, mainly the Free Syrian Army and contributed to the international coalition fighting ISIS. This had put more financial burden on the Emirates, not only because of the role in Syria but also because of the increasing activism of the UAE across the region. By 2015, the UAE joined Saudi Arabia in Yemen, which in fact led to a slow withdrawal by the UAE from various areas in the region. Second, both the UAE and Syria see great economic gains from this relationship. In particular, business elites from the two countries have been one of the driving forces behind the return of this relationship. Nada Ahmed (2020) highlights this clearly and argues that "the UAE's engagement with Syria began behind the scenes and was framed as an economic partnership. The Damascus trade fair presented an opportunity for businesses to play the role of intermediaries." She also adds that "because of the destruction in Syria, the country is in need of partners willing to implement reconstruction projects worth billions of dollars" (Ahmed 2020).

In addition, Santucci (2020) points out that "over the past two years, the UAE has made conciliatory advances toward Damascus. The benefits of Emirati and Syrian commercial ties have been a motivating force for the UAE to re-engage with President Assad." She explains that the UAE investors have always been attracted by the sizable financial gains that can be had from reviving Syria's economy in its post-conflict reconstruction phase (Santucci 2020). However, wealthy Syrians and businessmen have flocked to the UAE, oftentimes attempting to shield themselves from Washington's radar vis-à-vis profit-generating business fronts based in the Emirates (Santucci 2020). "The UAE is also using trade and investment to boost ties with Syria. In January 2019 the UAE hosted a visiting Syrian business delegation, and in August a delegation of 40 UAE business-people attended a state-backed trade fair in Damascus, in defiance of US warnings. Delegates included prominent UAE firms, such as a construction group, Arabtec Holding." Therefore, it is believed that the Emirates, over the past two years, preferred to influence al-Assad through economic ties rather than by military pressure.

UAE Foreign Aid to Syria and Syrian Refugees

Since the UAE's formation, foreign aid has been the most influential tool in its foreign policy. It has evolved over the past years from being a marginalized donor to one of the largest and most generous countries in the world. Its overall aid has been transformed from only being dedicated to Arab countries to including all countries in need. However, it has been criticized for providing most of its aid to Arab states, as well as for the politicization of aid. This has been perceived, nonetheless, from the UAE perspective as "Arab Solidarity." The Emirates is also one of the largest aid donors in the world in relation to its Gross Domestic Product (GDP). According to the UAE foreign aid report of 2017, it has provided about 1.18% of its GDP as foreign assistance and was ranked second after Sweden; it was ranked the first in 2016 by providing 1.21% of its GDP and also ranked first in 2017 by providing 1.03%. It is important to note, however, that this is for humanitarian aid only. The UAE has been named the world's largest donor of development assistance in proportion to its gross national income for the fifth year running, according to the Development Assistance Committee of the Organization of Economic Cooperation and Development (Reliefweb 2018).

During its early years, the UAE used aid as a tool to seek recognition and assist Arab states in the region. Syria has been one of the largest recipients of UAE aid since the 1970s. This is because the late Shaikh Zayed believed in Arab Nationalism and strong support for the Arab cause in general. Although aid to Syria was decreased in the 1980s due to Syria's position toward the Iraq-Iran war, it received more after standing against Saddam during the Iraqi invasion of Kuwait. In 2002, Syria received about one billion UAE dirham and about the same in 2007.[1] This is only from the Abu Dhabi Fund for development. Furthermore, in the 1970s, aid from all GCC states contributed significantly to the economic development of Syria. As mentioned earlier, Morris (1993) pointed out that

---

[1] About $300 US dollars.

following the Baghdad Summit of 1978, the Gulf states pledged a yearly stipend of $1.8 billion to Syria. During the 1980s, foreign aid was almost frozen, but by the early 1990s Gulf states resumed providing financial assistance to Syria due to its political position regarding Kuwait.

Since the start of the uprising, UAE aid to Syria has continued to flow but mainly as humanitarian aid. Between 2012 and 2019, the UAE provided about one billion US dollars to refugees scattered in areas around Syria. Although it was difficult to provide direct aid to Syrians within Syrian territory, the Emirates assisted countries hosting refugees, mainly Jordan and Lebanon. According to the UAE foreign aid report, the Syrian crisis has impacted Jordan's financial situation due to the influx of Syrian refugees, which it is estimated account for nearly ten percent of Jordan's total population (UAE Ministry of Foreign Affairs and International Cooperation 2019). In addition, *Khaleej Times* (2021) points out that "over the past 10 years, the UAE has provided more than $1.11 billion in relief aid to Syrian refugees in Syria, Jordan, Lebanon, Iraq, and Greece. These include the provision of food, shelter, and healthcare, as well as the establishment of field hospitals and refugee camps." The UAE is also a co-founding member of the Syria Recovery Trust Fund along with Germany and the United States. It has contributed about $23.4 million. Most of UAE humanitarian aid to Syrian refugees goes to Jordan and Lebanon, and therefore, the amount is much higher. For example, the UAE is the fourth largest humanitarian donor to Jordan, where it has provided about 6.4% of the total aid received by the Jordanian government. It also provided about 6% of the total humanitarian aid to Jordan in 2018, and 13.2% in 2016, as well as 6% in 2013 (Financial Tracking Service 2013b). Due also to the political importance and strong relations between the UAE and Jordan, humanitarian aid was much higher than to refugees in Lebanon. It provided aid worth Dh230 million to Syrian refugees between 2011 and 2015 (*Khaleej Times* 2015). However, the political instability in Lebanon has affected the flow of aid to Syrian refugees from the Emirates (Table 7.1).

Despite the enormous amount of humanitarian aid, the UAE and other Gulf states were criticized for not accepting refugees. In the Emirates, there is no refugee status, but most people who arrive come under different visa categories. In fact, the UAE is not a signatory to the UN Convention on Refugees. Ouaki (2016) points out that "one of the reasons that countries in the Persian Gulf—including Saudi Arabia, Kuwait, Bahrain, Qatar, the United Arab Emirates, and Oman—decided

Table 7.1 UAE
reported humanitarian
aid to Syrian refugees

Year	Amount
2020	$10,000,000
2019	$42,000,000
2018	$9,000,000
2017	$10,000,000
2016	$73,741,064
2015	$5,650,000
2014	$50,136,254
2013	$198,085,918

Source https://fts.unocha.org

to shut the door on Syrian refugees is because the concept itself of refugees isn't actually recognized in their politics." This means that the monarchies of the Gulf countries have no legal obligation toward refugees; they make no distinction between the statuses of migrants, therefore give no preferential treatment toward those with a "refugee" status and consider them as mere "residents" (Ouaki 2016). This is because non-nationals constitute about 85% of the total UAE population. Accepting refugees would create further demographic imbalance. In addition, there is a fear among all Gulf states that Arab refugees might bring with them various ideologies. This fear started at the end of the 1970s when all Gulf states preferred Asian migrants over people coming from the Middle East. Therefore, the number of migrants from Asia has increased significantly. For instance, in the Emirates there are over three million Indians out of the ten million population.

Nonetheless, in the UAE, there are about 115,000 Syrian residents, but not in the form of refugees. Many of them arrived before the uprising in 2011. In 2016 the Emirates announced that it would receive fifteen thousand Syrian refugees, but in 2019, the UAE accepted only twenty-six refugees from Syria, according to World Data source.[2] Despite the announcement in 2016, there are no sources to confirm that the UAE has welcomed fifteen thousand Syrian refugees. It has probably received them in the form of different visa categories, such as employment visa or resident visa. Therefore, due to the lack of available statistics, it is difficult to pinpoint that the Emirates has not welcomed Syrian refugees. The UAE

[2] https://www.worlddata.info/asia/arab-emirates/asylum.php.

and all other GCC (with the exception of Saudi Arabia) have received fewer refugees in comparison with many European countries.

CONCLUSION

During the past twenty years, UAE–Syria relations have been fluctuating. This is mainly due to regional dynamics and the changing behavior of the two states. Since the uprising in 2011, the UAE's regional role has increased significantly making it one of the most active states in the region. Its roles in different areas in the region and the changing foreign policies of different international powers such as Russia have influenced the UAE, moving from supporting opposition groups to re-opening its embassy in Damascus. It is also believed that the economic dimension played a role in the UAE's changing policies toward Syria. The Emirates regional activism has put more pressure on the UAE's financial capabilities. For a small state, it was difficult to engage in different conflicts in the region simultaneously. Therefore, the shift can be seen as a result of the UAE's priorities. In particular, the role of the UAE in Yemen, Libya, and the Horn of Africa has forced this small state to alter its behavior.

In the long term, the UAE sees relations with Syria in an economic dimension. There are more gains to be made in investments and trade between the two states. In addition, the Emirates prefers a secular—oriented government in Syria which can potentially improve relations. In the long term, the UAE assumes that it might be able to influence Syria to change some of its relations with some states in the region such as Iran. At beginning of the uprising, Iran played a major role in assisting al-Assad, which created a further fear that Syria would be under the influence of Tehran. Consequently, the rapprochement with Syria might lead to improving relations and give the UAE a part in a future Syria.

Russia's rising role in Syria has definitely changed the dynamics in the conflict. The Emirates' role was reduced and moved from being on the side of some opposition groups to supporting Russia as well as improving ties with al-Assad's regime. Therefore, there is no doubt that Russia has played an important role in bringing the two countries together. The UAE believes that supporting Russia's effort will reduce tension and promote regional stability.

Over the past ten years, the Emirates has enjoyed a unique relationship with Moscow that has led to both states cooperating to resolve some of the security challenges threatening their regional interests. This is because of the unpredictable US foreign policy toward the Middle East and the American pivot toward Asia. In other words, the UAE has certainly followed a strategic hedging approach, where it seeks to maintain good links with all regional and international powers regardless of their position on any issue in the Middle East. This approach by the Emirates has contributed to its increasing role in the region. From a neo-realist perspective, the UAE as a small power with some middle-power capabilities will use and adopt various foreign policy tools in order to achieve its regional objectives. The ability to influence and exert power in the region has been greatly engineered by the use of its financial capabilities and recently by its military power. Therefore, UAE–Syria relations will definitely improve, and the UAE will use its power to influence other states in the region to open more doors for Damascus and so reduce tension. It has, in fact, successfully managed to convince some of its allies in the region, where we have seen, for example, Bahrain restore its diplomatic mission to Syria.

REFERENCES

Ahmed, Nada. 2020. "It's Business, not Personal: In Syria, Russia and the United Arab Emirates are Collaborating and Competing at the Same Time." Carnegie Middle East Center, May 27. https://carnegie-mec.org/diwan/81912.

Aldardari, Sima. 2020. "Strategic Interests Drive Gulf Policy Toward Syria." The Arab Gulf States Institute in Washington, December 29. https://agsiw.org/strategic-interests-drive-gulf-policy-toward-syria/.

Aljazeera. 2018. "Syria's War Explained from the Beginning." April 14. https://www.aljazeera.com/news/2018/4/14/syrias-war-explained-from-the-beginning.

Al-Qasemi, Najla. 2020. *The UAE's Role in Syria's Stability.* Geneva: The Geneva Centre for Security Policy (GCSP).

Aydıntaşbaş, Aslı, and Cinzia Bianco. 2021. "Useful Enemies: How the Turkey-UAE Rivalry Is Remaking the Middle East." European Council on Foreign Relations, March 2021. https://ecfr.eu/wp-content/uploads/Useful-enemies-How-the-Turkey-UAE-rivalry-is-remaking-the-Middle-East.pdf.

Belcastro, Francesco. 2020. *Syrian Foreign Policy: The Alliances of a Regional Power.* London: Routledge.

Berti, Benedetta, and Yoel Guzansky. 2014. "Saudi Arabia's Foreign Policy on Iran and the Proxy War in Syria: Toward a New Chapter?" *Israel Journal of Foreign Affairs* 8 (3): 25–34. https://doi.org/10.1080/23739770.2014.11446600.

Daher, Joseph. 2019. "The Dynamics and Evolution of UAE-Syria Relations: Between Expectations and Obstacles." Technical Report, EUI RSCAS; Middle East Directions (MED); Wartime and Post-Conflict in Syria; 2019/14. European University Institute. https://doi.org/10.2870/40366.

El-Dessouki, Ayman, and Ola Rafik Mansour. 2020. "Small States and Strategic Hedging: The United Arab Emirates Policy Towards Iran." *Review of Economics and Political Science.* https://doi.org/10.1108/REPS-09-2019-0124.

Embassy of the United Arab Emirates in Washington DC. "Syrian Refugee Crisis – UAE Contribution." https://www.uae-embassy.org/syrian-refugee-crisis-%E2%80%93-uae-contribution.

Financial Tracking Service. 2013a. "United Arab Emirates, Government of 2013." https://fts.unocha.org/donors/100/summary/2013.

Financial Tracking Service. 2013b. "Jordan 2013." https://fts.unocha.org/countries/114/summary/2013.

Ghadban, Obaida. 2020. "Dynamics of Change in UAE Foreign Policy Towards Syria." Aljazeera Centre for Studies (Doha). December 31. https://studies.aljazeera.net/en/node/4881.

Karakoç, Jülide, and Fulya Doğruel. 2015. "The Impact of Turkey's Policy toward Syria on Human Security." *Arab Studies Quarterly* 37 (4): 351–366. https://doi.org/10.13169/arabstudquar.37.4.0351.

Katzman, Kenneth. 2014. "The United Arab Emirates (UAE): Issues for U.S. Policy." CRS Report RS21852. *Congressional Research Service.* September 25. https://www.everycrsreport.com/files/20140925_RS21852_3ae5d0a7444f6fed81a71c195d7d29ca2abc9f99.pdf.

Khaleej Times. 2015. "UAE's Aid to Syrian Refugees in Lebanon Touches Dh230m." September 13. https://www.khaleejtimes.com/region/mena/uaes-aid-to-syrian-refugees-in-lebanon-touches-dh230m.

Khaleej Times. 2021. "UAE Pledges $30 Million for War-torn Syria." March 30. https://www.khaleejtimes.com/news/uae-pledges-30-million-for-war-torn-syria.

Khatib, Line. 2019. "Syria, Saudi Arabia, the U.A.E. and Qatar: The 'sectarianization' of the Syrian Conflict and Undermining of Democratization in the Region." *British Journal of Middle Eastern Studies* 46 (3): 385–403. https://doi.org/10.1080/13530194.2017.1408456.

Morris, Mary E. 1993. *New Political Realities and the Gulf: Egypt, Syria and Jordan.* Santa Monica, CA: RAND. https://www.rand.org/pubs/monograph_reports/MR127.html.

Ouaki, Valentine. 2016. "Syrian Refugees: Why Won't Rich-Oil Gulf States Take Them In?" *Le Journal International,* January 30. https://www.lejournalint

ernational.fr/Syrian-refugees-why-won-t-the-oil-rich-Gulf-States-take-them-in_a3477.html.

Ramani, Samuel. 2019. "UAE and Russia Find Common Ground on Syria." The Arab Gulf States Institute in Washington, March 11. https://agsiw.org/uae-and-russia-find-common-ground-on-syria/.

Ramani, Samuel. 2020. "Russia and the UAE: An Ideational Partnership." *Middle East Policy* 27 (1): 125–140. https://doi.org/10.1111/mepo.12479.

Reliefweb. 2018. "UAE Named World's Largest Humanitarian Donor for Fifth Straight Year." April 10. https://reliefweb.int/report/united-arab-emirates/uae-named-world-s-largest-humanitarian-donor-fifth-straight-year.

Santucci, Emily. 2020. "The Caesar Act Might Alter the UAE's Normalization Policy with Syria." The Atlantic Council, August 24. https://www.atlanticcouncil.org/blogs/menasource/the-caesar-act-might-alter-the-uaes-normalization-policy-with-syria/.

Szymanski, Adam. 2017. "Turkish Policy Towards War in Syria." *Teka Komisji Politologii i Stosunków Międzynarodowych* 12 (1): 63–84. https://doi.org/10.17951/teka.2017.12.1.63.

The Economist. 2019. "UAE Engagement in Syria Grows." *The Economist – Intelligence Unit*, December 19. http://country.eiu.com/article.aspx?articleid=38838787&Country=United%20Arab%20Emirates&topic=Pol_2.

Todman, Will. 2016. *Gulf States' Policies on Syria.* Report. Center for Strategic and International Studies (CSIS). https://www.jstor.org/stable/resrep23307.

Uslu, Emrullah. 2016. "*Jihadist* Highway to *Jihadist* Haven: Turkey's *Jihadi* Policies and Western Security." *Studies in Conflict & Terrorism* 39 (9): 771–802. https://doi.org/10.1080/1057610X.2015.1119544.

United Arab Emirates Ministry of Foreign Affairs & International Cooperation. 2019. "UAE Foreign Aid Report 2019."

CHAPTER 8

New Regional Powers Confronting Uncertainties in the Middle East

Bertrand Badie

Traditional political science has always been dominated by an uncritical usage of the concept of power, to the point where it has embarked on using learned typologies that in particular put into perspective variable intensities, different institutional profiles and the nature of the resources mobilized, thereby distinguishing between different manifestations of a power presented as a single unit in the international game. Strangely enough, these classifications have very little to do with the reality of the function carried out no more than they have with the context in which this takes place. These classifications only incidentally ask questions about regional powers as such. The science of international relations was born in an extremely bipolar system and remains obsessed by the clash between the two superpowers that seemed to demote other forms of power evermore to a secondary rank and not worth bothering with. This dogma is no longer applicable today or, in any case, is significantly challenged:

B. Badie (✉)
Sciences Po Paris, Paris, France
e-mail: Bertrand.badie@sciencespo.fr

© The Author(s), under exclusive license to Springer Nature
Switzerland AG 2021
B. Balci and N. Monceau (eds.), *Turkey, Russia and Iran in the Middle East*, The Sciences Po Series in International Relations and Political Economy, https://doi.org/10.1007/978-3-030-80291-2_8

power is spread over different projects and with a variable range of actions, without totally respecting the old hierarchical logic. Such regional power, which once used to operate in the second division of a hierarchical world, is now taking on new meaning where the Middle East, in its current status of "*crater of the world*" is particularly significant.

COMPLEX DEFINITIONS

In the bipolar context that saw the generation of most theories of international relations, the very discrete notion of regional power gave way to the nevertheless uncertain notion of medium-sized power: in a world of power blocs confronting each other, regions had neither real autonomy nor their own political mode; they simply followed the binary game. What is more, middle powers, with their intermediate political capacities, took their place on a scale that, simply, defined them as superior to "small states" whether or not this superiority manifested itself within their own geographical zone. They belonged within a strictly hierarchical grammar: when he wished to define the status of his own country, the Canadian prime minister William Lyon Mackenzie King characterized it as a "middle power," too small to interfere in the Moscow-Washington confrontation, but too large to renounce playing any part on the global stage. It was evident that Canada could not compensate for its relative inferiority by playing the regional card, and so it took its place among those middle powers that sought to belie their lack of effective power by playing the multilateral card. The situation was different for European middle powers that willingly invested the Old Continent stage and institutions to give substance to their new status: even though France and Britain, permanent members of the Security Council, still hankered after power on a global scale, General de Gaulle very quickly grasped what diplomatic leadership role was open to him within the new "European Economic Community." France was joined in this by Germany as it emerged from the post-war shadow; London, however, hesitated for a long time between sustaining its former global status and that of a first-rank European power. Little by little, the idea of a regionalization of medium powers spread, affecting Japan in Asia, Brazil in Latin America, and, benefitting from decolonization, India, Indonesia, South Africa and Nigeria, in their own zones.

During the Cold War, all these powers were marked by their inefficacy. At best, they were considered as powers "by proxy," benefitting from a delegation of power reluctantly yielded by the superpowers. Hence the difficulties encountered by Gaullist diplomacy, which only succeeded in securing a basic autonomy thanks to a judiciously dissident diplomacy that went completely to ground when such vital issues came to the fore as the U2 incident (1960), the Cuban missile crisis (1962), or the matter of Berlin: thus the regional power remained more-or-less aligned and only weakly dissenting. This pattern was rapidly established in the Middle East (Beck 2014): as it was absorbed into the bipolar structure, it tended to model itself under the influence of the superpowers alone; those regional actors who still harbored some hegemonic inclinations, rapidly realized that it was at their own expense. Such was the case with Saudi Arabia, notwithstanding the Quincy Pact of February 14, 1945, when it had passively to accept Harry Truman's abandonment of promises conceded by his predecessor in respect of Palestine. This forced submission led to Riyadh's renouncing, at least for half a century, all aspiration to any real regional power and autonomy. Egypt seemed to hold the reins from then on, from the time of the revolution of the Free Officers. Despite his charisma and a made-to-measure pan-Arabist ideology, Nasser in his turn had to accept partial disappointment. While still in the ascendant, the President aspired to a new vision of regional power, emancipated from the great powers, suspicious of the Soviet Union, skeptical of and then disappointed by the United States, strongly centered on the region it wanted to shape, but with a global voice, notably among the states in the Non-Aligned Movement. In fact, Cairo had to lower its ambitions very rapidly, challenged as it was from its own side, and above all unable to act without Soviet support that grew ever stronger right up till Nasser's death in 1970. The notion of power by proxy had a troubled existence as was shown by Iran's rise in capacities under the Shah, as it was promoted to the role of Washington's lieutenant…

The decay and then the disappearance of bipolarity changed things: and these events inspired a substantial body of writings on the topic, that had scarcely existed before (Neumann 1992; Stairs 1998; Royds 1999; Hurrell et al. 2000; Pedersen 2002; Buzan and Waever 2003; Godehardt and Nabers 2011; Stewart-Ingersoll and Frazier 2012; Nel et al. 2012). This is as much about the causes as about the consequences: regional powers certainly saw their powers enhanced as bipolarity weakened, but this was in its turn rocked by the rise of emergent powers such as the "Asian dragons" and the Latin-American "jaguars" that, initially at least, were not envisaging displacing the superpowers, just dominating regional economies. These new powers were emerging from sometimes extreme poverty, while setting up inequalities that were sometimes increasing, in order to build in the heart of oriental Asia or Latin America new centers, alluring by virtue of their economic success and nationalist message, but somewhat disturbing to the older regional and global order (Nel et al. 2012). This capability was not just symbolic, but in reality was based on resources that counted for that much more as post-1989 neo-liberalism no longer accorded the military community the determining role it had held during the Cold War. On the model of India, Brazil and even South Korea and Indonesia, the New Regional Powers (NRPs) were thus gaining in real autonomy, and these were changes of a kind that were still at this time absent from the Middle East. Moreover, the rationale of interdependence that accompanied globalization precluded ignoring these new actors. Perhaps over-confidently, it was thought they could be analyzed by way of their systematic integration in accordance with the law of necessary cooperation articulated beforehand by Robert Keohane (Keohane 1969): the functional capacity of these new regional powers to promote a "cooperative regionalism" made them new potential stabilizers for regions not drawn to a center that no longer existed or at least that was weakened (Pedersen 2002). These new powers were henceforth reputed to be "stabilizers" of an order undergoing globalization, and their leadership manifested itself by producing new institutions, and by their entrepreneurial abilities and intellectual energy (Nel et al. 2012).

This functionalist optimism probably obscured a fundamental truth, that NRPs were not the fruit of an agreed law of evolution. On the contrary, their new history inhabited a conflictual ambiance that of securing for themselves a new status in the face of the old hegemons, of acquiring a role different from theirs and even superior to what it had been. Doing this involved dual activities: the effective displacement of the superpowers that formerly dominated the regions concerned, and getting both small and former major states to acknowledge the new role of NRPs, generated by new expectations and prerogatives never before conceded (Holsti 1970, 27). Recognizing this implied a break with the past, transcending juridical formalism and activating equality of respect, a sentiment of mutual esteem and trust (Iser 2015). This was in fact a conspicuously conflictual process, especially in zones marked by extreme rivalries. On the other hand, it is true that achieving it could appear functional: a region deprived of regional powers became inevitably liable to crises, while, on the global level, the old middle powers deprived of regional support (Canada, Australia ...) or where the institutional basis of regional support was uncertain (Europe) tended to decline (Østerud 1992).

THE MIDDLE EAST, TEST-BED OF GLOBAL CHANGE

The Middle East in fact followed exactly the sine-wave of regional power. Its particularly complex engagement in international affairs bestowed on it a changing political configuration, rendering the emergence of regional powers impossible, probable or conflictual in turn. The first sequence begins with the Ottoman Empire and presents us with pure geopolitical illusion: the weakening of the High Porte in the context of western European domination blocked the emergence of any new regional power and prepared the way for familiar regimes of concession and mandate. At most, the new Turkey that emerged from the treaties of Sèvres and Lausanne attained recognition of sovereignty, limited by the absence of any control over the Straits, while it found itself reduced to a modest size and incapable of accomplishing any real function as a regional power, faced with the pressure of the mandate in the Levant. In parallel, and from 1907 on, an Anglo-Russian agreement divided Persia into two zones of influence. This first sequence was therefore that of the *annihilation* of any regionalization of power in this part of the world where strict and direct surveillance was sought, considering its position as a geopolitical crossroads, its vocation to link or to oppose the Abrahamic religions and, obviously, the oil issue that had imposed itself on the strategic plan since before the First World War: William d'Arcy founded the Anglo-Persian Oil company in 1909...

This initial balance was tentatively modified following the Second World War. The game was changed by the end of the mandates, the constitution of a formally independent Arab world and, from 1945, the creation of the Arab League allied with the rise in militant nationalism, relayed in Iran by Mohamed Mossadegh: the regionalization of power became not only a possibility that already had potential vectors available but it also had a true function since it is true that a "geopolitical" space newly formalized is naturally on the lookout for leaders. The game of procuration did not really work: the states setup were too young to attract the trust of the powerful or else their loyalty was too uncertain, such as Iran, drawn between Washington and Moscow. The chosen solution was that of integrating the larger elements into transnational pacts, like Turkey joining NATO in February 1952, whereby it reinforced its power but at the same time was turned away from exercising true regional leadership. Three years later Ankara sided with Iraq, Iran and Pakistan in the Baghdad Pact, closely overseen by London and Washington: John Foster Dulles would have liked Egypt to have been included but Gamal Abdel Nasser refused that already began to threaten with failure this second sequence which was that of a political *domestication* of the regional power.

The Iraqi revolution of July 1958 put an end to the experiment: the Pact became the CENTO and obviously continued but without the participation of any Arab state, while several of them laid claim more or less secretly to the role of leading regional power. The candidacy of Nasser's Egypt was explicit, at a time when the country was ushering in the new United Arab Republic, in a union with Syria. The model is clear: it is composed of pan-Arabism, socialism and non-alignment! Not far away, Iraq was waiting on the side-lines dreaming of playing its own role, opposed to Persia and the Saudi monarchy, both of which were legitimist and pro-American. Finding its own existence following on from that, Ba'athist Syria swiftly had the same objectives: the three former caliphate capitals were then rivals for the same place. This opened the way to a third sequence, that of the *rebel and dissenting* regional power, which nevertheless met its limits under more or less forced Soviet tutelage, to which was opposed the system of American proxies given to Israel, to the Shah's Iran and to Saudi Arabia. Between *rebellion* and *proxy,* the new forms of regionalization seemed fragile.

In all these cases, the regional power broke through with difficulty in the Middle Eastern sphere, on bases that were in fact classic, conforming to a Westphalian model that was trying to become universal. Local states were simply making an effort to exist according to classic criteria defining a power that they identified with difficulty from their known assets but which were often contradictory: wealth found under the ground, "geopolitical" position, military resources, the capital of trust stored up with the superpowers that patronized them or ideological investment. This equation evolved in a decisive fashion as the world order shifted from bipolarity to that of globalization. The fall of the Berlin Wall brutally devalued classical power (Badie 2019) and the criteria that went with it and little by little it advanced another unit of account that was more subtle and more complex, as *status* gradually replaced *power.* In other words, facing a power whose efficacity was uncertain, states now sought to flag up a position that bore their identity and open up the rights and privileges of being recognized not only in their existence but also their accreditation to co-manage, if not the whole world, then at least their own region. During a transition period, this status was still appreciated in classic terms of material resources, economic or military, which thus did not change appearances: the new regional powers detached themselves from the old Westphalian power game without really becoming incarnated in new forms of expression (Parlar Dal 2019, 501). This was Turkey's gamble at the turn of the century up until the first period of the AKP, the Syria of Bashar al-Assad before 2011 and Egypt at the end of the presidency of Hosni Mubarak.

As the new century moved on, other parameters were affirmed, around which fresh competition for status was based: ideology, certainly once again, but also culture, religion "civilization," supposedly moral superiority (Parlar Dal 2019); even more deeply the tendency to manage social flows, to restructure the social order and to redefine the regional landscape would be highlighted. The change is easily understood: depolarization gives the region back its own history; it weakens the old powers, whether they had been vanquished, like the old USSR, or whether, like the United States, they had lost their rival and were now just posing in their imperial pretention. Globalization therefore played its role without the "geopolitical" constraints of the past: it accelerated interdependencies, re-evaluated economic and social parameters, shook up societies, densified communication, visibility and exchanges, reinforced the inclusion of regions previously marginalized, like the Sahel, Afghanistan and Yemen, and, finally, intensified the mobility of people, symbols and ideas.

In this new context there are not legions of candidates for the rank of regional power. Above all, they are rare within the Arab world itself: the American invasion of Iraq in 2003 and the fall of Saddam Hussein, the Arab Spring that swept away the Egyptian and Libyan leaders and abolished their position, the civil war in Syria, whose horrors have spread, have removed these four countries from the list, making Saudi Arabia the only candidate possible. A financial power, one of the top three oil producers in the world and the fourth power in terms of military spending, the kingdom has all the classic attributes of a power, even though it is seriously handicapped by its feeble capacity to make use of its presumed force, as indicated by its absence of reaction to the attacks on the oil processing facilities in Abqaiq and Khurais in September 2019. On the other hand, its symbolic resources flatter its pretensions to status: strong religious influence, ability to maximize control over holy sites, aptitude to forge a strict variant of Islam, to maintain networks, whether of preachers or of humanitarian aid NGOs, to hand out financial manna in the form of holy offerings as a source for retaining loyalty. These are all strong points capable of imposing the kingdom on neighboring states (Egypt, Sudan, a few of the Gulf principalities) but also, and maybe above all, of imposing itself on networks, parties, media, armed groups, entrepreneurs of violence who rage throughout all the Middle East and beyond ... Only Qatar in the Arab world appears as the only other possible postulant, partly served by the same material and symbolic resources as its mighty neighbor.

Outside of this world, two non-Arab powers can impose themselves in a more credible manner, one is Turkish, the other Persian. They can both deploy the classic criteria of power: population (each has over 80 million inhabitants, much more than Saudi Arabia, with only 33 million, a third of whom being foreigners), military capacities (in particular Turkey, even though it is only 15th in world rankings for military spending, Iran being 18th), while their economic level has pushed them into the status of emerging nations and places them just behind Saudi Arabia at the top of the list of GDPs in the greater Middle East (Turkey being 19th in the world ranking and Iran 28th, according to the World Bank in 2018). Above all, these two countries affirm their positions by emphasizing their symbolic and cultural capacities, as illustrated notably by the evolution of the AKP's foreign policy, investing more and more in religious *soft power*. Because of its attributes, its sources and its capacities, Israel could certainly be placed in the same category if its offer turned out to be attractive to the states in the region and if it was accepted as such: this is obviously far from being the case ...

THE FIGHT FOR RECOGNITION

These three "NRPs" (if we momentarily exclude the Qatari case that remains, as we shall see, in an uncertain state) are making a stand. Since at least the turn of the century and the definitive break with the bipolar or immediately post bipolar temporality the problem has lain in the subjective dimension of status and therefore of recognition by others. The stakes are sufficiently high that they in turn define the contours of the new regional conflictuality. This new sequence opened up after operation "Desert Storm" (1991) and the failure of the Madrid conference (October–November 1991) and when the Oslo Accords (September

1993) seemed to usher in a new age for the re-autonomization of the region.

In this context, the old powers were obliged to review their position in the region and to specify their degree of acceptance of these new regional partners. In fact, the lack of legal recognition has never been a real problem at this level since within the Middle East it has only affected the Palestinian state and this only upon the initiative of America: even if Washington and Tehran have broken off diplomatic relations since April 7, 1980, the current Iranian regime has always been recognized as such by the United States. The three other criteria suggested by Mattias Iser (recognition through respect, esteem and trust) are, however, much more problematical and they concern everybody, as much on the side of the old powers as on the side of the NRPs (Iser 2015). The Ottoman Empire already had to put up with, at least since the nineteenth century, all the characteristics of institutionalized scorn: considered as "the sick man of Europe," it was perceived as inferior in its economic, technological and military capacities, even if, on its side, the Sublime Porte itself tended to direct the same condescending gaze on its Arab provinces of the time (Herzog 2002). This developmentalist reading of the Middle East had, for a long time, been consecrated by the regime of Capitulations that, throughout the region, dispensed European residents from being subject to judgment by local courts. This arrangement was even confirmed by the Treaty of Sèvres (August 1920) that at the same time, through the institution of French and British mandates in the Levant, formalized the idea that Arab peoples were incapable of governing themselves. In a less formal fashion, from the end of the nineteenth century, the multiplication of British, Russian, French and Belgian concessions in Persia led to the same affirmation.

This hierarchical culture proved to be durable: it quickly became part of the ordinary social behavior forged on both sides. The arrogance on one side was matched by the feeling of humiliation on the other, giving rise to a long history made up of mutual distrust, of a desire for revenge and of protectionist sovereignty. These were all elements that lastingly hampered the process for recognition of the new regional powers that was beginning to break through and that increasingly worried the old powers, all the more so as their rise bore the increasingly clear signs of revanchism and symbolic affirmation! The Saudi exception was only partial: while enjoying a more favorable attitude from the Westerners linked to the alliance that had flourished since the Quincy Pact, the kingdom was suffering from the progressive conversion of its sources of power, which were more and more expressed around Islamic symbols that caused fear, even more, so as many Saudis were involved in the attacks of September 11. Turkey and Iran, each in their own way, raised the strongest fears. The former because it could only impose itself as a NRP by clearly dismantling the links that previously tied it to the Western camp, through NATO, from which it needed to distance itself in order to regain some kind of liberty, facing a Europe into whose core it had never been admitted and that it was no longer courting. Russia was not much more reassured although it in Ankara it saw the entry point to the Atlantic world and, even better, the multi-secular rival that was barring its route toward warm seas. Facing Iran, things were even worse; the shadow of grievances accumulated since the hostage crisis at the American embassy went beyond the United States and the Western states and even affected Russia that had its own history of distrust of the Islamic republic.

This distrust was in fact expressed in two ways: over the long term we observe a long-standing reservation regarding the cooperative strategies giving local actors in the Middle East too much latitude. One only needs to recall the difficulties met by Gamal Abdel Nasser when dealing with the two superpowers, the constant refusals by the American administration to allow him weapons or even to participate financially in the construction of the Aswan Dam. The welcome was not much more favorable in Moscow even though, following a reflex tested in the region and still very clear today, the Kremlin quickly understood the game that it could win by filling the place left vacant by Washington. The Memoirs of Mohamed Hassanein Heikal are, however, full of examples of misunderstandings and distrust between Khrushchev and Nasser (Heikal 1972). Regarding trust, this was more a case of simple instrumentality based more on the occasion than on the long term. Thus, later on, regional status was granted to Saddam Hussein to counter the Islamic Republic of Iran, or to Hafez al-Assad in order to contain Palestinian resistance at the beginning of the Lebanese civil war, just as the role of establishing links between Israel and the Palestinian resistance was delegated to Mubarak. It was never a question of long-term recognition covering all the diplomatic sectors as the status of a real regional power would have required.

A second factor has been the constant re-evaluation of the jihadist question on the international agenda that has reinforced distrust with regard to Middle Eastern regimes that were not (or were no longer) modelled on the old bipolar order. The states on the Arabian Peninsula where Jordan benefited from favorable preconceptions because of their pro-western stance: however, except for Riyadh, they did not have the scope of an NRP. States arising from the former Arab socialism and with a lay orientation, like Ba'athist Syria, even today are the object of distrust in the West although this was partly lifted during the first decade of the new century when Syrian power was once again delegated with a limited regional role that Russia, faithful to its own style, sought to widen while all the time tightly controlling. Finally, those dictatorships that displayed their anti-jihadist determination, like Marshall Sissi's Egypt, or, quite recently, the militia of Marshall Haftar in the east of Libya, saw themselves delegated a role for maintaining regional order that is, however, a long way off from covering all the functions proper to NRPs. On the other hand, the two potential main regional powers, Turkey and Iran, suffered from a confusion of registers: their religious orientation, by nature very different, was worrying and raised distrust of them, even though the former could not construct its regional dominance only by containing jihadist pressure, while the latter is, by identity, resolutely opposed to the state that remains its sworn enemy... The lesson is clear: the weight of representations is stronger than realistic perspectives, where the invention of NRPs is concerned... and my enemy's enemy is by no means necessarily my friend. Nevertheless, it is on this basis that in yesteryear, the status of regional power was acknowledged...

In this altogether naive game, the West has shown constancy, reinforced by the desire to not displease Israel. This naivety is all the more intensified in that the status of regional power is not decreed, cannot be the object of a ban nor of a quarantining: it is imposed by the resources accumulated and the level of capacity that is reached. At most, the actor who is outside it can try to arrange it, modulate it and accompany it; but in denying it they will surely lose, and the winners will be their own rivals, like Russia and China or even other emerging powers, that have known how to get the upper hand.

THE NEW MIDDLE EASTERN GAME

By its own insistent imposition, this new structure of regional power is dictating its law, organizing the region, its conflicts, its subtle coalitions, its apparent reversals of situation and the force play of the great powers, henceforth more reactive than proactive. In the first place, this new structure is generating a new conflictual configuration, putting the NRPs, real or potential, in contact, then positioning them in relation to other actors in the game, basically the old powers. In one case as in the other, two strategies stand out: hostile competition or cooperative competition. The first case illustrates Saudi-Iranian relations and, to a lesser degree, Saudi-Turkish relations, or even Saudi-Qatari. Undeniably, hostility lies in the fear felt in Riyadh of seeing Ankara or Tehran dominate the Arab world and in particular, in the second instance, of seeing the Shi'ite position shored up opposite Wahhabi fundamentalism. There is no doubt at all that the regionalization of politics, almost everywhere, drapes itself in cultural and religious emblems that exacerbate the logic of competition. Behind this flame, the main thing is still nevertheless a rivalry in the domination based on the conviction that this cannot accommodate association. Many factors play a role in this conviction: the physicality of the Gulf as a strategic stake, the uncertainty of the position of many intermediate players (Oman, Qatar and also Kuwait, even the emirate of Dubai under Iranian financial pressure, Yemen), the governance of OPEC and above all the clash of populations, Shi'ites in the north-east of Arabia, Sunnites and Arab-speakers in the south-west of Iran, heightened by the complex flows throughout the Gulf that are migratory, diasporic, commercial and financial. Less tense, the rivalry between Ankara and the Saudi kingdom is fed by their shared desire to restore, in their favor, the Sunnite caliphate of yesteryear... Conversely, the cooperative logics have won the day with Iran and Turkey: old rivals within the heart of the region, these two major players seem to consider that the antagonism of the past is no longer adapted to the situation of today. The reciprocal threats aimed at destabilizing the other are no longer valid, while their shared marginalization by the Western powers has created a solidarity reinforced by the need to cooperate economically.

At the international level and particularly on the Western side, everything seems to conflictualize the rise of the NRPs: an old commitment to the hegemonic game of alliances that is brought back with the Washington-Tel Aviv-Riyadh triangle, the substrate of suspicion already analyzed, and the well-known conviction that feeds the idea that only control, direct or indirect, by the global hegemon can ensure stability in a region in crisis. This dogma of "hegemonic stability," supported by the theories of Robert Gilpin (1987), leads now to making a delicate choice: either negotiate this gently, like Barack Obama who, however, got rebuffed by the Israeli ally; or enforce it, to the point of even stalling as soon as any military engagement is refused, as did Donald Trump; or reshape, as Joe Biden tries to do, with the risks of an uncertain success. In any case, the question of the Iranian nuclear program has suddenly risen to become the priority issue in a negotiation that is no longer really hegemonic, and in which the former superpower is clearly deprived of its traditional strategic assets. Faced with the impotence of the hegemon in thinking around efficient cooperative strategies with the NRPs, other powers have only to help themselves: Turkey and Iran thus see in this an activated cooperation with Moscow, the surest means to settle their regional range of influence. For its part, the Kremlin sees in this a relatively inexpensive way of gaining a foothold in the region while China carefully follows the Russian approach. A new conflictual configuration, with international pertinence, derives automatically from this, thereby offering Tehran and Ankara, global diplomatic status. The first game is "lose-lose," the second is "win–win"…

Beyond this unprecedented new conflictual configuration, the rise of the NRPs deeply modifies the very nature of coalitions. The superimposing of international and regional lines of division and the complexification of these make lasting and homogenous alliances impossible: the example of the Kurdish question is there to prove this, just like the great subtlety deployed by every player in the Syrian, Iraqi and then Lebanese conflicts. The Middle East is in no way more "complicated" than other regions of the world: the clash between the emerging NRPs and the declining world powers just simply breaks the continuities in alliance and sets up an extremely fluid game that should be defined as the proliferation of opportunities in which each actor sees the advantage of momentarily acting alone or stealthily with a view to carrying off an immediate advantage.

The third consequence is that NRPs have to negotiate their relations with the outside world. In a context of conflict, the game might prove costly although without necessarily leading to failure. Thus, Iran has to bear the pressure of brutal sanctions that have not had any decisive effect on the choices it makes however: at the same time, it is testing its impunity in the different actions of force that it has undertaken directly or not (boarding or even attacking boats in the Gulf, arbitrary arrests of foreign nationals and above all the attacks on Saudi oil installations in September 2019). As for Turkey, all it faces are painless verbal admonitions, with barely any link to a slight deceleration in military cooperation with Washington when it goes ahead and purchases Russian military hardware… In the cooperative game, one might even ask questions about the meaning

of this: Russia seemingly obliged to follow its Turkish and Iranian partners than to dictate their conduct. In any case, the cost of the cooperation
is higher, given that most of the strategic initiative comes from the NRPs.
However, this cost is much less than that paid by the Western powers
who pay a high price for the weakness of their regional cooperation and
therefore their relative isolation in the zone.

In the fourth place, proactiveness has changed sides. The troubled
arrival of NRPs has indubitably limited the margin for maneuver of the
older powers. Whatever the will of someone like Nasser might have
been in the past, he was limited by effective pressure from the superpowers: even if they had to face resistance from the old superpowers, the
current NRPs today possess a superior faculty for creating the event. It is
enough to just consider a few major episodes that have recently affected
the Middle East: the circumstances for the reconstruction of the Iraqi
state, the handling of the Kurdish issue, military and diplomatic developments in the Gulf and the development of Emirates' diplomacy obliged
to somewhat accommodate Iran… One of the most remarkable of these
diplomatic fulfilments is to be found in the Astana process talks, set up by
the summit talks held on May 4, 2017 in the Kazakh capital, establishing
four de-escalation zones in Syria. The talks brought Iran, Russia and
Turkey together thereby officializing a triangulation that has substituted
itself in fact for the other negotiation processes including those attempted
under the aegis of the United Nations. Even though the agreement was
not ratified by Damascus nor by the different combatant movements, it
has sketched the outlines of an "international community," significantly
reduced to three points of view, which is active and is presented as the
guarantor of the new regional order. The process has held as best it could,
through other summits (such as Tehran on September 7, 2018) followed
by other meetings, in Moscow, in Sochi… It has resolved nothing, except
momentarily, but its main effect has been to exclude all the other powers
and so it has fashioned a first and entirely original model of active regionalization… It is understood that henceforth nothing can be constructed
in the region without including these NRPs, while the exclusion of the
former powers is apparently becoming more commonplace. The Astana
triangle is just drawing conclusions from the existence of the complex
networks and connections set up by Tehran and Ankara, particularly in
Iraq (where Turkey is present, notably in Kurdistan, while Iran has a
strong influence on the government as well as on a number of militias), in
Syria, where Ankara has strong links with the Syrian National Army (SNA)

and also the National Front for Liberation (NFL) including notably the Islamist group *Ahrar al Sham*. Turkish influence is lesser in Lebanon though far from negligible, exercised through the Turkmen populations, in Baalbek and Akkar in particular but also through families living in the north of the country who have Ottoman origins; it is obviously less than that of Iran which is well-known.

However, it is advisable to be circumspect: an NRP is not a hegemon, which is a dominant and invincible actor responding to the appeal from its base and its allies (Badie 2019). In a significant manner, the circumstances surrounding its rise limit its capacities for domination. In former times, the regional power seemed to obey a geopolitical logic, linked almost exclusively to the positioning and the resources of states. Today, as we have seen, basically the NRPs feed off social resources, informal influence and networks of all kinds. Their capacity is all the more random and unnegotiated, subject to fluctuations, that no-one can control it or even less, master it, unlike the ordinary events of Westphalian diplomacy. In fact, any excessive exercise of different kinds of domination leads almost automatically to reactivating social behavior that can be violent: we only need to look for proof in the anti-Iranian social movements on the streets of Beirut and Baghdad, or even the burning of the Iranian consulates in the holy cities of Najaf and Kerbala, in November 2019.

Two important points need to be made. On the one hand, contrary to the received idea, religion is not sufficient for the weaving of links of allegiance that would be sufficiently durable to constitute a solid international divide. The Iraqi demonstrators in winter 2019 in no way forswore their Shi'ite faith but they were contesting the right of the Iranian regime to instrumentalize this orientation and identity for its own purposes. In other words, the political networks do not obey the mechanics of identity affiliation but rather they go with the encounter between this and the socio-political positioning of whoever bears this: one is "pro-Iranian" not because one is Shi'ite but because as a Shi'ite one is convinced that the backing from an older brother can help manage claims and expectations that one cannot satisfy on one's own. When practical matters give the lie to these hopes the allegiance drops away. In this the NRP is, by essence, fragile and unstable, at least in its cyclical short-term situations. On the other hand, another point is that the street demonstrations in the Iraqi and Lebanese capital cities have shown that social movements are perfectly able to do what a super power cannot do: to weaken significantly the capacities of a regional power and maybe to oblige it to rethink its strategy. Everything seems to happen as if the opposition of the strong was feeding the capacities of the NRP while the mobilization of the weak was likely to put an obstacle in the way.

There is certainly a sizeable kind of singularity in the Middle Eastern experience in this matter. Once again it is a question of greater degree rather than being an exception. The NRP creates, through its formation, higher tensions than elsewhere and even conflicts that organize the priorities of the international agenda, like the Iranian nuclear crisis seems to be suggesting. But for the most part, the basic process remains the same everywhere: new capacities, more social then "geopolitical," that make it indispensable for new states to take their place in a renewed regional game; a risk of conflict or destabilization should, the new reality, be denied; a capacity, definitely fragile but undeniable, to contribute, even more than the "world powers," to the stabilization of the area concerned.

Translation by Moya Jones

References

Badie, Bertrand. 2019. *L'hégémonie contestée. Les nouvelles formes de domination internationale.* Paris: Odile Jacob.

Beck, Martin. 2014. "The Concept of Regional Power: The Middle East as Applied to the Middle East." In *Regional Powers in the Middle East*, edited by Henner Fürtig, 1–20. New Yok: Palgrave.

Buzan, Barry, and Ole Waever. 2003. *Regions and Powers: The Structure of International Security.* Cambridge: Cambridge University Press.

Gilpin, Robert. 1987. *The Political Economy of International Relations.* Princeton: Princeton University Press.

Godehardt, Nadine, and Dirk Nabers, eds. 2011. *Regional Orders and Regional Powers.* London: Routledge.

Heikal, Mohamed Hassanein. 1972. *The Cairo Documents.* London: New English Library Ltd.

Herzog, Christoph. 2002. "Nineteenth Century Baghdad Through Ottoman Eyes." In *The Empire in the City*, edited by Jens Hanssen, Thomas Philipp, and Stefan Weber, 311–328. Beirut: German Orient Institute.

Holsti, Kalevi. 1970. "National Role Conceptions in the Study of Foreign Policy." *International Studies Quarterly* 14 (3): 233–309.

Hurrell, Andrew, Andrew F. Cooper, Guadalupe Gonzalez Gonzalez, Ricardo Ubiraci Sennes, and Srini Sitaraman. 2000. *Paths to Power: Foreign Policy Strategies of Intermediate States.* Washington, DC: Latin American Program, Woodrow Wilson Center for Scholars.

Iser, Mattias. 2015. "Recognition Between States? Moving Beyond Identity Politics." In *Recognition in International Relations. Rethinking a Political Concept in a Global World*, edited by Christopher Daase, Caroline Fehl, Georgios Kolliarakis, 27–48. Basingstoke, New York: Palgrave.

Keohane, Robert. 1969. "Lilliputians' Dilemmas: Small States in International Politics." *International Organization* 23 (2) (Spring): 291–310.

Nel, Philip, Dirk Nabers, and Melanie Hanif. 2012. "Introduction: Regional Powers and Global redistribution." *Global Society* 26 (3): 279–288.

Neumann, Iver. 1992. *Regional Great Powers in International Politics.* Basingstoke, New York: Palgrave.

Østerud, Øyvind. 1992. "Regional Great Powers." In *Regional Great Powers in International Politics*, edited by Iver Neumann, 1–15. Basingstoke, New York: Palgrave.

Parlar Dal, Emel. 2019. "Status Competition and Rising Powers in Global Governance: An Introduction." *Contemporary Politics* 25 (5) (December): 499–511.

Pedersen, Thomas. 2002. "Cooperative Hegemony: Powers, Ideas and Institutions in Regional Integration." *Review of International Studies* 28 (4): 677–696.

Royds, Mollie. 1999. "Canadian Security Policy Under Axworthy." *The Centre for Military and Strategic Studies,* April 8.

Stairs, Denis. 1998. "Of Medium Powers and Middling." In *Statecraft and Security: The Cold War and Beyond*, edited by Ken Booth, 270–286. Cambridge: Cambridge University Press.

Stewart-Ingersoll, Robert, and Derrick Frazier. 2012. *Regional Powers and Security Orders: A Theoretical Framework.* London: Routledge.

CHAPTER 9

The Iran-Russia Geopolitical Encounter: A Marriage of Convenience Rather Than a Strategic Alliance

Clément Therme

[The Russians] would be glad if Turkey, Persia, and Afghanistan ceased to exist as kingdoms but were maintained merely to be used as tools in the service of Russia herself.[1] As seen from the Kremlin, relations with Iran are closely bound up with perceptions of the West. Consequently, political parties have adopted positions on the Iranian issue that depend on their perception of the necessity or otherwise of making the search for alliances with Western countries in general and the USA in particular a foreign policy priority. On the bilateral level, the historical background

---

[1] Declaration by Amir Abdur Rahman Khan, who ruled Afghanistan from 1880 to 1901. See Sultan, Muhammad Khan, ed. Mir Munshi, *The Life of Abdur Rahman, Amir of Afghanistan*. London: John Murray, 1900, pp. 260 ff., quoted by Günther Nollau, Hans Jürgen Wiehe. *Russia's South Flank. Soviet Operations in Iran, Turkey, and Afghanistan*. London/New York: Frederick A. Praeger, 1963, p. 3.

C. Therme (✉)
Centre for Advanced Studies, European University Institute (EUI), Fiesole, Italy

© The Author(s), under exclusive license to Springer Nature Switzerland AG 2021
B. Balci and N. Monceau (eds.), *Turkey, Russia and Iran in the Middle East*, The Sciences Po Series in International Relations and Political Economy, https://doi.org/10.1007/978-3-030-80291-2_9

can be defined as short-lived ententes in a history of conflict until the Islamic Revolution of 1979. However, the main characteristic that unites these two states is, without a doubt, the fact that they are each the heir to a great historical legacy and are driven by the same will to reclaim an imperial past or, at least, to be a part of its heritage. Thus, the current diplomatic orientations of these two countries and even their military engagement in the war in Syria must be interpreted in light of this close link between imperial past and the ambition to become a new regional center of power.

SHORT-LIVED ENTENTES IN A HISTORY OF CONFLICT

The first Russian-Iranian relations at state level can be found dating from the Safavid (1502–1736) period. Nevertheless, the Volga opened up commercial contacts between the eastern Arab Caliphate and eastern Europe as early as the eighth century BCE. (Tikhomirov and Gafourov 1965, 20) The earliest commercial exchanges between Persia and Russia, along the Volga and across the Caspian Sea, (Andreeva 2007) took place against the background of these broader exchanges between the Slavic regions and the Arab Caliphate. They were interrupted by the Mongol invasions in the thirteenth and fourteenth centuries but started up again in the fifteenth with the rise of the state of Muscovy. It was not until the sixteenth century that diplomatic contacts were established between Persia and Russia, with the latter acting as an intermediary in the trade between Persia and Britain (Tereshchenko 2009, 88). Transporting goods across Russian territory meant the British could avoid the zones under Ottoman and Portuguese control. The Muscovy Company (also known as the Russian Company) was founded in 1553 to expand the trade route across the Caspian Sea. Moscow's role as an intermediary in exchanges between Britain and Persia led Russian traders to set up business in urban centers across Persia, as far south as Kashan. Commercial exchanges via Russia eventually came to an end in 1581 due to the increasing dangers faced by traders on the Volga. The route, taken six times by the Russian Company between 1560 and 1580, was a failed attempt to redirect trade with Persia from an east–west to a north–south axis via the river network connecting the Volga to the Caspian Sea (Lockhart 1986, 383). The alternative trading route fell victim to the combined opposition of the Ottomans, Venetians, and Armenians involved in trade with Persia via the Ottoman Empire. Though commercial exchanges between Russia and

Persia in the latter half of the sixteenth century were limited in scope, they nonetheless indicate that the fledgling entente between the two countries emerged as a result of opposition to the Ottoman Empire (Blow 2009, 85–98).

The end of the Safavid period saw an increase in trade between Persia and Russia. The exchange of ambassadors, which originally took place against a backdrop of wars between the Ottoman and Safavid empires, created the opportunity to strengthen bilateral trading links. Diplomatic relations between Iran and Russia date back to 1521, when the Safavid dynasty Shah Ismail sent an emissary to visit Czar Vasili III. As the first diplomatic contact between the two countries was being established, Shah Ismail was also working hard to "develop a dialogue with the Christians, the traditional or potential adversaries of the sultans of Istanbul, with the aim of joining forces against them" (Bacqué-Grammont 1987, 128). On several occasions, Iran offered Russia a deal exchanging territory (e.g., Darband and Baku in 1586) for its support in its wars against the Ottomans (Mahdavi 1996, 83). The issue of trade links was at the heart of the first diplomatic exchanges. Iranian traders sold fruits, spices, and silk—Persia's biggest export product in the sixteenth century in Russia, while Russia provided Iran with leather, furs, and metals (Matthee 2003, 105–106; Kazemzadeh 1991, 314–15). Even during these early contacts, diplomatic representatives and Russian traders were not hosted in accordance with the norms of Safavid hospitality—a sign of the Iranians' feeling of cultural superiority toward the religiously impure (*najes*) Russians they thought of as barbarians. (Matthee 2012, 99–125).

After the fall of Shah Hussain brought the Safavid dynasty to an end in 1722, the greatest threats facing Persia were Russian and Ottoman ambitions for territorial expansion in the Caspian region and north-western Persia respectively. The fall of the Safavid dynasty caused a major change in the history of bilateral relations between Russia and Persia. During the Safavid period, Russian and Persian power was relatively evenly balanced (Andreeva 2007, 13). Following Shah Hussain's fall, the relationship lost its symmetry as Russia gained a degree of domination over Iran, albeit one that varied over time. An almost equal relationship was, however, re-established under Nader Shah in the eighteenth century, when Iran negotiated with the Russian Empire on equal terms. The power relationship between Persia and Russia only came to a degree of stability after Persia suffered a series of defeats in the early nineteenth century.

The nineteenth century remains until today as a negative factor in the historical memory of the population of both countries. The second Russo-Persian war (1826–1828) was triggered by Persia, the main driving factor being the crown prince's thirst for military revenge after his defeat at the hands of the Russian army in 1812. The clergy was largely responsible for opening hostilities, but the army also had a role in influencing the decision by Fath Ali Shah and the crown prince, Abbas Mirza, governor of Tabriz. Other factors that came into play were the lack of precision over the border as defined in article two of the Treaty of Gulistan and the rivalry between the shah and his son, but it was the call to jihad by Aqa Sayyid Muhammad Isfahani that led Persia into conflict with Russia, reflecting anger over Russia's treatment of Muslims (Avery 1971, 17–23).

The 1828 Treaty of Turkmenchay formalized Persia's loss of its Caucasian territories, fixing the border between Russia and Persia along the Aras River, which has remained almost unchanged to the present day. Most of the clauses in the treaty were unfavorable to Iran. It forced the country to pay an indemnity of twenty million roubles and implemented a system of capitulation, depriving Iran of the right to sail its flotilla on the Caspian and repatriating all Russian prisoners of war, including those who wished to stay in Persia, while giving all Russian citizens resident in Iran the opportunity to return to their home country.

After this nineteenth-century experience of war and imperialism, the birth of a state-centered Iranian nationalism under the Pahlavi dynasty (1925–1979) is key to understanding the new Iranian foreign policy toward Moscow. This pragmatic foreign policy was based on an alliance with Washington to counter the perceived hegemonic and revolutionary ambitions of the Soviet Union. This does not mean a conflictual relationship with Moscow was sought but rather a pragmatic partnership based on neighboring relations, and after 1962, on the construction of a bilateral economic partnership. Indeed, after this date, Iranian-Soviet relations entered a phase of detente facilitated by the establishment of bilateral economic and military cooperation. But, as the former minister of the Shah, Dariush Homayun, pointed out it was the refusal of the Shah to welcome American missiles on Iranian territory that allowed the process of rapprochement between the two neighbors to be launched.[2] At the

---

[2] Personal interview with Dariush Homayun, Geneva, June 17, 2010.

same time, the Soviet authorities gave their support to the White Revolution initiated by the Shah while inside the country this aroused the opposition of the reactionary clerics. Seen from Moscow, the referendum of January 26, 1963, on the question of agrarian reform was perceived positively because the latter went against the interests of the Iranian feudal lords "supported by the Western colonialists". As a consequence of this rapprochement, Moscow also decided to stop its radio programs and the publication of the Soviet press in Persian hostile to the Shah's regime.

It was in 1967 that the major economic and military agreements with Moscow were signed, allowing the Shah to assert his independence on the regional scene by rebalancing his diplomacy between the two superpowers. An arms contract was signed with Moscow for $110 million resulting in the arrival of the first Soviet military experts in Iran. These supplies of military equipment were intended exclusively for defensive and light weapons. Therefore, this purchase of Soviet arms then reflected the Shah's dissatisfaction with the American aid policy. In addition, the main industrial achievements resulting from this partnership were the construction of the Isfahan steel plant, which amounted to approximately $600 million. Moscow's interest in Iranian gas resources allowed the Shah to negotiate a barter deal with Moscow.[3] Thus, the contract for the construction of the Isfahan steel plant, signed in January 1966, would be settled by exports of Iranian gas to the Soviet Caucasus. These exports began in the early 1970s, the day after the gas pipeline connecting Iran to the Soviet Caucasus was inaugurated by the Shah and Podgorny. With the improvement of bilateral relations, the USSR decreased its support for the Toudeh party. In 1971, the Soviet premier, along with many leaders of Communist bloc countries such as Tito, participated in the commemorations to mark 2,500 years of the Iranian monarchy.

THE ISLAMIC REPUBLIC'S IDEOLOGICAL CHALLENGE TO SOVIET RUSSIA

Despite the rapprochement during the last two decades of the Pahlavi dynasty, it was the conflictual historical background that was one of the main explanations behind the Pahlavi dynasty's choice to favor an alliance with the UK until 1953 and the fall of Mossadegh. After that date, the

[3] See Renaud Sivan, French Ambassador in Iran to his excellency the Minister of Foreign Affairs in Paris "Construction éventuelle d'une acierie en Iran par l'URSS: réactions de la presse iranienne", Tehran, July 10, 1965. French Embassy in Tehran, Diplomatic Archives, La Courneuve.

USA would step in as the Shah's main international ally. During the revolutionary period (1977–1979), Moscow maintained cordial relations with the regime of the Shah, perceived as a factor of stability on the 2000-kilometer southern border of the Soviet Union. The main feature of Moscow's Iranian policy, then, is ambiguity. Indeed, on the one hand, the Soviet authorities supported the Iranian left's movements in general, and the Toudeh party in particular, which was then engaged in an alliance of circumstance with the Islamist groups, until the fall of the Shah. On the other hand, the presence of Muslim minorities in the border regions between the USSR and Iran (Central Asia and the Caucasus) prompted Moscow to be cautious about the plan to establish an Islamist theocracy on its southern border. The ideology of political Islam promoted by the new Khomeinist political elites was perceived in Moscow as a challenge to Marxist-Leninist ideology, hence the mistrust, even the contradictions of Soviet policy vis-à-vis the Islamic revolution. Subsequently, the Soviet occupation of Afghanistan further complicated relations between the USSR and the Islamists. In his letter to Gorbachev, Khomeini highlighted the theoretical incompatibility between Marxist and Khomeinist ideologies. To convince Gorbachev of the overwhelming need for his understanding of the world to "study Islam", the Ayatollah advised him: "A true understanding of Islam may forever release you from the problem of Afghanistan and other similar involvements".[4]

This argument of Iranian-Soviet ideological tension exacerbated by the Afghan question deserves to be qualified. Indeed, if the Soviet occupation of Afghanistan was a point of divergence between the Islamic Republic and the USSR, Tehran's Afghan policy remained a rhetorical opposition, even if the presence of many refugees and Afghan exiles sometimes constituted an obstacle to Tehran's moderate diplomacy on the Afghan question. In 1981, the Soviet authorities issued a warning to the authorities of the Islamic Republic following a demonstration by Afghan exiles in front of the Soviet embassy in Tehran:

> Following the demonstration of the Afghani exiles in front of the Soviet Embassy in Tehran, the Soviet government, not satisfied with the sending of a strong-worded note, called for the Iranian ambassador, Dr. Mokri, and announced to him the "strong warning" which was in effect an official threat against Iran. In this warning, the Soviet government called the

---

[4] http://en.imam-khomeini.ir/en/n29222/Imam-s-letter-to-Gorbachev.

just rage of Afghanis whose country is still occupied by Russian forces, a "criminal act" and demanded that the Iranian government protect the "security of Soviet establishments and personnel in the Islamic Republic" and that it compensate for the damages done to the Soviet embassy in Tehran.[5]

The Afghan example shows that after the Islamic Revolution, despite the slogan "neither East nor West, Islamic Republic", it has always been more East than West. This is significant because the Soviet Union and then Russia were perceived after 1979 as an eastern country by the Islamic Republic. Faced with the economic consequences of Western containment, Iran put aside its historic rivalry with Russia and included it in its Look East policy—referring to China, Russia and India. Iran's inclusion of Russia in its Eastern vision is a political maneuver made by the Iranian clerical establishment in general, and the Supreme Leader in particular (Ganji 2016). It is worth mentioning that there has been political infighting in Iran regarding both the rapprochement with Russia and the Iranian role in the Syrian war since 2011 (Brumberg 2018).

TEHRAN'S DEPENDENCY ON POST-SOVIET RUSSIA

To achieve foreign policy independence, the Islamic Republic not only became more dependent on Russia and China, but also relied on the theocratic state's harsh anti-US ideological rhetoric; an ideological dimension that presents a strategic disadvantage for Iranian diplomats when negotiating with non-Western countries, impeding their ability to leverage Tehran-Washington relations in an attempt to balance increasing partnerships with eastern countries. While the Islamic Republic's anti-US slogans make it almost impossible to normalize ties with Washington, Moscow is more flexible in balancing its geo-economic interests between the USA and Iran. More broadly, the Iranian search for strategic partnerships with Russia and China is also part of a broader project to integrate Asian regional organizations such as the Shanghai Cooperation Organization (SCO) and the Association of Southeast Asian Nations (ASEAN). Until now, this Iranian strategy has only been partly successful because Iran was able to secure observer status in the SCO in 2005 and to sign a

---

[5] "The Russian bear grinds his teeth" in *Iraninform. A Marxist-Leninist Review*, Vol. 2, No. 5, March 1981.

friendship treaty with the ASEAN in 2018. However, Iran is still not a full member of the SCO—despite Russian diplomatic support—because of Chinese reluctance to transform the SCO into an anti-US US regional organization. Given the asymmetry in the bilateral relationship between Russia and Iran, Iranian policymakers have proclaimed that the relationship has become an alliance or even a strategic partnership. Indeed, there is a gap between the discourse and the reality of bilateral cooperation in the economic sphere. For instance, in 2015, the two governments set an unrealistic target for trade at between ten and fifteen billion dollars per year, with both parties boasting joint-projects with financial targets set at forty to fifty billion dollars according to Iranian sources. These political statements do not reflect the current level of bilateral trade between the two countries, which has oscillated between one and three billion dollars annually since 2011. This economic cooperation is driven by political will rather than economic convergence (Therme 2018, 549–562).

The war in Syria since 2011 has brought the two countries nearer to a military entente despite growing differences (Dekel and Valensi 2019). Nevertheless, there are varying narratives regarding the amount of economic benefit that Iran is receiving from its involvement in Syria. One narrative comes mainly from Iranian sources claiming that Iranian government officials are frustrated by the dearth of reconstruction contracts awarded to Iranian companies when compared to those awarded to Russian entities benefiting from Chinese financial support. The other narrative comes from Western sources claiming that Iranian involvement in post-war Syrian reconstruction is massive and is evidence of Iranian self-interest in its involvement in Syria. The Islamic Republic, however, continues to argue that Syria has sidelined Iranian companies and products despite the immense support offered to Syria by the Iranian government and Iranian non-state actors since 2014. Iran has indeed provided political, economic and military support to the Syrian regime since the beginning of the Syrian civil war. It began by providing two credit lines for the import of Iranian goods for more than two billion US dollars (Westall and Al-Khalidi 2015). Iran also transferred about sixty thousand barrels of oil per day to Syria for a total value of around six billion US dollars (Philips and Lee 2015). In return, it is expected to be Syria's most important economic partner moving into the reconstruction phase of Syria's development. It asked for rights to construct a sea port in Syria mainly for commercial use. It also signed five major trade deals in 2017, one of which was to the Telecommunications Company of Iran (ITC), which is affiliated with the Islamic Revolutionary Guard Corps (IRGC), to become a mobile service provider in Syria. (*Reuters* 2017a). The Iranian energy company MAPNA also signed a memorandum of understanding with Damascus to restore a main control center for the Syrian power grid (*Reuters* 2017b). Iran's Research Institute of the Petroleum Industry has declared plans to build an oil refinery in Syria with a capacity to produce seventy thousand barrels per day once the war ends (Iran Front Page 2017), and several entities close to the IRGC have signed a memorandum of understanding to cooperate in a phosphate mine in Syria's al-Sharqiya area (Islamic Republic News Agency 2017).

Despite all of this, Salah Serzi, the Vice Chairman of Iran's Chamber of Commerce stated that Syria "continues to create restrictions on Iranian exports" (Deutsche Welle 2018). This dissatisfaction with the current state of trade relations between Syria and Iran mostly stems from unrealized expectations as an agreement reached between Syria and Iran sought to increase Iranian exports to Syria to about one billion US dollars, but according to Iranian officials only a quarter has been achieved thus far. This is not necessarily the fault of the Syrian government nor does Iran blame Bashar al-Assad himself. Ali Asghar Jumaee, the vice Chairman of the Joint Iran-Syria Chamber of Commerce, says that the problem of transferring money between Iran and Syria is the main obstacle to the expansion of trade relations, which, together with the lack of infrastructure and equal conditions for Iranian exporters and their rivals, have weakened the link between Syria and Iran (Taajeraan 2017). The need to increase bilateral trade and benefit from Syrian reconstruction contracts is further exacerbated by the immense pressure placed on Iran to expand its non-oil economic trade due to the downturn in the oil trade because of US sanctions, as well as the massive inflation and domestic turmoil that troubles the Iranian domestic economy. As a result, Iran is seeking to maximize its economic benefits from its involvement in the region. This policy is the product of an internal debate both inside the Islamic Republic system (*nezam*) and inside Iranian public opinion.

Iran's Regional Policy: Between Internal Debates and Revolutionary Ambitions

Indeed, popular, institutional, and Islamist factions in the Islamic Republic of Iran all have different opinions on how and why the Iranian state should be involved in the affairs of its neighboring countries. Iran's support of its regional allies, in particular through its use of proxies, is highly debated. The debate revolves around whether involvement with the proxies is the means to an end or the end in and of itself for Iranian foreign policy. The most conservative elements of the Islamic clerical establishment view the proxies as ends in themselves (exporting the Islamic Revolution), (Khomeini 2001) whereas for the moderate and so-called reformist factions, these proxies are a defensive means to protect the country (known as the theory of forward defense). While the political establishment reacts to public opinion and domestic tensions, the ideological Islamo-nationalist synthesis promoted by the (quasi)elected institutions (especially the presidency and the government since 2013) does not appear to have convinced a significant enough segment of the Iranian population of the benefits of its investment in its regional strategy nor of the transnational dimension of "Islamic internationalism" that is at the center of Khomeini's ideological proposition. While traditional supporters of the clerical regime in Tehran continue to support a narrative of Iranian participation in the region as an ideological and religious imperative, support for Iranian participation among other sections of society, particularly among the urban middle class, appears to be waning. While there appeared to be cross-societal support for Iranian participation in the fight against so-called Islamic State in Iraq and Syria in 2016, following the group's collapse support for regional intervention seems to have been in decline in 2018. There have been several incidents of dissent in the past year which have included criticisms of Iran's support, particularly financial support, for its regional allies. For example, in May 2018, there were in Iran, on average, 17 protests or strikes per day all over the country (BBC Persian 2018). Many slogans challenged the official narrative regarding Tehran's support for proxies all over the Middle East and asked the establishment to focus on internal challenges rather than on external military adventurism.

The more sectarian regional policy Iran has pursued since 2011 can therefore be described as a product of the dual nature of the Islamic Republic's institutions. On the one hand, since the election of President Hassan Rouhani, the elected institutions have tried to protect Iranian national interests by using Tehran's participation in regional conflicts not only as an element of national security (i.e., the fight against terrorism), but also as a bargaining chip with Washington and Moscow that enables Iran to present itself as a partner in the fight against ISIS. On the other hand, the hardline factions believe there is an existential battle with the

West and that Iran should side with the "oppressed" ("axis of resistance") as well as any non-Western international power (such as China and Russia). For example, the Office of the Supreme Leader and the Revolutionary Guards give priority to the promotion of the values of the Islamic Revolution and the defense of Shi'ite communities in Muslim countries as well as an alliance with Russia.

After 2013, the rise of Shi'ite paramilitary forces in Syria and Iraq demonstrates that beyond the use of religion for recruitment purposes, the ethno-nationalist factor remains a hurdle for Tehran in its attempt to export the Islamic Revolution. This limit has not been a hurdle to rising security cooperation between Iran and Russia in the Middle East. This new relationship with Moscow became more visible given the new relationship between Iran, Russia and some Shi'ite militias especially in Syria after 2012. The two countries used think tanks' platforms to promote their own vision of the Middle East and their common opposition to US policy in the area.[6]

The Failure of Multipolar Ententes Strategy

Beyond the regional cooperation with Moscow, the Islamic Republic's failure in building a network of multipolar ententes to counterbalance the negative impact of its hostility toward the USA could be best explained by the revolutionary dimensions of Iranian foreign policy. Indeed, Tehran has an ability to transform potential partners into adversaries due to a lack of flexibility in defining the interests to be pursued. The partnerships between Iran, China, and Russia should not be understood as predominantly anti-Western, or viewed as an anti-Western block, but as the manifestation of the will of these countries to appear as independent on the international stage. The aspiration toward international independence further explains the resilience of Russia and China in the face of US economic and political pressures aimed at thwarting their cooperation with Iran. At the same time, these countries adopt flexible diplomatic approaches that are centered around challenging US unilateral policies; their respective relationships with the Islamic Republic can be tools in achieving this goal.

---

[6] See for instance: http://www.iras.ir/www.iras.iren/doc/interview/3330/anton-mardasov-the-deterioration-of-relations-between-russia-and-the-us-is-in-interests-iran.

The Iranian clerical establishment is weakening the Islamic Republic's standing both regionally and internationally, in part, because the Khomeinist worldview is still dominating the decision-making process of Iranian foreign policy. The Revolutionary ideological dimension remains a formidable hurdle to transforming Iran into a truly emerging country. This also explains the inability of Iranian decision makers to defend the national interests of their country while dealing with non-Western international powers such as Russia and China. Because of their anti-US strategy, they are more dependent on their Russian partners in order to guarantee the survival of the Islamic Republic and to resist US and European pressures for behavior changes regarding its regional policies and ballistic program. Due to the Iranian decision makers' anti-US strategies, and in order to thwart US and European pressures for behavior change, to pursue a ballistic program and ultimately to ensure the survivability of the Islamic republic, Iranians are pivoting toward their Russian partners now more than ever.

CONCLUSION

Russian policy in Iran differs between the period of Muhammad-Reza Pahlavi's reign (1941–1979) and that of the Islamic Republic (1979–). The Islamist oligarchs do not perceive the powerful neighbor from the North as the main threat to the national security of the Islamic Republic which, in their view, comes from the USA. Moreover, the last Shah considered that the Soviet superpower constituted not only the main risk for the territorial integrity of the country but also a threat to the ideology of his regime by using the Toudeh party as a Trojan horse inside the monarchical state apparatus. Ultimately, the Shah showed great political lucidity in the face of the fear of an alliance between "red (communist) and black (Islamist)" (*ettehad sork-o siah*) since it was ultimately the main external factor explaining the fall of the monarchy. Paradoxically, relations with the USSR were on a better level in the period preceding the Islamic Revolution (1962–1979) than in the first revolutionary decade (1979–1989). More surprisingly, there is a continuity in Tehran's vision of its relations with Moscow before and after the Islamic Revolution. Regardless of the regime in power and the ruling faction in the Islamic Republic, the keyword remains the need to establish "good neighborly" relations with Russia. However, regime change in Iran has had a negative effect on Iranian-Soviet relations, despite the participation of the Tudeh communists in the Islamic revolution. It was therefore necessary to wait, another paradox, for the period after the end of the USSR in 1991 for the relations between Tehran and Moscow to recover their level of the pre-revolutionary period (before 1979).

BIBLIOGRAPHY

Andreeva, Elena. 2007. *Russia and Iran. Travelogues and Orientalism.* London: Routledge.

Avery, Peter W. 1971. "An Enquiry into the Outbreak of the Second Russo-Persian War, 1826–1828." In *Iran and Islam. In memory of the late Vladimir Minorsky*, edited by C. E. Bosworth. Edinburgh: Edinburgh University Press.

Bacqué-Grammont, Jean-Louis. 1987. *Les Ottomans, les Safavides et leurs voisins. Contribution à l'histoire des relations internationales dans l'Orient islamique de 1514 à 1524.* Istanbul: Nederlands Historisch-Archaeologisch Instituut in het Nabije Oosten.

BBC Persian. 2018. "rouzi hivdah ehteraz dar iran az rouz-e karegar ta rouz-e karegar." May 1. http://www.bbc.com/persian/43947490.

Blow, David. 2009. *Shah Abbas. The Ruthless King Who Became an Iranian Legend.* London/New York: I.B. Tauris.

Brumberg, Daniel. 2018. "Iran's Hardliners and Reformists and the Syria Gambit." December 27. http://arabcenterdc.org/policy_analyses/irans-hardliners-and-reformists-and-the-syria-gambit/.

Dekel, Udi, and Carmit Valensi. 2019. "Russia and Iran: Is the Syrian Honeymoon Over?" *INSS Insight* 1171, May 27. https://www.inss.org.il/publication/russia-iran-syrian-honeymoon/.

Deutsche Welle. 2018. "به حاشیه رانده شدن ایران در بازسازی سوریه" January 19. https://p.dw.com/p/2r8yA.

Ganji, Akbar. 2016. "Can Iran Trust Russia?" *Foreign Affairs*, May 3. https://nationalinterest.org/feature/can-iran-trust-russia-16027.

Iran Front Page. 2017. "Iran to Build Oil Refinery in Syria." *IFP News*, September 27. https://ifpnews.com/exclusive/iran-build-oil-refinery-syria/.

Islamic Republic News Agency. 2017. "Iran, Syria Ink 5 Cooperation Documents." January 17. http://www.irna.ir/en/News/82390694.

Kazemzadeh, Firuz. 1991. "Iranian Relations with Russia and the Soviet Union, to 1921." In *The Cambridge History of Iran. Vol 7. From Nadir Shah to the Islamic Republic*, edited by Peter Avery, G. R. G. Hambly, and C. Melville, 314–315. Cambridge: Cambridge University Press.

Khomeini, Ayatollah Ruhollah. 2001. *Imam Khomeini (s.a.) On Exportation of Revolution.* Tehran: International Affairs Department, The Institute for Compilation and Publication of the Works of Imam Khomeini (s.a.).

Lockhart, Laurence. 1986. "European Contacts with Persia." In *The Cambridge History of Iran. The Timurid and Safavid periods*, edited by Peter Jackson and Laurence Lockhart. Cambridge: Cambridge University Press.

Mahdavi, 'Abdol Reza. 1996. *Ravabet khareji-e Iran. Az ebtedaye doran-e safavie ta payan-e jang-e dovom jahani* [Iran's Foreign Relations. From the Safavid Period to the Outbreak of World War Two]. Tehran: Mo'hasese' entesharat Amirkabir.

Matthee, Rudi. 2003. "Anti-Ottoman Concerns and Caucasian Interests. Diplomatic Relations between Iran and Russia. 1587–1639." In *Safavid Iran and Her Neighbors*, edited by Michel Mazzaoui. Salt Lake City: The University of Utah Press.

Matthee, Rudi. 2012. "Facing a rude and barbarous neighbour: Iranian perceptions of Russians from the Safavids to the Qajars." In *Iran facing Others: Identity boundaries in a historical perspective,* edited by Abbas Amanat and Farzin Vedjani, 99–125. New York: Palgrave Macmillan.

Philips, Mathew, and Julian Lee. 2015. "How Iranian Oil Tankers Keep Syria's War Machine Alive." *Bloomberg*, June 24. https://www.bloomberg.com/news/articles/2015-06-24/how-iranian-oil-tankers-keep-syria-s-war-machine-alive

Reuters. 2017a. "Iran to Operate Mobile Service Network in Syria." January 17. https://www.reuters.com/article/us-mideast-crisis-syria-telecoms-idUSKBN1511QE.

Reuters. 2017b. "Syria Producing More Energy After Army Recaptures Gas Fields – Ministry." September 26. https://www.reuters.com/article/us-mideast-crisis-syria-electricity-idUSKCN1C12JY.

Taajeraan. 2017. "تعامل ها و تقابل ها بین المللی در بازاسازی سوریه", November 15. http://www.taajeraan.com/index.php/otaghebazargani-list/3281-2017-11-15-16-16-02.

Tereshchenko, Alexey. 2009. "Le tournoi des ombres." In *Le Grand Jeu. XIXème siècle, les enjeux géopolitiques de l'Asie centrale*, edited by Jacques Piatigorsky and Jacques Sapir. Paris: Autrement.

Therme, Clément. 2018. "Iran and Russia in the Middle East: towards a regional alliance?" *The Middle East Journal* 72 (4) (Autumn): 549–562.

Tikhomirov, Mikhail, and Babadjan Gafourov. 1965. *Les Slaves et l'Orient*. Paris: UNESCO.

Westall, Sylvia, and Suleiman Al-Khalidi. 2015. "Syria Ratifies Fresh $1 Billion Credit Line from Iran." *Reuters*, July 8. https://www.reuters.com/article/us-mideast-crisis-syria-iran/syria-ratifies-fresh-1-billion-credit-line-from-iran-idUSKCN0PI1RD20150708.

CHAPTER 10

Relations Between Turkey and Russia: Between Strategic Partnerships and Regional Rivalries

Nicolas Monceau

On January 8, 2020, the opening ceremony for the TurkStream gas pipeline in Istanbul—the symbol of energy cooperation between Russia and Turkey—brought the Russian President Vladimir Putin and the Turkish President Recep Tayyip Erdoğan together for the eighth time in a year. In comparison, the last visit made by the Turkish president to Brussels in order to meet European leaders dated back to October 2017. This imbalance highlights the now central position that Russia enjoys in Turkish foreign policy. Long defined as a main objective, full membership of the European Union (EU) now seems relegated to the background or even ignored by Turkey in favor of a deepening of new partnerships where the multidimensional cooperation with Russia is emblematic.

N. Monceau (✉)
University of Bordeaux, Bordeaux, France
e-mail: nicolas.monceau@u-bordeaux.fr

© The Author(s), under exclusive license to Springer Nature Switzerland AG 2021
B. Balci and N. Monceau (eds.), *Turkey, Russia and Iran in the Middle East*, The Sciences Po Series in International Relations and Political Economy, https://doi.org/10.1007/978-3-030-80291-2_10

167

This revival of relations between Russia and Turkey is taking place in a national, regional and international context which has changed profoundly over the last few decades. The end of the Cold War in the early 1990s then the coming to power of the Party of Justice and Development (AKP) in 2002 have brought about a growing development in bilateral exchanges in the political, economic, commercial, and military fields.

This recent rapprochement between Russia and Turkey has, however, raised a range of questions about its validity and whether it will last. In fact, both countries are the heirs to empires and have maintained historical and political rivalries down the centuries on the regional as well as the international scale. They share several points in common in their respective histories, in particular the existence of an age-old imperial heritage which has played an important role in shaping the national memory. But the weight of a past shaped by many conflicts—around fifteen, up until the First World War, between the Tsarist Empire and the Ottoman Empire—and regional rivalries have opposed them for a long time.

During the Cold War, the two countries remained adversaries because of the Soviet policies which led Turkey to belong to the Western bloc. As a member of NATO and an ally of the United States with close relations at economic, political, and military levels, Turkey was against Soviet expansion in the region, and in particular against Stalin's policy regarding the Turkish Straits, and was responsible at the time for the security of south-east Europe. The Straits issue has remained as one of the basic issues between Russia and Turkey since that time. In the 1990s, several factors caused tensions to flare: the reinforcement of Russian influence in the Caucasus region, the pan-Turkic policies carried out by Ankara in former Soviet spaces, and also the reciprocal accusations of support for terrorist groups. In the latter years, the two partners went through periods of tension and even of diplomatic crises because of their diverging opinions on the conflict in Syria.

It would thus be opportune to examine the scope and the limits of this reinforced cooperation in the geopolitical context of the region as well as the conditions for a lasting alliance between the two countries while taking into account their old and current rivalries and the consequences of these at regional and international level.

How should the recent developments in relations between Russia and Turkey be understood and interpreted? These evolutions have raised growing interest over the last few years. A range of special issues and reports have focused on the development in relations since the end of the Cold War (Bazoğlu Sezer 2000, 2001; Insight Turkey 2002; Aktürk 2006; Kınıklıoğlu and Morkva 2007; Aras 2009; Bölme 2009; Öniş and Yılmaz 2016; Kortunov and Erşen 2018; Balta and Çelikpala 2020). Some approaches have addressed the historic dimension, others have insisted on economic and energy cooperation while some have looked at the military cooperation between the two countries. Since the Syrian conflict broke out (2011) and then with Russia's military intervention in the conflict from 2015, a growing number of studies have examined the relations between the two countries in the context of the Syrian conflict.

Besides the fighting in Syria, this chapter aims at taking a wider look at this "ambiguous partnership" (Baev and Kirişçi 2017) or this "adversarial collaboration" (Yıldız 2021) by presenting an overview of relations between Russia and Turkey as well as their cooperations and/or rivalries in an effort to impose themselves as regional powers. Conditions for rapprochement between Russia and Turkey are recalled in the first part. Then, different aspects—economy, energy, and military—of the Russia-Turkey partnership are discussed in the second part. Finally, the convergences and divergences in interests in the two countries are examined in the last part.

THE CONDITIONS FOR RUSSIAN-TURKISH RAPPROCHEMENT

Russian-Turkish rapprochement has been set in a more favorable context marked by the end of the Cold War and has been manifested in different ways, ranging from official visits to setting up new instruments for cooperation.

A More Favorable Context Marked by the End of the Cold War

In the early 1990s, following the collapse of the Soviet Union, the end of the Cold War ushered in a new phase in the history of Russia-Turkey relations. The emergence of a new world order in which the two countries were no longer adversaries as they had been in the past favored the appearance of a climate of more consistent bilateral cooperation in economic and commercial terms. They both shared common stakes in the new international configuration while also facing several challenges regionally which helped toward their rapprochement.

In a context perceived to be more favorable for deepening bilateral relations, the factors for rapprochement between the two countries turned out to be many (Aktürk 2006). On the political front, Russia and Turkey shared common disappointments regarding Western countries, in particular in Europe, to the point of forming an "axis of the excluded" (Hill and Taspinar 2006; Kınıklıoğlu 2006). On the Russian side, the long-term complex relations with European countries and the consequences of the collapse of the USSR and then the reunification of Europe featured among the reasons that were advanced first of all. The expansion of NATO to include former Warsaw Pact members (such as Hungary, Poland, and the Czech Republic in 1999 and the three Baltic countries, Bulgaria, Romania, Slovakia as well as Slovenia in 2004) aroused deep concern in Russia. On the Turkish side, the multiple and regular obstacles encountered on the path to EU membership cooled relations between Turkey and its European partners, as for example in 1997, when the Luxembourg European Council did not grant it candidate country status.

From a security point of view, the attacks on the United States on September 11, 2001 and their consequences (American interventions in Afghanistan and Iraq) created more propitious conditions for a Russian-Turkish rapprochement. In March 2003, the Grand National Assembly of Turkey refused to allow American soldiers to invade Iraq from across its northern territory. This unprecedented decision reinforced Turkey's credibility as an independent actor in the Russian authorities' perceptions and encouraged the development of bilateral political dialogue. Turkey remembered the Western military intervention led by the United States against Iraq in 1991 and faced the consequences (such as the risk of destabilization of south-east Anatolia following the arrival of Iraqi refugees many of whom were Kurds). By refusing American military intervention from its territory since 2003, Turkey's intention was to protect itself against new waves of refugees and against the prospect, which became real with the new constitution of Iraq in 2005, of the creation of an Iraqi Kurdistan on its borders.

Moreover, the two countries faced security issues whose growing importance led them to grow closer after several years opposing each other. Since the first Chechen war (1994–1996), Russia had been fighting Islamist and separatist movements in the north Caucasus, in particular on Chechen territory, while Turkey had been combatting Kurdish separatism following the move to armed conflict by the PKK (Kurdistan Workers' Party) from 1984.

After having long accused each other of supporting terrorist organizations, the two countries decided to alter their respective stances with a view to fighting terrorism and begin a rapprochement to cooperate over security. The turning point came in November 1999, when the Turkish Prime Minister Bülent Ecevit visited Moscow. When the second Chechen war broke out in August 1999, Turkey recognized the Chechen question as being an internal problem for Russia and declared that henceforth it would exercise stricter control over pro-Chechen activities on its national territory. As for Russia, an undertaking was made to ban or to limit the activities of pro-Kurdish organizations along its borders including the Kurdish House in Moscow, considered as a front for the PKK (Olson 1996, 106–118, 1998, 209–227; Gudiashvili 2002, 72–79).

In the past few years, the two countries have grown closer in their fight against terrorism: Turkey offered to cooperate with Russia in order to protect the winter Olympic Games at Sochi in February 2014. Attacks committed in Turkey and attributed to Islamic State of Iraq and Syria (ISIS)—including the bombing at Suruç on the Syrian border in July 2015, those in Ankara in October 2015 and the one at Atatürk international airport in Istanbul in June 2016—were condemned by President Putin who called for stronger cooperation with Ankara in the fight against terrorism.

For those who supported this political and security approach, the convergence between Russia and Turkey was the expression of a defensive position shared by both states, faced with the formation of a new Europe from which they were excluded as well as shared apprehensions about the United States' foreign policy in the Middle East and in Europe. The factor deemed the most important in the development of Russia-Turkey relations would be determined by their respective relations with Western countries.

However, other factors contributed equally to bring the two countries together in particular in the fields of economics and energy. In fact, Russia and Turkey shared growing ambitions in the economic and energy realms while experiencing economic crises at very close periods at the end of the 1990s. Numerous trade and energy agreements were signed between the two countries, shoring up the bases of the Russia-Turkey partnership.

Opinions differ on the causes of rapprochement and the importance of these. Two main approaches are preferred in the interpretations put forward. For some, economic cooperation—trade exchanges and energy relations—constituted the foremost and the dominant factor which guided the decisive impulse for rapprochement between the two countries from the end of the 1990s. In this version, Ankara undertook to strengthen economic and energy ties to open the way for cooperation on policy and security issues. The Kremlin, for its part, intended to take advantage of bilateral economic links to encourage the Turkish authorities to adopt more independent positions in international politics, in particular with regard to the United States and the EU. In this view, the intergovernmental agreement on construction of a subsea pipeline ("Blue Stream" project), signed in 1997, is considered as the foundation of a strategic partnership aiming to develop energy cooperation between the two countries in a climate of restored trust.

For others, in particular those who believe in the realist approach in theories of international relations, the renewal of Russia-Turkey relations is explained above all by changes in the way that reciprocal threats were viewed after the collapse of the USSR. These fresh perceptions would have preceded and facilitated the development of trade exchanges and the intensification of economic cooperation. According to this analytical perspective, two principal factors have led Russia and Turkey to stop seeing each other as a threat: on the Turkish side, the disappearance of the looming "Soviet threat" which had weighed on Turkey since Stalin's territorial claims in 1945; on the Russian side, the failure of pan-Turkic policies in the former Turkish-speaking Soviet republics in the Caucasus and Central Asia which revealed the limits of Turkey's strategic capabilities in the region (Torbakov 2007). This modification in reciprocal perceptions represented an initial and necessary condition for future cooperation and the identification of common geopolitical interests. Consequently, the success or the failure of the Russian-Turkish partnership has depended greatly on the perception of the other as a direct threat or not.

The Stages of Rapprochement: Official Visits, New Implements for Cooperation

From the mid-1990s, a range of bilateral, official visits took place and they helped to re-launch Russian-Turkish relations. The first official visit, by Russian Prime Minister Viktor Chernomyrdin to Turkey in December 1997 and then that of his Turkish counterpart Bülent Ecevit to Russia in November 1999, played an important part in easing new approaches to common issues such as energy security, economic and trade exchanges as well as regional security. The prospect of a "strategic partnership" between the two countries was mentioned for the first time during Chernomyrdin's visit to Turkey, during which an agreement was signed on the Blue Stream project to build a gas pipeline in Turkey (passing under the Black Sea) which opened the way to an increase in bilateral energy exchanges.

After the bilateral meetings in 1997 and 1999, several major stages marked the Russian-Turkish rapprochement. From 2002, relations between the two countries gained a new lease of life with the coming to power of the AKP. The improvement in relations with Russia was then identified as a priority by the new Turkish Prime Minister Recep Tayyip Erdoğan. Whereas the last visit to Turkey by a Soviet head of state dated back to 1972, official bilateral visits by heads of state and government—Vladimir Putin and Dimitri Medvedev, Ahmet Necdet Sezer then Abdullah Gül—multiplied all through the 2000s. Erdoğan made official visits to Moscow as a leader of the AKP then as prime minister and finally as president of the Republic.

From the early 2000s, Russia and Turkey signed many agreements in the economic, political, and energy fields. In November 2001, one of the first action plans aimed at developing cooperation in Eurasia. When Russian President Putin visited Turkey in December 2004, the signing of a "Joint Declaration Between the Republic of Turkey and the Russian Federation on Deepening Friendship and Multi-Dimensional Partnership" marked an important step in the bilateral rapprochement. This declaration restated the shared common interests of the two countries while underlining the growing trust established over recent years. Russia and Turkey are presented as Eurasian powers which grant strategic importance to security and stability. Six agreements were signed covering economic and military issues. Afterward, the two countries' leaders— Erdoğan and Putin—met up on over ten occasions in five years, including four meetings in 2005.

In 2010, the launching of a "strategic partnership" between Russia and Turkey was the apex of the rapprochement between the two countries. This made provision for the establishment of a high-level Cooperation Council, the organization of annual summits, and the construction of a strategic planning group whose mission was to develop economic, political, cultural, and security cooperation. The Council's meetings, which brought together the leaders of both countries, led to the signing of more than thirty agreements. Some of the important decisions adopted during these meetings included agreement on waiving visas and the plan to build a nuclear power station in Turkey (Kanbolat 2012).

THE DIMENSIONS OF THE RUSSIAN-TURKISH PARTNERSHIP

The partnership between Russia and Turkey is part of a multidimensional approach, with economic, trade, energy, and military aspects.

Economic and Commercial Cooperation

During the Cold War, trading exchanges between Soviet Russia and Turkey were fairly limited because they each belonged to opposing blocs. In 1984, the two countries signed a first trade agreement on the purchase of natural gas. Then, after the collapse of the USSR, trading relations developed quite rapidly. From 2008, Russia became Turkey's top trading partner, after all the EU Member States together. The total volume of commerce between the two countries grew significantly, reaching 37.9 bn USD in 2008 (compared to 500 million in 1988) and over 33 bn USD in 2012. Because of the Russian sanctions against Turkey implemented in 2015, exchanges diminished after that, falling to 16.9 bn USD in 2016 and then 22.3 bn USD in 2017. In 2019, trade volume between Russia and Turkey has reached 26.3 bn USD, with Turkey's 3.8 bn USD worth of exports and 22.4 bn USD imports (TÜIK).

The development of bilateral commercial relations was characterized by a large imbalance in favor of Russia. Turkish imports from Russia represented about 80% of this trading volume. In November 2013, Russia was the first country for Turkish imports with goods worth 2,340 million dollars (data from the Turkish Institute for Statistics). In 2019, Russia remained Turkey's main supplier (22.5 bn USD, 11.1% of Turkish imports), followed by China (18.5 bn USD, 9.1% of imports), Germany (17.9 bn USD, 8.9% of imports), the United States (11.2 bn USD, 5.5% of imports), Italy (8.6 bn USD), and India (6.6 bn USD). In January-March 2021 period, the top country for Turkey's imports was China (7.2 bn USD, 11.9% of imports). The country was followed by Russia (6.7 bn USD, 10.7% of imports), Germany (5.4 bn USD, 9.5% of imports), Italy (2.6 bn USD, 4.6% of imports), and the United States (2.6 bn USD, 4.5% of imports). Regarding exports, for several years, Russia was the third or fourth largest market for Turkey, in particular for textiles and certain consumer goods before dropping down the list, overtaken by European countries. In 2019, Turkish exports to Russia increased (+13.4%) which then ranked eleventh among Turkey's customers (data from the Turkish Ministry of Trade).

The asymmetrical nature of the Turkish-Russian economic interdependence was very apparent with the economic sanctions implemented by Russia in 2015–2016 which exposed Turkey's vulnerability (Bilgic-Alpaslan et al. 2015). In parallel, the bilateral economic relations had been influenced by a series of other international factors: the global financial crisis and the economic sanctions imposed by the West on Russia weakened the potential for Turkish-Russian economic cooperation, and also the inability of the economic interdependence between the two countries to quickly change itself into the complex interdependence which characterizes bilateral relations in the advanced capitalist world (Köstem 2018, 10–32).

The economic sectors which benefited the most from the development of exchanges between Russia and Turkey were in construction, agri-food, services, textiles, and telecommunications on the Turkish side and hydrocarbons, tourism, and telecommunications on the Russian side. The "suitcase trade"[1] between the two countries and Russian tourism in Turkey (seven million Russian tourists in 2019) as well as the presence of Turkish workers in Russia have grown substantially over the last twenty years, all enjoying visa exemptions for trips between the two countries since April 2011.

Energy Cooperation

The energy issue has been one of the most determining aspects of the revival of Russian-Turkish relations (Winrow 2017). Cooperation over energy between the two countries has been focused on three main resources: natural gas, oil, and nuclear energy.

The first deliveries of natural gas to Turkey took place in 1987 following a Turkish-Soviet intergovernmental agreement signed in 1984. Over the years, the Russian Federation has become one of Turkey's

---

[1] Suitcase trade is "a form of unrecorded (or under-recorded) international transactions in goods that is currently existent at the edges of formal trade" (International Monetary Fund [IMF] 1998: 6).

main suppliers, providing the largest volume of energy imports. In 2017, most Turkish imports of gas, 51.93%, came from Russia with the next suppliers being Iran (16.74%), Azerbaijan (11.85%), and Algeria (8.36%) (EMRA 2018a). In 2013, Alexey Miller, CEO of the Russian consortium Gazprom, declared that Turkey might become the chief importer of Russian gas in the coming decades, overtaking Germany (Voice of Russia, June 28, 2013). The importance of the level of bilateral exchanges in this field has brought about a situation where Turkey is energy dependent on Russia. As a consequence, the diversification of energy resources is one of the major issues which Turkey will face in the decades to come (Winrow 2009).

Apart from natural gas, Russia and Turkey are also closely linked over the supply of crude oil. For years, Russia has been one of the most important suppliers of crude oil to Turkey. The year 2010 marked a turning point: for the first time, Iran overtook Russia as the top supplier. Whereas in 2009, 41% of imported oil came from Russia, and 23% from Iran, the proportions were reversed in 2010 with 43% coming from Iran and 20% from Russia. In 2017, Russia was Turkey's second supplier of oil (crude and diesel) (18.87% of imports), after Iran (26.94%) and ahead of Iraq (16.55%), India (8.23%), and Saudi Arabia (5.34%) (EMRA 2018b).

The energy issues between the two countries, involving hydrocarbons, are concentrated in the region of the Black Sea where there are several projects for regional cooperation. For Russia, Turkey remains a top-ranking strategic partner in its energy diplomacy regarding the EU. In Russia's energy policy, Turkey is a prime importer of hydrocarbons and its energy needs are growing but Turkey is also seen as a transit area where supply routes for Europe can be diversified, in particular by going around Ukraine, where Russia has experienced several crises (notably the "Orange Revolution" of 2004 and the gas crisis of 2006), and where sanctions, imposed on Russia by the EU after the Ukrainian crisis at the beginning of the 2010s, can be avoided.

Since the first deliveries of gas in 1987, commercial supplies of gas via the Blue Stream pipeline started in 2003 and have been one of the major achievements, with a maximum flow of 16 billion cubic meters per year. Several projects have been set up subsequently. Blue Stream 2, an extension of the first pipeline, was started in 2002 with the aim of building a second pipeline under the Black Sea in order to join the Samsun-Ceyhan line in Turkey and supply countries bordering the southern Mediterranean (Israel, Lebanon, and Cyprus). Blue Stream 2 was then replaced by South

Stream, a new gas pipeline project launched in 2007. This project was in direct competition with the Nabucco pipeline, backed by the EU, because it would have controlled a large part of the deliveries from gas deposits in the Caspian Sea and in Kazakhstan. EU sanctions against Russia after the Ukrainian crisis as well as opposition from the European Commission to bilateral agreements deemed to be contrary to European legislation for the proposed route between Russia and Bulgaria led to the project being abandoned by Russia in December 2014. It was then replaced by the new Turkish Stream project (subsequently renamed TurkStream). Its route linked Russia and the European part of Turkey by crossing the Black Sea before reaching several southern European countries (Greece, Macedonia, and Serbia). After many technical and political difficulties, and delayed by the diplomatic crisis between Russia and Turkey in 2015, the agreement for the TurkStream project was signed in Istanbul on October 10, 2016 by presidents Putin and Erdoğan. The opening ceremony took place in Istanbul on January 8, 2020.

Among the other projects for cooperation between Russia and Turkey in energy issues, a project to build an oil pipeline in Turkey, begun in 2007, had a planned route to cross Turkey in order to link the port of Samsun on the Black Sea coast to the Mediterranean port of Ceyhan. It was designed to carry 60–70 million tons of crude oil a year and this project should have meant opening up an alternative route for conveying Russian and Kazakh oil as well as avoiding the overloaded straits of the Bosporus and the Dardanelles (Country Analysis Brief: Turkey 2017). The straits in Turkey are among the busiest maritime passages in the world. Tankers carrying oil from Russia and the Caucasus regularly pass through these straits heading for international markets. According to estimations by the U.S. Energy Information Administration, over two million barrels of crude per day passed through these Turkish straits in 2015. Along with the two other active pipelines at the oil port of Ceyhan, this project should have made Turkey a hub for oil supplies (Flanagan 2012). In 2013, the project for the Samsun-Ceyhan oil pipeline was judged to be too costly and unprofitable and was cancelled.

Lastly, Russia and Turkey have developed significant cooperation over nuclear energy. The first nuclear power plant in Turkey, located at Akkuyu (a place in the province of Mersin on the Mediterranean coast) was the subject of a call for tenders in 2008 which was won by Atomstroyexport, a Russian consortium and a subsidiary of the Russian Federal Agency on Atomic Energy (then called Rosatom State Atomic Energy Corporation).

Following the cancellation of the call for tenders, the Turkish-Russian nuclear partnership was re-launched in May 2010 when Russian president Medvedev was on an official visit to Turkey, and this resulted in the signing of a bilateral political agreement. Despite the doubts about the feasibility of the project, raised after the catastrophe at Fukushima in 2011 and the completion of an impact study for the power station, as well as opposition from environmental activists mobilized in Turkey, and also numerous criticisms in the media, building work was begun in 2018 and it is expected to become operational in 2023 for the celebration of the 100th anniversary of the Turkish Republic. In March 2021, presidents Erdoğan and Putin remotely inaugurated the construction of a third nuclear reactor at the Akkuyu power plant. However, Russia is not Turkey's only partner in nuclear energy matters. In May 2013, a cooperation agreement was signed with Japan with a view to building a second nuclear power plant in Turkey (Dünya Gazetesi 2014).

Military Cooperation

Military cooperation between Russia and Turkey has mostly developed along two main lines. Working groups on military and defense issues were set up with regular meetings between the two partners. Following the 2004 joint declaration, an intergovernmental commission was established to ensure military and technical cooperation and in the defense industry. Apart from the working groups, the arms market is another field for cooperation between Turkey and Russia. Over several decades, the Russians had not managed to enter the Turkish market in the defense industry but the situation evolved in the early 1990s when Russia succeeded in selling Turkey military armaments (several helicopters, infantry weapons, and armored tanks). Turkey then became the sole NATO member with whom Russia had made close ties in the field of military and technical cooperation. In 1994, Turkey signed an agreement for military cooperation with Russia in order to acquire the military hardware that European countries refused to deliver. This equipment was used by Turkish security forces in the fight against the PKK. After that, military cooperation continued between the two countries. After the Russian-Georgian crisis in summer 2008, Russia began negotiating arms sales to Turkey and developed technical cooperation with the Turkish defense industry. The negotiations were about the supply of Russian systems of air defense.

At the start of the 2010s, Russia answered Turkey's calls for bids for the supply of a long-range air defense system (T-LORAMIDS program—Turkish Long-Range Air and Missile Defense System) with the offer of S-400 missiles. Among several proposals, negotiations began with a Chinese company but this eventually withdrew its offers when faced with pressure on Turkey from the West and from NATO in particular. The Chinese exit opened the way for the reinforcement of Turkish-Russian military and technical cooperation with the Russian offer of S-400 missiles (Kibaroğlu 2019). The desire for closer military cooperation between the two countries was announced by President Erdoğan during a meeting with his Russian counterpart in Saint Petersburg on August 9, 2016. This announcement came at a time of high tension between Turkey and the EU because of the migrant refugee crisis and also the Turkish-Russian rapprochement after several months of diplomatic crisis.

In September 2017, Turkey signed a contract for 2.5 billion dollars with Russia for the supply of a Russian air defense system, made up of S-400 surface to air missiles, which proved to be incompatible with the NATO defense system. This initiative aroused debate in the international arena, marked by sharp criticism from the NATO member countries. Despite American warnings, the Turkish authorities defended their choice on account of Turkey's requirements regarding an air defense system (rapid operational deployment, technologies shared with Turkey to allow co-production of the system, affordable cost) which the American offer of Patriot missiles did not fulfil.

The Turkey-Russia "S-400 deal" caused a major crisis with Turkey's Western allies. Some NATO members, and firstly the United States, declared that purchasing the S-400s would have negative consequences on bilateral relations between the United States and Turkey, and they threatened to impose military and economic sanctions on Turkey. Among the reprisals, the Trump administration excluded Turkey from the F-35 program (stealth fighters) (Kasapoğlu 2017; Kirişçi and Köstem 2018; Kasapoğlu and Ülgen 2019; Johnson and Gramer 2019). Regardless of the growing tensions between the United States and Turkey, the first delivery of Russian missiles arrived in the summer of 2019, before their operational activation, which was planned for April 2020, but then postponed because of the health crisis in Turkey due to coronavirus.

Despite the "S-400 deal," the prospects of deepening Turkish-Russian military cooperation seem, however, to be limited because of Turkey's membership of NATO and the competition with other Western actors who share the Turkish armament market. Many interpretations have been put forward over the "S-400 deal" and its potential consequences. According to some analysts, this agreement would allow Russia to gain advantages from the tensions between Turkey and the United States to endanger the NATO alliance (Kibaroğlu 2019). For Turkish officials, the military cooperation with Russia would also be instrumentalized by Turkey in order to negotiate better conditions from its Western suppliers.

PARTNERS AND/OR RIVALS? CONVERGENCES AND DIVERGENCES OF INTERESTS BETWEEN TURKEY AND RUSSIA

The Converging Interests of Turkey and Russia on the Regional Scale

The contexts of the main common interests between Turkey and Russia, developed earlier, are the economic, trade, and energy sectors and the two countries also converge on the geopolitical plan, in particular in their respective relations with Europe as well as close shared interests in several issues to do with regional security.

In March 2003, the refusal by the Grand National Assembly of Turkey to authorize U.S. soldiers to invade Iraq from across Turkish territory greatly weakened the relations between these two allies. This decision made a positive modification to the Russian perception of Turkey which now appeared to be a more independent actor in its foreign policy as compared to its loyalty to the United States during the Cold War. The Turkish refusal reinforced Russian confidence in Turkey's ability to no longer align itself systematically with American interests in the region and to free itself from its main ally inside NATO (Özdal et al. 2013, 21).

Apart from the question of Turkey's autonomy in the region facing the Western powers, in particular the United States, Russia, and Turkey had a common appreciation of several regional issues until the middle of the 2000s, which may have seemed divergent from or even opposed to the United States' foreign policy in the region: the Israeli-Palestinian conflict, the need to preserve territorial integrity and the political unity of Iraq, the maintenance of stability in the Caucasus as well as security in the Black Sea zone by coastline states (Kınıklıoğlu 2006, 3).

More recently, the two countries have grown closer in their positions over two regional crises: in Syria and in Libya. During the battle for Tripoli between April 2019 and June 2020, Russia and Turkey supported opposing sides—for Russia, the dissident marshal Khalifa Haftar, head of the Libyan National Army and for Turkey, the Fayez Mustafa al-Sarraj's Government of National Accord—by providing them with various kinds of military support (weapons, drones, mercenaries). However, the two countries found some common interests, as was demonstrated in the call for a cease-fire in Libya made by presidents Putin and Erdoğan in Istanbul on January 8, 2020. For many observers, this Russian-Turkish rapprochement over the Libyan crisis was a repeat of the "Astana Process" begun for Syria, where the two partners positioned themselves as mediators in the civil war and sponsors of a future political solution in Libya by sidelining the efforts of the international community and the UN and trying to replicate the model of cooperation and mutual accommodation that they developed in Syria (Zharov 2020). Abdul Hamid Dbeibah, the new Libyan prime minister, elected on February 5, 2021, enjoys the support of Turkey and Russia, leading some observers to fear that the military division of Libya between Russian and Turkish zones of influence will be confirmed and the Turkish-Russian condominium in Libya will be maintained in the future (Bobin 2021).

Without referring to convergences, Turkey adopted a prudent position on a range of regional questions when facing Russia. On several occasions, the Turkish authorities avoided taking a stand on the conflicts and tensions where Russia might have opposed Western countries. During the summer of 2008, and despite the good relations with Tbilisi, Turkey did not directly denounce the Russian military intervention in Georgia, choosing to position itself as a mediator among the belligerents without taking sides. The Turkish authorities then proposed setting up a regional platform to stabilize the Caucasus and to find joint solutions. Although a NATO member Turkey nevertheless strictly applied the Montreux Convention to its Western allies, in particular the United States, whose warships were going through the Straits to supply Georgia (Özdal et al. 2013, 22). During this crisis, Turkey seemed to submit to Russian pressure that increased warnings on this matter. In July 2008, Russia had thus decided to slow down Turkish trade imports, mentioning technical reasons.

Similarly, Turkey remained prudent regarding the crisis in Ukraine that erupted in 2013. The positions adopted by Ankara demonstrated its desire to maintain a balance between the solidarity with Western countries and the necessity of not ruffling Russia on whom it depends economically and for energy. With a view to preserving its economic interests, in particular the continued energy exchanges via Ukraine, Turkey called for the political crisis in Ukraine to be settled in line with international law and on the basis of the country's territorial integrity. Turkey was also concerned about the situation in Crimea, and more particularly about the fate of the Muslim Tatar minority. It condemned the persecutions suffered by the Tatars in Crimea since it had been annexed by Russia in March 2014, and was also opposed to the decision made by the Parliament of the Autonomous Republic of Crimea to organize a referendum on the status of the peninsula. Likewise, Turkey was careful not to openly criticize Russia following the incident in the Kerch Strait opposing the Russian and the Ukrainian navies in November 2018. During the ninth meeting of the Turkish-Ukrainian High-Level Strategic Cooperation Council, which was held in Istanbul on April 10, 2021, the two presidents, Erdoğan and Volodymyr Zelensky, issued a joint declaration in which they pledged to continue "coordinating steps aimed at [...] the de-occupation of the Autonomous Republic of Crimea and the city of Sevastopol, as well as territories in the Donetsk and Luhansk regions." This statement was made as Moscow had been amassing troops on the Ukrainian-Russian border since the end of March 2021. A day before the meeting in Istanbul, President Putin called President Erdoğan in order to inform him that Russia was going to restrict flights to and from Turkey from April 15 to June 1 as new coronavirus infections were rising very quickly in Turkey. For many observers, this decision was also a warning to Turkey not to go too far in the support for Ukraine.

Finally, a convergence between the two countries can be observed on the international stage where there is mutual support in regional and international organizations. Russia looks favorably on Turkey's joining the EU while Turkey has supported Russia gaining observer status, in 2005, within the Organisation of the Islamic Conference, as well as Russia's 2012 membership of the World Trade Organisation. Similarly, in October 2010, the Turkish authorities decided to remove Russia from the list of states that threatened the country in the "national security policy document." Lastly, in November 2013, Turkish Prime Minister Erdoğan expressed Turkey's wish to join the Shanghai Cooperation Organisation, of which Russia was a founder member. When he visited Uzbekistan in November 2016, President Erdoğan spoke of this prospect as an alternative to joining the EU as Turkey was going through a tense period with Europe in the context of the migrant crisis.

The Diverging Interests of Turkey and Russia on the Regional Scale

Beyond trade and energy issues, the strategic partnership between Turkey and Russia seems nevertheless to have reached certain limits because of divergences where their respective national interests are concerned. In the early 1990s, both countries faced a dilemma in their bilateral relations. Although they were partners in a growing commercial and economic cooperation, they nevertheless remained rivals in the emerging geopolitics of Eurasia (Kelkitli 2017). We can identify more broadly seven main areas of divergence.

The Question of NATO and Its Expansion

Since the end of the Cold War, the question of NATO and its expansion have been one of the persistent points of divergence between Turkey and Russia. In the early 2000s, the two countries were defending opposed positions on the issue of NATO's expansion to include Central and Eastern European countries that were former Soviet Socialist Republics. Turkey defended this process while Russia was strongly against it, seeing this as a threat to its geopolitical interests. During the NATO summit in Bucharest, in April 2008, Turkey aligned its position with the organization's main members: the United States, Germany, France, and the United Kingdom. They were committed to the principle of eventual membership for Georgia and the Ukraine but in the face of opposition from Russia did not launch a "Membership Action Plan" (Bucharest Summit Declaration 2008). Since then, Turkey has reaffirmed its initial position and regularly defended membership for Georgia. During the World Economic Forum in Davos, in February 2020, the Turkish foreign minister, Mevlüt Çavuşoğlu, reiterated Turkey's support for NATO expansion, especially for Georgia. During the ninth meeting of the Turkish-Ukrainian High-Level Strategic Cooperation Council, which was held in Istanbul on April 10, 2021, President Erdoğan claimed again that he was supporting Ukraine's membership of NATO. Military cooperation has been strengthening between Turkey and Ukraine following the purchase of armed Turkish drones by Ukraine in 2019. The supply of armed Turkish drones and joint military cooperation projects were at the top agenda of the Ukrainian president's visit to Turkey in April 2021. By exporting the products of its defense industry to Ukraine, Turkey has been strengthening its influence in the region. Providing support for Ukraine allows Turkey to side with the United States and its NATO allies, as the relationship between Turkey and NATO has deteriorated in recent years after Turkey's purchase of Russian military S-400 missiles.

The Fight Against Terrorism

The fight against terrorism is another major point of opposition between Russia and Turkey. For decades, restoring bilateral political relations were delicate because of the unstable security situation in the two countries: the "Kurdish question" in Turkey and the "Chechen problem" in Russia. The authorities in both countries accused each other of backing terrorist organizations and cited the security situation in the other country in order to demand that there be no interference in their own domestic problems (Kelkitli 2017, 77–85).

The Caucasian diaspora in Turkey actively supported the Chechen rebels against the Russian army and was suspected by Russia of being supported by Turkey. For the Turkish authorities, the Russians seemed to be tolerant with regard to the activities of the PKK in Russia, and in 1994, the Russians authorized the establishment of the Confederation of Kurdish Organisations in the Commonwealth of Independent States. According to some analysts, Russia may have had an interest in supporting the PKK in order to encourage internal conflict within Turkey and weaken its influence in the Caucasus and in Central Asia (Mincheva and Gurr 2013, 59). At the end of the 1990s, with bilateral visits by the Turkish and Russian prime ministers, the position of both countries evolved toward more convergence on the issue of combatting terrorism (Olson 1996).

The Question of the Armenian Genocide and Its Recognition

As a traditional partner of Armenia in the Caucasus region, Russia had taken several initiatives on the issue of the Armenian genocide that was poorly received in Turkey, stoking a certain distrust or even tensions. Whereas the Turkish authorities did not recognize the Armenian genocide, but rather used other terms such as "relocation" in the context of the First World War, Russia took up a differing position on this question of memorialization. In April 2005, the resolution adopted by the state Duma of the Russian Federation Federal Assembly on the recognition of the Armenian genocide brought a reaction of protest from the Turkish minister of foreign affairs.

In April 2015, in Erevan, Russian president Putin took part in ceremonies to mark the centenary of the Armenian genocide, during which he mentioned the genocide in his speech. The Turkish president Erdoğan replied, expressing his "sadness" with regards to Putin's stance and called on Russia to "give an account of its actions in Ukraine and Crimea" before applying the term "genocide" to the events that had occurred in the Ottoman Empire (Toksabay and Gumrukcu 2015).

Energy Cooperation in Competition

Energy cooperation between Russia and Turkey is an indicator of mutual interests, but it is also competitive. Despite the special trading relations between the two countries, Turkey has been deploying an energy strategy that aims at reducing its heavy dependence on natural gas and crude oil from Russia by diversifying its sources of supply. While granting priority to relations with Russia, Turkish authorities have made the strategic choice of developing partnerships with Iran and the Middle East. The final aim is to impose itself as an energy hub—gas and oil— against the supremacy of Russian energy (Ögütçü and Arinç 2010). The challenges for Turkish energy policy in making a space for the redistribution of hydrocarbons lie in using Russian supplies while limiting their importance by turning to other additional suppliers, whether this is Azerbaijan (oil and gas), Iran (gas), Iraq (oil and gas), or even Syria (gas). The new position of Iran, which became Turkey's prime supplier of crude oil in 2010, to the detriment of Russia, might be interpreted as an indicator of this new strategy.

In the energy sector, Turkey is a transit territory for several gas pipeline projects—Blue Stream, Nabucco, South Stream, TANAP—managed by the EU or by Russia, and it plays a central role in these projects in determining the routes. Turkey and Russia have sometimes found themselves in competition over international projects in which they were involved. Turkey invested heavily in the Nabucco project, backed by the United States and the EU, where the Russian consortium Gazprom was not involved. This project was launched in 2002 and its aim was to diversify sources of energy and delivery lines in Europe in order to reduce European dependence on Russia. At the beginning of this project, successive gas crises between Russia and Ukraine persuaded the EU to seek other suppliers and alternative itineraries. The Nabucco project was planned to be operational from 2017 and a gas pipeline was to be built in order to link Iran and countries bordering the Caspian Sea (Azerbaijan, Turkmenistan) to countries in south-east and central Europe, crossing through Turkey. Ultimately, the gas line was to be hooked up to the Syrian and Iraqi gas transport system (Demiryol 2013).

The construction of Nabucco was brought into question by the launching of two competing projects: the TANAP gas pipeline (Trans Anatolian Pipeline), begun in 2011 in order to take the Azerbaijani gas initially earmarked for Nabucco via a south-European gas corridor (*Southern Gas Corridor*) that crosses the Caucasus region and then Anatolia, going as far as Greece. The other was the Turkish-Russian South Stream gas pipeline that was planned to cross Turkish territorial waters between Russia and Turkey. The international sanctions over the nuclear question that isolated Iran for about ten years also slowed the project. In June 2013, the consortium exploiting the gas reserves at Shah Deniz (Azerbaijan) chose the TANAP gas pipeline over Nabucco and this brought the project to a halt.

The Geopolitical and Security Issues in the Eastern Mediterranean:
The Cyprus Question
In the geopolitical and security sector, Russia and Turkey also diverged at a regional level. This opposition was manifested in particular in the eastern Mediterranean and focused on Cyprus where the northern part of the island has been occupied by the Turkish armed forces since 1974 and which joined the EU in 2004. Russia and the Republic of Cyprus have had close links for decades in numerous areas, economic, financial, cultural, and linguistic as well as in political and security matters. In this framework, Russia has regularly supported the Cypriot government in order to defend its own security and geopolitical interests in the eastern Mediterranean (Sakkas and Zhukova 2013). Russia's plan to sell S-300 missiles to the Republic of Cyprus caused a passing crisis with Turkey in 1997–1998 (Bazoğlu Sezer 2001). Similarly, Russian stances on the Cypriot issue have raised tensions between the two countries. In April 2004, the Russian Federation vetoed a UN Security Council resolution on a plan for the reunification of Cyprus that called on the Greek and Turkish Cypriot communities to vote in favor of this in referendums held on April 24 while Turkey, for its part, supported these referendums.

Geopolitical and Security Stakes in the Caucasus Region
In the post-Soviet space, in particular in the Caucasus region, rivalries between Russia and Turkey had long hampered any attempt at cooperation. The main source of tensions crystallized around the conflict between Armenia and Azerbaijan in the Nagorno-Karabakh region. After the collapse of the USSR, Moscow, and Ankara, respectively, backed

Armenia and Azerbaijan politically. Tension reached its height in 1992 when Armenia launched a military attack on the Nagorno-Karabakh enclave. Ankara threatened reprisals to support Azerbaijan, causing an immediate reaction from Russia that declared itself ready to use force against Turkey. Since a ceasefire was signed in May 1994, marking the end of military operations in the Nagorno-Karabakh, Turkey has backed Baku, condemning the Armenian occupation of part of Azerbaijani territory and refusing to establish diplomatic relations with Armenia where the shared border was closed in 2010. Turkey and Azerbaijan signed a strategic partnership agreement that included a clause on mutual defense. For its part, Russia has remained Armenia's main ally in the region even though it maintains links, particularly economic, with Azerbaijan (Kuchins and Mankoff 2013, 12–22). Moreover, Russia was co-president of the Organization for Security and Cooperation in Europe (OSCE) Minsk Group, thereby intervening officially as one of the actors in search of a solution to the Nagorno-Karabakh issue. During the 45-day war between Azerbaijan and Armenian forces in September–November 2020, Turkey stepped up its support for the Azeri offensive against the Armenians leading the Armenian government to turn to Russia for help. Turkey also benefited by increasing its influence over Azerbaijan and in the region, whereas Russia consolidated its position as the dominant external power over Armenia (Yıldız 2021, 2).

Despite repeated Turkish requests, Russia does not seem to have exerted any significant influence on Armenia with a view to accelerating the protocols that Ankara and Erevan had signed in October 2009, to normalize their diplomatic relations (International Crisis Group 2018).

Regional and International Crises: The Iranian Nuclear Question and the Syrian Conflict

Apart from conflicts in the post-Soviet space, since the end of the Cold War several regional and international crises have estranged Russia and Turkey because of their diverging positions. In the 1990s, the two countries supported opposite sides during the conflict in Bosnia (1992–1995) and Kosovo (1999). Regarding the Iranian nuclear program and the international crisis raised by this issue, in June 2010, Russia voted in favor of resolution 1929 of the UN Security Council that concerned a series of stronger sanctions against Iran. Turkey rolled out a strategy that clashed with the international community: it was then the only member of the Security Council, with Brazil, to vote against the resolution, after having

reached an agreement with Iran and Brazil in May 2010, about transferring 20% enriched uranium from Iran to Turkey in a swap for highly
enriched uranium for a medical research reactor in Tehran (Gürzel 2012;
Brannen 2013, 9–11; Pieper 2019).

But the uprisings of the "Arab Spring," in particular the conflict in
Syria, were undoubtedly one of the major factors of dissension. The Syrian
crisis highlighted the limits if not the failures of the "good neighbor
policy" (Aliriza and Flanagan 2012, 28–29) advocated by Turkey since the
mid-2000s by marking a sharp break in the rapprochement between the
two countries (Oktav 2013, 193–203). But it also contributed indirectly
to a deterioration in relations with other partners of Turkey's, including
Russia and Iran, which led many observers to ponder about the changing
dynamic within the Turkey-Iran-Russia triangle. Russia and Turkey had
in fact defended positions on the Syrian conflict that were totally opposed
because they had diametrically opposed interests.

In the 2000s, Turkey began a spectacular rapprochement with Syria in
the framework of its "zero problems with neighbors" policy. This shift led
to an intensification of economic exchanges, the removal of visas between
the two countries and also joint military exercises. The close personal
relationship between the Turkish and Syrian leaders, Erdoğan and Bashar
al-Assad, eased this rapprochement. The popular Syrian uprising, in
March 2011, and its subsequent repression by the regime entailed a significant evolution in the bilateral relations. Firstly, the Turkish authorities
tried to persuade Syria to set up a transition government. Faced with
Syria's refusal and intensification of the repression, the Turkish leaders—
with Erdoğan in the lead—then called for the fall of the Ba'athist regime,
denouncing the Syrian government's role in the violence. This stance
marked a brutal breach between the two countries. Since then, Turkey has
supported all of the opposition forces in Syria, leading some to denounce
this position as ambiguous with regard to ISIS. This strategy proved to be
at odds with the orientations of Russian foreign policy, leading to tensions
and incidents between the two countries.

Remembering the 2011 NATO military intervention in Libya, to
which it had been opposed, Russia backed Bashar al-Assad's regime politically and militarily. This Russian support for the Syrian regime can be
explained most notably by its strategic interests in the region, including
the presence of a Russian military base inside Syria. During the autumn
of 2013, on President Putin's initiative, Russia engaged in mediation with
the Syrian regime in order to prevent any Western military intervention

after the use of chemical weapons by Damascus. In September 2015, it intervened militarily in Syria with air strikes against the Syrian and ISIS opposition forces as well as having troops on the ground. This decision marked a strong comeback by Russia in the Middle East.

In this new regional configuration, the increasing number of incidents helped to weaken, if not to jeopardize, relations between Russia and Turkey. The crash of a Russian bomber, shot down close to the Syrian border on November 24, 2015 by a *Turkish* Air Force F-16 fighter jet after several violations of Turkish airspace, was the cause of the most serious diplomatic row between the two countries since the Cold War. This incident aroused the strongest reactions from the Russian authorities who imposed economic sanctions on Turkey in the tourism, energy, construction, and agriculture sectors.

After several months cooling off, marked by tensions, the two countries renewed contact at the highest level in June 2016, after President Erdoğan expressed his "regrets" over the destruction of the Russian bomber. President Putin's condolences after the attack on Istanbul's international Atatürk airport on June 28 and the support conveyed to the Turkish president after the failed military coup in Turkey on July 15 and 16 also helped in the process of normalizing bilateral relations. The meeting between presidents Erdoğan and Putin in Saint Petersburg, on August 9, 2016, marked the official restart of discussions between the two countries following by the lifting of Russian sanctions and the progressive normalization of relations. Since then, the two leaders have met up on several occasions.

Since 2016, Russia and Turkey have been engaged in an amazing rapprochement over the conflict in Syria after having adopted antagonistic positions since the start of the uprising in 2011 (Köstem 2020). This Turkish-Russian rapprochement can be explained by the security challenges facing Turkey in the Syrian crisis. When attacks occurred in Turkey in 2015–2016 and the United States was keeping its distance regarding Turkey's appeals to establish a buffer zone in northern Syria, Russia stepped forward as the only viable partner for Ankara (Kirişçi and Köstem 2018).

Russia and Iran, allies of Bashar al-Assad's regime, and Turkey, supporting the rebels, were behind the introduction of a ceasefire in Syria starting from December 30, 2016, and then of the organization of the Astana conference (Kazakhstan), in January 2017, which inaugurated direct talks between the Syrian regime and the rebel groups.

Between January 2017 and April 2019, twelve sessions for peace talks have been organized in Astana. In May 2017, the three mentor countries of the "Astana Process" adopted an agreement in principle over the creation of four "de-escalation zones" in Syria. On the military side, Russia and Turkey signed a memorandum of understanding on January 13, 2017, in order to coordinate Russian, Turkish, and Syrian regime flights over Syria. Joint airstrikes against ISIS positions in the region of Aleppo were carried out for the first time on January 18, 2017. The assassination of the Russian ambassador to Turkey, on December 19, 2016 in Ankara, by a policeman protesting against the Russian bombing of Aleppo, and the deaths of three Turkish soldiers during a Russian bombardment in northern Syria, in early February 2017, which led President Putin to present his condolences to his Turkish counterpart, did not lead to renewed tensions between the two countries (Đidić and Kösebalaban 2019, 123–138). With Russian permission, Turkey launched military operations on three occasions in northern Syria—the last being in October 2019—to fight ISIS and the People's Protection Units (YPG) () pro-Kurdish militia.

Reasons for dissension have nevertheless remained intense between the two partners. The Idlib crisis in February–March 2020 caused an escalation between Russia and Turkey risking a direct clash before the two countries managed to calm the situation. In the long term, Russia is still backing the Syrian Kurds and has allowed a Democratic Union Party (PYD) bureau in Moscow since 2016. It wants to include the PYD as a Kurdish political party in negotiations, in the face of opposition from Turkey. Lastly, Ankara and Moscow continue to disagree about the future of the Syrian Bashar al-Assad. Unlike Putin, Erdoğan defends the prospect of a Syria without al-Assad (Kirişçi and Köstem 2018).

Conclusion

In conclusion, the development of relations between Russia and Turkey over the last few decades has reflected the dilemma that the two countries are facing, as partners and rivals. On one side, bilateral economic and energy exchanges have undergone an unprecedented intensification in the context of a multifunctional partnership. The energy issues, at the heart of which lie major projects for the construction of gas pipelines, now constitute a vital dimension to Russia-Turkey relations. Similarly, the two countries have established a new political cooperation marked by regular summit meetings between the national leaders. On the other hand, despite this rapprochement, viewed as spectacular, Russia and Turkey remain in competition or even in an adversarial situation as they face several regional and international issues, notably in the region of the Caucasus. The excuses of the "good neighbor policy" promoted by Turkey, which has led to its adopting positions opposed to those of Russia over several regional crises, bear witness to the difficulties and the limits that the Russia-Turkey partnership faces. Even if Russia-Turkey relations remain extremely important, this did not prevent strategic disagreements between the two countries expanding into real diplomatic crisis over the incident where the Russian bomber was downed by Turkish air forces in November 2015. However, the importance of these relations explains the limited scope of Russian sanctions, in so far as these could also have harmed Russia.

Also, the recent evolution of Russia-Turkey relations has raised several questions, in particular over the temporary or lasting character of the partnership set up by the two countries. The rapprochement with Russia has not in fact led to Turkey altering the basically pro-Western orientation of its policies even if Turkey's purchase of Russian military S-400 missiles has provoked a deep crisis with the United States and its NATO allies. Likewise, a clear and sufficiently attractive alternative to its alliance with Western countries has not been suggested to Turkey. In this view, even if the idea of a Russia-Turkey alliance on the frontiers of Europe has been mentioned by some analysts, the rapprochement between Turkey and Russia could appear to be more tactical than strategic, as being selective according to the stakes and motivated by conjunctural circumstances.

The future of Russia-Turkey relations and the many scenarios possible (reinforcement of the bilateral partnership, or deepening of regional and international rivalries) that can be envisaged, will in the end show how far the recent bilateral rapprochement has contributed to reinforcing the regional power status of the two countries.

Translation by Moya Jones.

REFERENCES

Aktürk, Şener. 2006. "Turkish-Russian Relations after the Cold War (1992-2002)." *Turkish Studies* 7 (3): 337–364.

Aliriza, Bulent, and Stephen Flanagan. 2012. "The End of Zero Problems? Turkey and Shifting Regional Dynamics." In *2012 Global Forecast. Risk,*

Opportunity, and the Next Administration, edited by C. Cohen and J. Gabel, 28–29. Center for Strategic and International Studies.

Aras, Bülent. 2009. *Turkey and the Russian Federation: An Emerging Multidimensional Partnership.* SETA Policy Brief no. 35, August 2009.

Baev, Pavel K., and Kemal Kirişçi. 2017. *An Ambiguous Partnership: The Serpentine Trajectory of Turkish-Russian Relations.* Turkey Project Policy Paper 13. Washington, DC: Brookings.

Balta, Evren, and Mitat Çelikpala. 2020. "Turkey and Russia: Historical Patterns and Contemporary Trends in Bilateral Relations." In *The Oxford Handbook of Turkish Politics*, edited by Güneş Murat Tezcür. https://doi.org/10.1093/oxfordhb/9780190064891.013.12.

Bazoğlu Sezer, Duygu. 2000. "Turkish-Russian Relations in the 1990s: From Adversity to 'Virtual Rapprochement'." In *Turkey's New World: Changing Dynamics in Turkish Foreign Policy*, edited by Alan Makovsky and Sabri Sayari, 92–115. Washington, DC: Washington Institute for Near East Policy Papers.

Bazoğlu Sezer, Duygu. 2001. "Russia: The Challenges of Reconciling Geopolitical Competition with Economic Partnership." In *Turkey in World Politics: An Emerging Multiregional Power*, edited by Barry Rubin and Kemal Kirişçi, 151–172. London: Lynne Rienner Publications.

Bilgic-Alpaslan, Idil, Bojan Markovic, Peter Tabak, and Emir Zildzovic. 2015. "Economic Implications of Russia's Sanctions Against Turkey." *European Bank for Reconstruction and Development*, December 7. http://www.ebrd.com/news/2015/economic-implications-of-russias-sanctions-against-turkey.html.

Bobin, Frédéric. 2021. "En Libye, l'ombre de la Turquie et de la Russie plane sur le compromis politique," *Le Monde*, February 8.

Bölme, Selin M., ed. 2009. *Türkiye-Rusya ilişkileri Çalıştayı raporu.* SETA, Kafkasya Çalışmaları, December 4.

Brannen, Samuel J., ed. 2013. *The Turkey, Russia, Iran Nexus. Evolving Power Dynamics in the Middle East, the Caucasus, and Central Asia.* Center for Strategic and International Studies. Lanham: Rowman & Littlefield Publishers.

Demiryol, Tolga. 2013. "The Geopolitics of Energy Cooperation Between Turkey and the European Union." *L'Europe en Formation* 367 (1): 109–134. https://doi.org/10.3917/eufor.367.0109.

Đidić, Ajdin, and Hasan Kösebalaban. 2019. "Turkey's Rapprochement with Russia: Assertive Bandwagoning." *The International Spectator* 54 (3): 123–138. https://doi.org/10.1080/03932729.2019.1627070.

Dünya Gazetesi. 2014. "Türkiye ile Japonya arasındaki nükleer anlaşmaya ilişkin kanun Resmi Gazete'de yayımlandı," January 18.

Energy Market Regulatory Authority (EMRA). 2018a. *Turkish Natural Gas Market. Report 2017.* Ankara.

Energy Market Regulatory Authority (EMRA). 2018b. *Turkish Petroleum Market. Report 2017*. Ankara.

Flanagan, Stephen J. 2012. *The Turkey, Russia, Iran Nexus: Economic and Energy Dimensions. Proceedings of an International Workshop*. Ankara, March 29, Center for Strategic and International Studies, May 24. https://doi.org/10.1080/0163660X.2013.751656.

Gudiashvili, David. 2002. "Turkey and the Russo-Chechen War of 1994-1996." *Central Asia and the Caucasus* 5 (17): 72–79.

Gürzel, Aylin. 2012. "Turkey's Role in Defusing the Iranian Nuclear Issue." *The Washington Quarterly* 35 (3) (Summer): 141–152.

Hill, Fiona, and Omer Taspinar. 2006. "Turkey and Russia: Axis of the Excluded?" *Survival: Global Politics and Strategy* 48 (1): 81–92.

Insight Turkey. 2002. "Turkey and Russia: from Competition to Convergence." Special issue. *Insight Turkey* 4 (2) (April–June): 3–189.

International Crisis Group. 2018. *Russia and Turkey in the Black Sea and the South Caucasus, Europe Report* 250, June 28.

International Monetary Fund. 1998. *International Monetary Fund Annual Report 1998*, September 13.

Johnson, Keith, and Robbie Gramer. 2019. "Who Lost Turkey?" *Foreign Policy*, July 19.

Kanbolat, Hasan. 2012. "Davutoğlu in Moscow: New Era in Turkish-Russian Relations." *Today's Zaman*, January 23.

Kasapoğlu, Can. 2017. "Turkey's S-400 Dilemma." *EDAM Foreign Policy and Security Paper Series 5* , July. http://edam.org.tr/wp-content/uploads/2017/10/s400en.pdf.

Kasapoğlu, Can, and Sinan Ülgen. 2019. "Strategic Weapons Systems in the Turkey-Russia-US Triangle." *EDAM Foreign Policy & Security Report 2*, January 16. http://edam.org.tr/en/strategic-weapons-systems-in-the-turkey-russia-us-triangle/.

Kelkitli, Fatma Aslı. 2017. *Turkish-Russian Relations: Competition and Cooperation in Eurasia*. London: Routledge.

Kibaroğlu, Mustafa. 2019. "On Turkey's Missile Defense Strategy: The Four Faces of the S-400 Deal between Turkey and Russia." *Perceptions* 24(2–3) (Autumn-Winter): 159–174.

Kınıklıoğlu, Suat. 2006. "Turkey and Russia: Partnership by Exclusion?" *Turkish Policy Quarterly* 8 (2) (Summer): 1–17.

Kınıklıoğlu, Suat, and Valeriy Morkva. 2007. "An Anatomy of Turkish-Russian Relations." *Southeast European and Black Sea Studies* 7 (4): 533–553.

Kirişçi, Kemal, and Seçkin Köstem. 2018. *Don't Let Russian S-400s Peel Turkey away from the West*. Order from Chaos, Brookings Institution, December 18. https://www.brookings.edu/blog/order-from-chaos/2018/12/18/dont-let-russian-s-400s-peel-turkey-away-from-the-west/.

Kortunov, Andrey, and Emre Erşen, eds. 2018. Deepening Turkey-Russia Relations. special issue. *Perceptions* 23 (2) (Summer): 1–3.

Köstem, Seçkin. 2018. "The Political Economy of Turkish-Russian Relations: Dynamics of Asymmetric Interdependence." *Perceptions* 23 (2) (Summer):10–32.

Köstem, Seçkin. 2020. "Russian-Turkish cooperation in Syria: Geopolitical Alignment with Limits." *Cambridge Review of International Affairs*. https://doi.org/10.1080/09557571.2020.1719040.

Kuchins, Andrew C., and Jeffrey Mankoff. 2013. "Turkey, Russia, and Iran in the Caucasus." In *The Turkey, Russia, Iran Nexus. Evolving Power Dynamics in the Middle East, the Caucasus, and Central Asia*, edited by S. J. Brannen, 12–22. Center for Strategic and International Studies. Lanham: Rowman & Littlefield Publishers.

Mincheva, Lyubov Grigorova, and Ted Robert Gurr. 2013. *Crime-Terror Alliances and the State Ethnonationalist and Islamist Challenges to Regional Security*. London: Routledge.

NATO. 2008. Bucharest Summit Declaration, Press Release, April 3. https://www.nato.int/cps/en/natolive/official_texts_8443.htm.

Ögütçü, Mehmet, and İbrahim Arinç. 2010. "Turkey's New Geopolitics of Energy." *Insight Turkey* 12 (3) (July–September): 33–236.

Oktav, Özden Zeynep. 2013. "The Syrian Uprising and the Iran-Turkey-Syria Quasi Alliance: a View from Turkey." In *Turkey-Syria Relations. Between Enmity and Amity*, edited by Raymond Hinnebusch and Özlem Tür, 193–203. London: Routledge.

Olson, Robert. 1996. "The Kurdish Question and Chechnya: Turkish and Russian Foreign Policies since the Gulf War." *Middle East Policy* 4 (3): 106–118.

Olson, Robert. 1998. "Turkish and Russian Foreign Policies, 1991-1997: the Kurdish and Chechnya Questions." *Journal of Muslim Minority Affairs* 18 (2): 209–227.

Öniş, Ziya, and Şuhnaz Yılmaz. 2016. "Turkey and Russia in a Shifting Global Order: Cooperation, Conflict and Asymmetric Interdependence in a Turbulent Region." *Third World Quarterly* 37 (1): 71–95.

Özdal, Habibe, Hasan Selim Özertem, Kerim Has, and M. Turgut Demirtepe. 2013. *Turkey-Russia Relations in the Post-Cold War Era:Current Dynamics, Future Prospects*, USAK Report, no. 13, July 6.

Pieper, Moritz. 2019. *Hegemony and Resistance around the Iranian Nuclear Programme. Analysing Chinese, Russian and Turkish Foreign Policies*. London: Routledge.

Sakkas, John, and Nataliya Zhukova. 2013. "The Soviet Union, Turkey and the Cyprus Problem, 1967-1974." *Les cahiers Irice* 10 (1): 123–135. https://doi.org/10.3917/lci.010.0123.

Toksabay, Ece and Tuvan Gumrukcu. 2015. "Turkey's Erdogan Criticises Putin over Armenian "Genocide" Comments." *Reuters*, April 27.

Torbakov, Igor. 2007. *Making Sense of the Current Phase of Turkish-Russian Relations*. Occasional Paper. Washington, DC: The Jamestown Foundation, October.

Türkiye Istatistik Kurumu (TÜIK), data. http://www.tuik.gov.tr.

U.S. Energy Information Administration. 2017. *Country Analysis Brief: Turkey*, February 2.

Yıldız, Güney. 2021. *Turkish-Russian Adversarial Collaboration in Syria, Libya, and Nagorno-Karabakh*. SWP Comment 2021/C 22, March.

Winrow, Gareth M. 2017. "Turkey and Russia: The Importance of Energy Ties." *Insight Turkey* 19 (1): 17–32.

Winrow, Gareth M. 2009. *Problems and Prospects for the 'Fourth Corridor': the Positions and Role of Turkey in Gas Transit to Europe*. Oxford Institute for Energy Studies, NG 30, June.

Zharov, Kirill. 2020. "Can Russia and Turkey Bring Peace to Libya?" Carnegie Moscow Center, January 13. https://carnegie.ru/commentary/80779.

CHAPTER 11

From Obama, to Trump, and on … Durable Changes, Durable Continuities?

Joseph Bahout

The end of Barack Obama's first term and the totality of his second presidential mandate, as well as part of President Trump's, were all spent while some of the most historically important events were unfolding in the Middle East. Arab revolutions started before Obama's second presidential campaign, and these same revolutions—and their various mutations— were in the background of the foreign policy debate surrounding Trump's time in office.

If one were to go back even farther, American foreign policy toward the Middle East was already in question, and sometimes deep and painful questioning, since the aftermath of the Iraq invasion—or even before that, since the shock of 9/11.

All throughout this long period, conceptual as well as policy revisions were continually at play in foreign policy circles, in what now resembles a long period of American soul-searching, one where, above and beyond

J. Bahout (✉)
American University of Beirut, Beirut, Lebanon

© The Author(s), under exclusive license to Springer Nature Switzerland AG 2021
B. Balci and N. Monceau (eds.), *Turkey, Russia and Iran in the Middle East*, The Sciences Po Series in International Relations and Political Economy, https://doi.org/10.1007/978-3-030-80291-2_11

changes in administrations and undertones, continuity and change have been in dispute, with no resolution, not yet at least.

An Elusive Middle East

Costly Rebalancing Acts

"In the beginning was Iran," Obama could have said very soon after the start of his presidency. In 2008, in the new president's mind was the wish to extricate America from a region where it has too often paid high prices for too little, by supporting unstable friends. The desire to turn the page of the traumatic Iraq war and devote the nation's wealth and resources to building the nation at home also added to the necessity of a "rebalancing act" between Sunni and Shia powers, and to adopting a posture equidistant between them in the wake of what seems to be a new "thirty years war." More strategically, this is articulated by a reading of a world that is increasingly Asia-centered, requiring America to "Pivot to the East," and in order to do so, needing to discharge itself of most of its Middle Eastern burdens. Such a strategy has moreover been eased by the new energy landscape, and the United States' decreasing dependency on Gulf oil. However, such a pivotal move has one inescapable condition, which is that of assuaging what remains of the wide-reaching conflicts in the region. Since the Arab–Israeli one has started to wither away by itself, the contentious one remains Iran with its nuclear project and its geopolitical expansionist appetite (Vakil 2014, 8–13).

Reality has proved to be much more vicious, however. While reaching an understanding with Iran was the key point for an orderly withdrawal from a reorganized Middle East, quite the contrary actually happened. The Joint Comprehensive Plan of Action (JCPOA) and what it revealed in terms of perception widened the mistrust between Obama's United States and the Sunni Gulf States; then, all trust was shattered by Trump who pushed for an unprecedented convergence and quasi-collusion between the two parties.[1]

The feeling of neglect by the United States that many of its traditional Arab allies were starting to resent after they discovered that negotiations

---

[1] For a full and informed account of the negotiations with Iran, from the opening of the secret channel in Oman to their conclusion, see the memoirs of then Deputy Secretary of State and now Director of the CIA, William J. Burns (2020).

with Iran were well under way suddenly came to echo the trauma left by the abandonment of rulers like Hosni Mubarak, at the very early start of the Arab uprisings in 2011. It was then to increase when faced with American passivity in Syria, where Iran—later on relayed by Russia—was filling the void left by Assad's crumbling regime.

The price to be paid for the twist toward Iran was to be much higher regarding the main pillar of U.S. Middle Eastern policy, namely Israel. Early signs were given of Obama's intentions as soon as he was elected, when the United States' protégé was challenged on the sensitive issue of colonization. Then came a similar discovery that Washington was determined to normalize with Tehran. Netanyahu's riposte was then hard-hitting when he landed in DC to deliver a defiant speech in front of the American Congress totally ignoring the President sitting in the White House. This was something that Trump found easy to reverse later on, by reestablishing ties with the Israeli Prime Minister up to the level of personal and familial intimacy, tasking his son-in-law with a file he pompously labeled a "Deal of the Century." Here again, nevertheless, deep trends were only recognized in the long run: Trump's announcement of the recognition of Jerusalem as the Israeli capital, the transfer of the United States embassy there, as well as the practical closure of any serious track toward Palestinian statehood, were all only frank acknowledgments that the "Two States Solution" was in fact dead, and only awaiting burial. In a prospective reading of this situation, one can thus only expect the new Biden administration to continue a verbal support for this equation, while concretely only focusing on the living conditions of Palestinians in the Territories, and on adapting to an ever-volatile Israeli domestic scene, while exploiting Trump's main "successes" on this question, those being the Abraham Accords and the long-awaited and hoped-for normalization between Arab Gulf States and Israel; here again, with the United States' phobia regarding Iran in the background.

The Arab Revolts Seen from Washington—A Historical Misunderstanding

Much more fundamentally, however, and what will remain striking in U.S. policy toward the Middle East, from Obama to Trump and then onward, is the United States' deep misapprehension of what the long—and still ongoing—cycle of Arab uprisings has really represented in terms of being historical phenomena. It is more so when put in contrast with Obama's

Cairo speech wherein, like many other Western leaders, he seemed to be embracing the aspirations of the region's peoples and their quest for change, regretting previous apathy toward political expression and participation, only to turn a blind eye, when this all started, not just to the moment itself, but to the structural transformations it was encompassing and inaugurating (Obama 2009). Of course, for a more vivid difference, one could also contrast this with G. W. Bush's promotion of democracy and the discontent it caused, to see where America was coming from and where it was again heading in the region, exclusively perceived and understood through the lens of stability and hard security (Tovar 2017).

In this sense, both Obama's and Trump's postures were much more in line with the Reagan era classical realism, expressed by then NSC head Brent Scowcroft, rather than with a Democratic tradition incarnated by Jimmy Carter—or even by Bill Clinton's "liberal interventionism" school—or with a Republican one borne by G. W. Bush and the neo-conservative movement.

In the situation under discussion there is, and in the future, there will probably be, a high price to be paid for U.S. foreign policy in the Middle East, a price that is much more conceptual and philosophical than simply political. It is not only that of misunderstanding the historicity of the moment, but also of helping to abort it, even though the probabilities of failure were intrinsic in what was happening. This is the price for entertaining the vicious circle in which Arab societies have been locked for more than half a century, that of a deadly and sterile choice between an inefficient and increasingly bloody authoritarianism and an Islamist trend increasingly pushed toward nihilistic radicalization and violence. Furthermore, by freezing Arab societies' dynamics in such a fatal dichotomy between autocrats and terrorists, the United States—and behind them the West more globally—have been putting themselves almost willingly in a situation where they are becoming prisoners of this same alternative in terms of policy choices, thus more solidly enforcing the idea that nothing good nor interesting could ever be expected from a doomed Middle Eastern region (Hamid 2015; Murray 2013, 146–166).

Here, Syria is a perfect case in point, illustrating both the demise of a coherent U.S. grand strategy toward the region and the high liabilities American contradictions would eventually entail for Washington for decades to come.

Since 2014, and after a few months of empty verbal posturing on the necessity for the Assad regime to undergo "reforms" and open up to more political inclusivity, U.S. policy toward Syria ended up simply prioritizing occasional counterterrorism operations against the Islamic State, culminating in 2015 with the deployment of forces—alongside other allies—to train, equip, and advise local partners in order to roll back ISIS.

With Trump's accession to power, the U.S. line toward Syria became defined as threefold: "the enduring defeat" of the Islamic State; a political settlement to the Syrian war; and the withdrawal of Iranian-commanded forces.

At the end of 2020, with about 600 American troops remaining in Syria, only the first of these objectives had been attained (Humud and Blanchard 2020). The second one was still subcontracted to Russia, willingly or not. The United States was hoping either that Moscow would itself ultimately get rid of Assad because of his unmanageable personality and the obstacle he and his clique represented to any viable reconstruction of the country, or it was betting that a more solid Russian presence in Syria would mechanically evict the Iranians, thus indirectly fulfilling the third American aim. Once again, none of these points were to even come close. With the arrival of the Biden administration in office, the Syrian conundrum is still undiminished for Washington, and what is more, to it is now added the rise to preeminence of new actors and factors weighing much more heavily on the new president's agenda.

One of these is the Kurdish aspect; another is the difficult and sensitive relations with Turkey; and both are obviously related.

If one is to draw a line of contrast between Joe Biden and his predecessors, it would be that of his clearly stated Kurdophilia, at least one already expressed in Iraq, where the then Senator and leader of the powerful Foreign Affairs Committee sketched (in co-authorship with Leslie Gelb at that time) a partition plan for the country in three components, essentially aimed at providing Kurdish society with the embryo of statehood (Biden and Gelb 2006). It is not yet clear to what extent he, as Vice-President to Barack Obama, pushed to help sanctuarize Syria's north-eastern regions, under the strengthened authority of Kurdish factions perceived as a lethal danger to Turkey.

It is no anodyne coincidence that Obama's—and briefly Trump's—United States Special Envoy for the anti-IS Coalition is Brett McGurk, himself a self-proclaimed friend of the Turkish PYD. He is back in business under Biden, in an upgraded capacity, that of NSC Director for the Middle East, and more directly in charge of the Syrian file.

In that regard, Trump's presidency will have been a brief parenthesis of better relations with Ankara and with Erdogan, who was disliked by Obama but probably despised by Biden. There is probably another fascinating chapter of America's relation to the Middle East to be written, that of its dealings with Turkey, and the drifting toward Russia of what was not so long ago the most solid NATO military pillar after the United States. When faced with the question about this turnaround, it is frequent to hear Turkish policy-makers citing Syria as a traumatizing episode in Ankara's relation with the West and the United States in particular—one where Erdogan saw, through Russia's unhinged behavior, the confirmation of his belief that only brutal strength ultimately pays off.

This is why, and paradoxically, it is still an old and quite rotten Middle Eastern region that any new American president will have to deal with, today and probably tomorrow. One where their administration will still have to make choices between Sisi's authoritarian-like restoration, Erdogan's Islamist-like autocracy, or civil-war quagmires such as the ones developed and entrenched in Syria or Yemen. We are speaking of an Arab world where old questions are still on the table and without a hint of resolution, generational reshufflings in the Maghreb, dysfunctional rentier-State economies out of order and looking for a second lifeline in the Gulf, resilient and mafia-structured military cliques defending clannish regimes in the Mashreq, and, across this board, an unstoppable and growing human drain in the form of migration toward Europe or other remote havens.

In parallel to that, and enhancing the U.S. foreign policy's quest for answers, a changing geopolitical landscape is on the way, where new regional powers are rising to affirm themselves, while global power-competition has returned to challenge America's might (Singh 2020).

A DOUBTING AMERICA IN A TRANSFORMING WORLD

Back to the "Great Game" and to Big Powers Competition

If one of the United States' competitors was to be singled out as a net beneficiary of the past decade of American hesitations, questionings, and setbacks in the Middle East, it would be Putin's Russia.

Already under way to being fully reintegrated in the global power game on the eve of Obama's election, Russia would turn down the "reset" offer made in what Moscow perceived as a condescending tone, to then twist the power dynamics and the balance in its favor exploiting what the regional evolutions would soon offer cynical and opportunistic Putinian tactics. After the Libyan episode, probably the last occurrence where Russia considers itself to have been bluffed and cheated on, Moscow would play hard and never concede anything anymore to a playbook it perceives as fundamentally antagonistic to its new official international doctrine, set of rules and codes of behavior. Here, it was Syria that would quickly appear for Putin as the privileged theater and point of application—through blood and fire—of his own playbook in international affairs (Wyne and Clark 2020).

From this international doctrine, especially applied to the Middle East, comes "anti-revolutions" as point one. A belated revenge on the "colored revolutions" that some decades ago dismantled the Soviet empire and a principle that Putin hides behind a formalistic defense of legalism and international law. Any international move, even in the form of humanitarian protection, is countered and labeled as an attempt to push for "regime change," a fear rooted in the Kremlin's mind by the Libyan precedent.

Then comes the staunch need to affirm and consolidate, in the minds of third parties, the idea of a loyal Russia, supporting its allies and protégés to the end and without hesitation. In a Middle East where Sunni autocratic powers are still feeling the trauma of the ousting of Hosni Mubarak in record time by the American administration, this gains immense value and allows Putin to counterbalance the suspicion of his anti-Islamism (or, in this case, anti-Sunnism) since the Chechen war. It also allows him to incrementally gain the confidence and sympathy of Gulf rulers, avid to start a diversification of their security guarantee arrangements, away from the exclusivity with the United States and increasingly seduced by Russian weaponry, especially its anti-air defense, well deployed and abundantly showcased in terrains like Syria.

Lastly, and in other constituencies of the region, Putin's posture meets the rising fear that radical and violent Islamist movements have sown, a stance that simultaneously allows Russia to appear as the ultimate defender of minorities in the Middle East, while at the same time talking to Western European opinions equally afraid of the changes in their social fabric induced by a flow of refugees fleeing the Arab chaos.

Indeed, Putin is first and foremost a cold geopolitical player, and the playbook serves this design well. When one looks at the points where Russia's efforts to regain a foothold in the Middle East are deployed, the map is quite obvious: Syria, as a centerpiece, Libya as a wider proxy war theater where the ties with Sisi's Egypt are also strengthened, and Yemen where Moscow has gained additional points in the political solution that will ultimately be back on stage. By connecting the dots, what is revealed are the Arab footholds lost by the former Soviet Union at the height of the Cold War for which Putin is so nostalgic.

Besides geopolitics, the other war Putin also seeks to win is that of the narrative. Against the liberal West he so despises, the aim is to demonstrate that in the Middle East there are only binary and simplistic choices to be made, between brutal and authoritarian regimes offering iron-fisted stability but fighting against frightening jihadist terror, exactly like the war he himself fought in Russia's southern periphery. What one is appalled to see, however, is that this narrative is in turn confirmed by the drift of the West, that has adopted almost the same talking points, either through fear or lack of means and imagination, or by neglect and passivity. If this started under Obama, it was further enhanced by Trump who even inserted this rhetoric into the domestic American political scene itself.

What Can America Still Do (or What Should It Do) in the (Arab) World?

The United States' interrogations about the world and about its role and place within it are also sometimes interrogations about America itself and its evolution. The rise to prominence of a new generation, much less impregnated than its elders by the sense of "American exceptionalism" or by the messianic character of its projections abroad, is much less familiar with the military tool and its use and is much more focused on domestic dynamics of greater social and societal equality, on environmental safety and durability and on well-being and what technology can bring to it. All this has increasingly led to a deep and fundamental questioning about the feasibility of keeping on under-writing the world's prosperity, security, and liberal order, and about the use and pertinence of this when these values are simply seen as being eroded and threatened at home.

This debate about the notion and concept of power and the interrogation about whether the twenty-first century will still be an American one or not is open and feverish; it will most probably remain so for a while. It traversed Obama's two terms, Trump's term, and will very surely endure in the Biden era. It focuses on fundamentals and legacies, on what should be kept and what could be let go; on what is structural and what is contingent, and what the priorities will be if the trap of overstretching and exhaustion is to be avoided. It is this set of new approaches that Obama was probably exhorting what has been called—with some disdain—the "Beltway Blob"[2] to embrace or at least to consider, in order to start new thinking, taking better into account the adequacy of ends and means, far from what the 44th President considered as an "old and inefficient playbook." It is striking to see that, even after a disruptive Trump presidency whose tone and style took the United States and its foreign policy to the extreme opposite of the pendulum swing, some of the fundamentals of what an American policy toward the Middle East will presumably be are by now more or less fixed around this same set of new notions.[3]

As a general principle, "restraint" will come, a concept that was well developed and theorized by MIT's Barry Posen, one of the main proponents of a thriftier use of American power (Posen 2015). A self-control mainly exerted toward the uses—or abuse—of military power, but that was to evolve, after Obama's preference for drone-operated targeted killings, into Trump's excessive manipulation of two other—more modern and less lethal—weapons, that of sanctions and of cyberwarfare (Lynch 2016, 127–144). In Obama's words, and they seem to have endured well after his presidency, the United States would be more advised to "use a scalpel instead of a hammer" (Brands 2016, 101–125).

This helps support the second notion, that of "sustainability," far from one-shots, despite those that Trump sometimes indulged in, like the killing of the master-operator of Iran in the Levant, Qassem Soleimani. And it also serves the longer-term aim, one that, after Obama, both Trump and his opponent Bernie Sanders were unanimous about adopting, that of "home rebuilding instead of nation-building abroad."

The most obvious underpinning of this strategic reorientation of U.S. foreign policy toward the Middle East during the last decade is undoubtedly the strong desire and necessity to purge the Iraq trauma and to heal the wound left by a disastrous—albeit easy—invasion and to resorb the trillions of dollars it cost, with no real result, except that of sowing durable chaos in the region and seeing Iran filling the many voids opened by states failing here and there. The lesson from Iraq was learned; one

[2] It refers to the microcosm of pundits and think-tanks within the DC area, often accused of group-thinking and of disconnect from other realities.

[3] For a synthetic reading on this topic, Jeffrey's Goldberg's long interview in *The Atlantic* is a must-read: Goldberg (2016).

has to wonder however if it was not over-learned. From this introspection and reflection on the takeaways of the last of real American wars, what was retained was the idea that nothing durable, if nothing good at all, could be designed in and for the Middle East. Moreover, America's interests in this region are diminishing by the day, and from now on, it can adopt a new approach by sub-contracting the region's problems to others—regional or other contending powers—in order to prepare for the new challenge rising in the East as well as aiming at sharing, if contesting, supremacy in the coming century. In his own way, this is what Trump was also ultimately doing, leaving to Russia the task of micro-managing the Syrian file—with the marginal solace of expecting it to get sunk in its quagmire; or relying on a transactional convergence between Israel and the Gulf States to increase the pressure on Iran; or leaving the Europeans to sort out their difficult proximity problems with Turkey.

We have yet to see whether the Biden presidency will confirm and pursue the track inaugurated by the president under whom he served as vice-president, a policy then exacerbated by his rival and nemesis, Donald Trump. But what is to be expected is that an "American return" will not place the Middle East at the top of its agenda priorities.[4]

What to Expect Next?

Biden's Presidency—To Heal and to Restore

Joe Biden's first instincts as expressed during the campaign and in the first months of his presidency suggest that he will take a more classical road in terms of foreign policy, much more in line with the fundamentals of a blend of common-sense realism with some eruptions in the defense of values and principles. Most of Biden's foreign policy team come from that tradition although the Obama years moved away from it and many of the team now express regret over some of the shortcomings or mistakes made on various issues (Lynch et al. 2020).

The Iran Deal will thus be the pillar to resurrect, but lessons learned will dictate that it should include the sub-chapters that led to its demise—the ballistic capacity of Iran and its Islamic Revolutionary Guard Corps

---

[4] Many of these actors have written extensively; a good glimpse at this literature can be found in the following: Bacevich (2016), Miller and Sokolsky (2020), Karlin and Cofman Wittes (2019), and Simon and Stevenson 2015.

(IRGC)'s nefarious actions in the region. The Iran Deal would also be better protected if the United States joined the absentee regional powers, Israel and the Gulf States, which led to its being wrecked. Regarding the latter, Biden's prize will be to acknowledge, praise, and nurture the Abraham Accords hastily arranged by Trump in his last days. The new administration will also keep a verbal stance on a two-state solution for the Palestinian issue, while not doing much to change the status quo that undermines this same solution, and while building on the outgoing administration's fait accompli that recognized Jerusalem as the definitive capital of the State of Israel. While Biden will be tempted to give his presidency tonalities of human rights defense and more strictly follow rules of law by adopting a firmer stance on Egypt—toward Sisi, Trump's "favorite dictator"—or on Saudi Arabia—toward Crown Prince Mohammad Bin Salman, Jared Kushner's best friend in the region—he will maintain the Syrian political solution design that is in the hands of Russia, hoping its influence on the regime in Damascus will tame that of Teheran. It is sure, here and elsewhere, that much will depend on the nature of relations with Russia and on the extent to which the new administration's ambition to recreate a "consortium of democracies" will not trigger a new round of animosity from Vladimir Putin.

But there again will come limits and constraints from the close circles and advisers and also from domestic politics, and those of the Democratic Party itself, one much more "to the left" than the President himself and most of his principals (Wallace-Wells 2019; Petti 2020). Biden's election was the result of a wide compromise between the various wings of the liberal and progressive camps and the President also knows that his presidency is a one-mandate term, after which the party will be deeply reshaped to prepare for a new durable leadership. As a result, the cursor of many of his foreign policy choices, and essentially those relative to the Middle East, will have to reflect this astute balance and diversity reflecting the constituency that led him to the White House. This constituency is much more domestically focused, all the more in the aftermath of the COVID pandemic that has fragilized America's economy and its social fabric, in a country polarized like never before and where healing and reconciliation have risen to the level of a national interest. It is not to be forgotten that the new President's National Security Advisor, Jake Sullivan, notably identified these parameters a few months before the transition, in a noticeable series of papers that he coordinated for the think tank where he spent his political parenthesis, entitled "A Foreign Policy for the American Middleclass" (Ahmed and Engel 2020).[5]

Trump is indeed gone, but Trumpism is here to stay, for a while at least, both in America's politics and in a largely "Trumpized world" (Rose 2020). With a blend of old-style isolationism, apparently muscled and armed with a verbal big stick, cynical and transactional, placed at the service of a hollow slogan, "Make America great again," Trump moved the United States more to the side of thuggish strongmen on the international scene, more to the side of a sort of global populist anti-liberal and authoritarian new age, where values and norms, beginning with multilateralism, are increasingly becoming secondary.

This is why the presidency that is starting will also confront the limits of reality itself, a reality paradoxically shaped by both Obama's and Trump's presidencies across which continuities are almost as evident as ruptures— a reality that has left America lingering in doubt, in the middle of an uncertain and transforming world.

A Tentative Conclusion

For years now, most of the U.S. policy-making debate about the Middle East has been revolving around the idea of "ending the American purgatory" (Karlin and Cofman Wittes 2019) or of putting a halt to "the endless, costly and useless wars" (Bacevich 2016) in this region. It is mostly a debate about ends and means, about investment and returns, and about calibration with respect to the next century's challenges in the light of what the previous one brought to America, both good and bad, coming from a region increasingly perceived as cursed.

On the path to ending war, most often cited are: the need to solve long-lasting and festering conflicts like the Israeli/Palestinian one, Iran's nuclear and geopolitical ambitions, the attempt to rebalance imbalanced relations and to redefine friendships and alliances, and the imperative of no longer being at the heart of newly triggered frictions as well as those contentions that have dragged on. However, as it pivots eastward toward new challenges, Washington could well encounter new rivals in the very region it is aiming at leaving, and this is a Catch-22 with which Biden and subsequent presidencies will have to come to terms. Can the United

---

[5] For a more Middle East focused reading of the new NSC head's vision, see Benaim and Sullivan 2020.

States both prepare to confront a rising China and an emboldened Russia, while not seeing the latter's infiltration of the Middle East as a zero-sum process that is done at its expense? If there is a challenge to new thinking in Washington regarding the Middle East, it should be exactly this one, and it is both geopolitical and conceptual.

REFERENCES

Ahmed, Salman, and Rozlyn Engel, eds. 2020. "Making U.S. Foreign Policy Work Better for the Middle Class." Report. *Carnegie Endowment for International Peace,* September 23. https://carnegieendowment.org/2020/09/23/making-u.s.-foreign-policy-work-better-for-middle-class-pub-82728.

Bacevich, Andrew J. 2016. "Ending Endless War: A Pragmatic Military Strategy." *Foreign Affairs*, September/October. https://www.foreignaffairs.com/articles/united-states/2016-08-03/ending-endless-war.

Benaim, Daniel, and Jake Sullivan. 2020. "America's Opportunity in the Middle East." *Foreign Affairs,* May 22. https://www.foreignaffairs.com/articles/middle-east/2020-05-22/americas-opportunity-middle-east.

Biden Jr., Joseph R., and Leslie H. Gelb. 2006. "Unity Through Autonomy in Iraq." *The New York Times*, May 1. https://www.nytimes.com/2006/05/01/opinion/01biden.html.

Brands, Hal. 2016. "Barack Obama and the Dilemmas of American Grand Strategy." *The Washington Quarterly* 39 (4): 101–125. https://doi.org/10.1080/0163660X.2016.1261557.

Burns, William J. 2020. *The Back Channel: A Memoir of American Diplomacy and the Case for Its Renewal*. New York: Random House.

Goldberg, Jeffrey. 2016. "The Obama Doctrine." *The Atlantic*, April. https://www.theatlantic.com/magazine/archive/2016/04/the-obama-doctrine/471525/.

Hamid, Shadi. 2015. "Islamism, the Arab Spring, and the Failure of America's Do-Nothing Policy in the Middle East." *The Atlantic*, October 9. https://www.theatlantic.com/international/archive/2015/10/middle-east-egypt-us-policy/409537/.

Humud, Carla E., and Christopher Blanchard. 2020. "Armed Conflict in Syria: Overview and U.S. Response." CRS Report RL33487. *Congressional Research Service*, July 27. https://fas.org/sgp/crs/mideast/RL33487.pdf.

Karlin, Mara, and Tamara Cofman Wittes. 2019. "America's Middle East Purgatory." *Foreign Affairs*, January/February. https://www.foreignaffairs.com/articles/middle-east/2018-12-11/americas-middle-east-purgatory.

Lynch, Marc. 2016. "Belligerent Minimalism: The Trump Administration and the Middle East." *The Washington Quarterly* 39 (4): 127–144. https://doi.org/10.1080/0163660X.2016.1263920.

Lynch, Colum, Robbie Gramer, and Darcy Palder. 2020. "Inside the Massive Foreign Policy Team Advising Biden's Campaign." *Foreign Policy,* July 31. https://foreignpolicy.com/2020/07/31/inside-biden-campaign-foreign-policy-team/.

Miller, Aaron David, and Richard Sokolsky. 2020. "The Middle East Just Doesn't Matter as Much Any Longer." *Politico,* March 9. https://www.politico.com/news/magazine/2020/09/03/the-middle-east-just-doesnt-matter-as-much-any-longer-407820.

Murray, Donette. 2013. "Military Action But Not as We Know It: Libya, Syria and the making of an Obama Doctrine." *Contemporary Politics* 19 (2): 146–166. https://doi.org/10.1080/13569775.2013.785827.

Obama, Barack. 2009. "Remarks by the President on a New Beginning." Speech, Cairo University, Cairo, Egypt, June 4. https://obamawhitehouse.archives.gov/the-press-office/remarks-president-cairo-university-6-04-09.

Petti, Matthew. 2020. "Bernie Sanders' Foreign Policy Advisors Invited to Biden Camp." *The National Interest,* April 14. https://nationalinterest.org/feature/bernie-sanders-foreign-policy-advisors-invited-biden-camp-144257.

Posen, Barry. 2015. *Restraint: A New Foundation for US Grand Strategy.* Cornell Studies in Security Affairs. Ithaca, NY: Cornell University Press.

Rose, Gideon, ed. 2020. "The World Trump Made." *Foreign Affairs special issue,* September/October. https://www.foreignaffairs.com/issue-packages/2020-08-11/world-trump-made.

Simon, Steven, and Jonathan Stevenson. 2015. "The End of Pax Americana." *Foreign Affairs,* November/December. https://www.foreignaffairs.com/articles/middle-east/end-pax-americana.

Singh, Mike. 2020. "U.S. Policy in the Middle East Amid Great Power Competition." In *The Future of Conservative Internationalism: A Collection of Essays from the Reagan Institute Strategy Group,* edited by Rachel Hoff. *Reagan Institute Strategy Group.* https://www.reaganfoundation.org/media/355589/risg-2019-essays.pdf.

Tovar, Juan. 2017. "The Foreign Policy of the United States Following the Arab Spring." In *Political Change in the Middle East and North Africa: After the Arab Spring,* edited by Inmaculada Szmolka. Edinburgh: Edinburgh Scholarship Online. https://doi.org/10.3366/edinburgh/9781474415286.003.0015.

Vakil, Sanam. 2014. "Obama's Iranian Gamble." *The International Spectator* 49: 8–13. https://doi.org/10.1080/03932729.2014.952980.

Wallace-Wells, Benjamin. 2019. "Bernie Sanders Imagines a Progressive New Approach to Foreign Policy." *The New Yorker,* April 13. https://www.new

yorker.com/news/the-political-scene/bernie-sanders-imagines-a-progressive-new-approach-to-foreign-policy.

Wyne, Ali, and Colin P. Clarke. 2020. "Assessing China and Russia's Moves in the Middle East." *Lawfare Blog,* September 17. https://www.lawfareblog.com/assessing-china-and-russias-moves-middle-east.

CHAPTER 12

Syria, the Kurds and the End of the Turkish-American Alliance

Ömer Taspinar

Decades from now, history books dissecting what went wrong in Turkish-American relations will dedicate a special chapter to Syria's civil war. This chapter will analyze how American military support for a Syrian Kurdish militia group in the fight against the Islamic State (IS) unraveled Turkish-American relations. As Syria's descent into a gruesome war approaches its tragic ten-year anniversary, it is important to remember that Syrians have perished in their hundreds of thousands and remain displaced, brutalized and traumatized in their millions. Less noticed collateral damage of the Syrian civil war, however, has been relations between Ankara and Washington.

Before the civil war in Syria, Ankara and Washington could still pretend to be strategic allies and NATO partners. As of 2021, Turkey has been subject to military sanctions by the United States and a newly confirmed US Secretary of State has called Turkey a "so-called strategic partner"

Ö. Taspinar (✉)
National Defense University, Washington, DC, USA
e-mail: taspinaro@ndu.edu

© The Author(s), under exclusive license to Springer Nature
Switzerland AG 2021
B. Balci and N. Monceau (eds.), *Turkey, Russia and Iran in the Middle East*, The Sciences Po Series in International Relations and Political Economy, https://doi.org/10.1007/978-3-030-80291-2_12

(*Reuters* 2021). The resentment against Washington in Turkey is even more acute. An overwhelming majority of Turks see the United States as a national security threat.[1] The drivers of anti-Americanism in Turkey have become increasingly multifaceted with the failed coup attempt of July 2016. The Turkish government believes the US-based Turkish cleric Fethullah Gülen and his secretive network within the civilian and military bureaucracy was behind this bloody attempt to overthrow the government (Yavuz and Balcı 2018). Yet, more than the issue of Fetullah Gülen's presence in the United States and Washington's refusal to extradite him, it is America's partnership with Syrian Kurds that fuels Turkish anger. This is hardly surprising for two main reasons.

First, Turkish political culture has always displayed strong nationalist traits and a deep suspicion of Western involvement in the Kurdish question. Second, America's Kurdish partners in Syria are undeniably linked to a Kurdish rebel group designated as a terrorist organization by both Ankara and Washington. As this chapter will explore, Washington's decision to support the YPG (People's Protection Units)—a Kurdish militia in Syria—has had three major consequences. First, a devastating impact on Turkey's Kurdish policy at home. Second, a major deterioration in Turkish-American relations, and third, a military rapprochement between Ankara and Moscow.

The Kurds and the West: A Very Turkish Predicament

Turkey's fear of dismemberment by Western forces has deep imperial roots and is today mostly manifested in Ankara's insecurity vis-à-vis Kurdish demands for ethnic, cultural and political recognition at home. It is important to remember the obvious fact that Turkish nationalism came of age fighting Western powers. Both during World War I and

---

[1] A 2019 survey by Kadir Has University found that 81.9% of the Turkish public view the US as a threat. See Soylu, Ragıp, "Anti-US Sentiment in Turkey Reaches a New High, Poll Shows," *Middle East Eye*, February 1, 2019. https://www.middleeasteye.net/news/anti-us-sentiment-turkey-reaches-new-high-poll-shows. Accessed on April 7, 2021. For Anthony Blinken's confirmation statement on Turkey, see "U.S. Secretary of State Nominee Calls Turkey a So-Called Strategic Partner" *Reuters*, January 19, 2021. https://www.reuters.com/article/usa-biden-state-turkey/u-s-secretary-of-state-nominee-calls-nato-ally-turkey-a-so-called-strategic-partner-idUSL1N2JU2Z6. Accessed on April 7, 2021.

the National Independence Struggle (1919–1922) the enemies of Turkey were European countries—UK, France, Italy, Greece and to a lesser degree the United States with its support for Greek, Armenian and Kurdish self-determination.

The clauses of the 1920 Sèvres Treaty signed by a defeated Ottoman Empire under British, French, Italian and Greek occupation envisioned the creation of a Kurdish state in eastern Anatolia, in addition to the partitioning of Asia Minor among these occupying forces. "Sevrephobia" is today part of the Turkish lexicon and strategic culture. Ingrained in the deeply nationalist education system, it still triggers an intensely resentful fear and suspicion of Western imperialist intentions (Jung 2003). The fact that an independent, sovereign and modernized Turkish Republic has become part of the transatlantic alliance by joining NATO has done little to change this deep suspicion of the West in the Turkish nationalist psyche.

The pre- and post-Cold War developments on the Kurdish front—both at home and at the regional level—played a critical role in the persistence of this Turkish anger regarding the West. The geographic distribution of Kurds, stretching across five states in the region, has had important implications for Turkish foreign policy since the inception of the republic in 1923. In 1925, the Sheikh Said rebellion became the first in a long series of Kurdish uprisings—almost two dozen until the late 1930s—that ended up traumatizing Kemalist founding fathers and creating their suspicion of all things Kurdish. Not surprisingly, these developments tempered Kemalist territorial ambitions over the British mandated province of oil-rich Mosul.

In the 1920s and 1930s, during rebellions in southeastern Anatolia, Turkish leaders were convinced that it was Britain that incited the Kurds. London, they believed, fomented Kurdish nationalism in an attempt to show Ankara that it would face tremendous challenges controlling the Kurds within Turkey, let alone in northern Iraq. The difficulties involved in ruling over a large Kurdish area thus deterred Ankara from pursuing territorial demands over Mosul (Olson 1989, 52–80). Prudence, realism and suspicion of the West thus came to characterize Kemalist foreign policy in modern Turkey. The scars left by this pre-Cold War Kurdish trauma in Turkey's infancy endures to this day. The re-emergence of Kurdish nationalism in the post-Cold War era, both at home and in the context of US military adventures in Iraq and Syria, partly explains such tenacity.

Are such historic Turkish fears of Western instigation of Kurdish nationalism justified? There is little doubt that British officers supported anti-Ankara Kurdish tribes during the War of Independence led by Mustafa Kemal. Moreover, it is hard to deny that the Kurdish uprising led by Sheik Said in 1925 influenced the League of Nations' final recommendation for the inclusion of the Mosul province in Iraq. Kemalist suspicion of British imperialism is thus understandable. What is highly debatable, however, is whether the more than a dozen Kurdish rebellions of the 1920s and 1930s were all instigated by Britain. Kurdish nationalism was not something Britain particularly wanted to encourage. After all, Iraq had its fair share of Kurds with 20% of the country's total population. And the territorial integrity of Iraq was a British priority since official commitments were made in this direction.

Finally, the fact that Kurdish rebellions within Turkish borders continued long after the resolution of the Mosul question in 1926 supports the view that Kurdish insurrections have erupted as a result of domestic dynamics rather than external provocation. It was only natural that the goal to create a centralized, secular and homogenous "Turkish" nation-state would meet opposition from ethnic and religious Kurds who had enjoyed semi-autonomy during the Ottoman centuries. Nevertheless, the alleged British role in the Sheik Said uprising continues to historically legitimize the conspiratorial views of many Turks regarding the role of Western actors in fomenting Kurdish nationalism. Fast forward to contemporary Turkish problems with the United States and one can understand why the sight of American soldiers training Syrian Kurds or Kurdish-American cooperation in Iraq is a nightmare for Turkish nationalists who still believe Western powers are determined to harm Turkey's territorial integrity.

In analyzing Kemalist foreign policy and strategic thinking, it is critical to understand that this instinctive distrust of the West stands in sharp contrast to the positive image of revolutionary Russia under Bolshevik rule providing military support to Mustafa Kemal during the National Independence Struggle. These fond memories of anti-imperialist Turkish-Russian solidarity in the early 1920s partly provide some historic inspiration for a "Eurasian" strategic alternative to Ankara's current troubles with both the United States and the European Union (Tobakov 2017, 125–145).

All these factors should help us understand not only why Turkey remains highly suspicious of Western intentions vis-à-vis the Kurds but also why Ankara denied the very existence of Kurds within its borders from the 1920s until the end of the Cold War. The Kurdish challenge, simply put, was existential for the territorial and national integrity of the republic. This also explains why, for decades, Turkey sought to assimilate its sizable Kurdish minority, called "Mountain Turks" by authorities. Kurdish ethnicity and cultural rights were brutally suppressed in the name of building a secular nation-state.

At this point, it is important to note that such Kemalist sensitivities are not always shared by Islamist Turkish politicians who blamed the Kemalist republic's radical secularism and nationalism for the loss of religious solidarity with the Kurds. The corollary is that religious conservatives in Turkey believe there is an Islamic solution to the Kurdish question: rejection of ethnic, divisive, Turkish nationalism in favor of embracing the Islamic solidarity and Muslim brotherhood of Ottoman times. It is partly for such reasons that Turkish politicians who are sometimes associated with neo-Ottomanism are also the ones who have tried to pursue a political solution to the Kurdish conflict in Turkey with some room for decentralization and multiculturalism. Yet, it remains the case that the Kemalist paradigm, defined by assimilationist nationalism, has dominated the republic's approach to the Kurdish question. Similar Kemalist dynamics applied to how the republic dealt with Islamic identity. While assimilationist Turkish nationalism suppressed Kurdish resistance, militant secularism subdued Islamist opposition parties.

Cold War Turkish Dynamics: Ideology Trumps Identity

After Turkey joined NATO and multi-party electoral democracy began, the Kemalist generals favored a praetorian system and did not hesitate to intervene in politics in almost every decade—in 1960, 1971, 1980–1983 and 1997. Yet, they also made sure not to stay in power for any prolonged period of time. There was to be no Turkish equivalent of a leader like Franco, Salazar, Pinochet, Suharto, Nasser, Assad or Musharraf who ruled the country by establishing a military dictatorship.

The Turkish General Staff (TGS) never wanted to govern openly and directly because it saw itself above politics, as the protector of the state and the guardian of the Kemalist system. Having played a major role in drafting the 1961 and 1982 constitutions, the top brass believed each intervention had constitutional legitimacy in terms of safeguarding the

Turkish Republic. The TGS's role was to make sure that the realm of the state would not be harmed by the political and ideological competition in the realm of politics. Such duty-bound professionalism and reluctance to stay in power distinguished Turkish military interventions from their Latin American, Middle Eastern, African, Pakistani, East Asian and Southern European equivalents.

Despite the military's reluctance to exert direct rule, this system of guardianship was highly problematic and failed to turn Turkey into a liberal democracy. Individual right and liberties, effective institutional checks and balances, the independence of the judicial system, freedom of speech and assembly remained either absent or in their infancy. Instead of protecting the citizens from a powerful state the system was designed to protect the state from its citizens. Despite such illiberalism, however, Turkey maintained a system of electoral democracy. The will of the people came to be represented in power by competing political parties. Elections took place regularly and governments changed regularly within the realm of politics.

During the 1960s and 1970s the country witnessed considerable ideological polarization. Kurdish and Islamic dissent were no longer high on the political agenda. They certainly did not disappear but rather came to be absorbed by the new political divisions of Turkey. Kurdish discontent found its place within radical left-wing politics with a socialist agenda, while Islam became part of the anti-communist struggle as it converged with Turkish nationalism. A Turkish-Islamic synthesis against the left thus emerged. Of all military interventions, the 1980 coup had particularly long-lasting consequences, some continuing to this day. The most important factor has no doubt been the worsening of the Kurdish problem. The alliance between left-wing groups and Kurdish nationalists was an existential threat in the eyes of anti-communist generals who embraced conservative Turkish nationalism. Instances of torture and killings in the Diyarbakir military prison under the 1980–1983 Kemalist junta helped plant the seeds of Kurdish ethnic separatism. The PKK (Partiya Karkeran Kurdistan, Kurdish Workers Party) gained stronger regional following and launched a separatist insurgency in the mid-1980s.

By the late 1980s, after the long Cold War interlude of ideological polarization, it was as if Turkey was back in the 1930s with a dangerous return to identity polarization over Kemalism. What followed during the 1990s1 was very detrimental for Turkish democracy. Turkish versus

Kurdish polarization on the one hand, and Islamic versus secularist polarization on the other, revealed an acute sense of a Kemalist identity problem in the country (Taşpınar 2005).

Between 1984 and 1999, during its most intense years, the war against the PKK caused tens of thousands of deaths and cost close to $200 billion in military spending alone (Mandıracı 2016; Bilgel and Karahasan 2017, 457–479). At the height of the insurgency in the mid-1990s almost half of Turkey's large army (around 400,000 troops) was deployed in the Kurdish southeast. As the Cold War was coming to an end, the Kurdish problem that had traumatized the early decades of the republic was back with a vengeance.

Post-Cold War Blues with Washington

The bipolar configuration of the Cold War provided a mental map dividing the world into two neat blocs: East and West. Within this straightforward division, Turkey was unproblematically placed in the Western camp. As the southern bastion of NATO against the Soviet Union, Turkey's Western credentials went undisputed. In a world dominated by nuclear threats and a delicate balance of power, thorny questions concerning Turkey's military interventions, human rights standards, the Kurdish problem or Muslim identity were rarely raised. Simply put, Cold War realpolitik dictated Turkey's inclusion in the West.

The Turkish Republic was perfectly content not to face questions regarding its self-proclaimed Western identity. The Turkish governing elite, in accordance with its Kemalist upbringing, had neither Islamic nor Ottoman imperial nostalgia. The security alliance forged with the United States and Western Europe in the framework of NATO came to be seen as being in perfect continuity and harmony with the Kemalist cultural revolution of the 1920s and 1930s. As the Cold War came to an end, however, Turkey increasingly looked to its Western allies as if it were a problematic country fighting its own ethnic and Muslim identity. The Leninist extinction therefore had major consequences for both Turkish domestic and foreign policy.

To be sure, there were some problems in Turkey's relations with the West even during the Cold War. Turkish-American relations in particular witnessed their fair share of ups and downs mostly in the form of Cyprus-centered episodes. These problems occasionally escalated to "crisis" level, as in the case of the "Johnson letter" in 1969 and the weapons embargo in 1974. However, it is important to remember such turbulence always took place always within the contours of a bipolar world where Turkey remained anchored in NATO. Turkey sometimes threatened to adopt a more independent foreign policy. For instance, one can hardly forget the words uttered by Prime Minister İsmet İnonu in reaction to President Lyndon B. Johnson's letter (warning that a Cyprus invasion would leave Turkey alone against the Soviet Union): "If conditions change and events make a new order necessary, Turkey will certainly find its place in this new global order" (Bölükbaşı 1993). Yet, Turkey stayed in NATO and anti-Americanism in the country at that time never reached its post-Cold War levels.

All this would change in the post-Soviet era. There are in fact two fundamental problems that have exacerbated tensions between Ankara and Washington since the demise of communism. First and foremost is the absence of a common enemy. In the post-Soviet regional and global order, Turkey and the United States no longer share an existential threat perception. Despite its identification as a common threat, "terrorism" has proved to be a highly generic concept and a poor substitute for the Soviet Union. To this day, and especially since the emergence of Al Qaeda and ISIS, the two countries have strongly differed on who they primarily identify as terrorists. For Ankara, the top priority was and remains ethnic terrorism in the form of Kurdish nationalism and sepa-ratism associated with the PKK. For Washington, particularly after 9/11 and with the Islamic State in Iraq and Syria, ideological terrorism with its violent jihadist variant has emerged as an existential threat. Moreover, even though anti-terrorism cooperation gained some traction in Turkish-American relations, it failed to provide the same sense of "strategic partnership" that existed when the threat perception was genuinely shared and when it consisted in containing a nuclear-armed Soviet Union.

ENTER THE MIDDLE EAST

The second and more critical issue that has come to haunt the Turkish-American partnership since the 1990s is the fact that center of gravity for the relationship has shifted from Eurasia to a much more difficult region: the Middle East. In the post-Cold War disorder, Turkey's geostrategic relevance for the United States increasingly came to be seen in the context of its borders with the Arab world and Iran, where Washington perceived an Islamist threat. Washington was bureaucratically and strategically ill prepared for this new era in its relations with Turkey in the context of its military interventions in the Gulf and Iraq.

As former Ambassador to Turkey Mark Parris perceptively argued:

> For reasons of self-definition and Cold War logic, Turkey is considered a European nation. It is therefore assigned, for purposes of policy development and implementation, to the subdivisions responsible for Europe: the European Bureau (EUR) at the State Department; the European Command (EUCOM) at the Pentagon; the Directorate for Europe at the [National Security Council (NSC)], etc. Since the end of the Cold War, however, and progressively since the 1990–1991 Gulf War and 9/11, the most serious issues in U.S.-Turkish relations—and virtually all of the controversial ones—have arisen in areas outside "Europe." The majority, in fact, stem from developments in areas which in Washington are the responsibility of offices dealing with the Middle East: the Bureau for Near East Affairs (NEA) at State; [CENTCOM] at the Pentagon; the Near East and South Asia Directorate at NSC. (Parris 2008)

Given this bureaucratic dilemma, American officials who focus on Turkey are often experts on Western Europe, NATO, Russia, the EU and the Mediterranean. With high expectations and mental habits established during the Cold War, they often tend to look at Turkey exclusively as a member of the transatlantic alliance and a Western state. Their level of disappointment is therefore much stronger when Turkey acts in defiance of transatlantic and Western norms (Shapiro and Aydintasbas 2020). Similarly, there is a tendency to see any deviation from these norms as Islamization instead of nationalism and the quest for "strategic autonomy." In short, not only have Turkey and the United States had diverging threat perceptions in the post-Cold War era but also the shifting center of gravity in bilateral relations toward the Middle East has created more room for faulty analysis and mutual misunderstanding.

Several problems began to emerge in this new Middle Eastern paradigm challenging the stability of the Turkish-American strategic partnership. These challenges can be classified in three broad categories. First and foremost was the emergence of the Kurdish question as a major bone of contention. As we will analyze shortly, Iraq and Syria were the external epicenters of Turkey's Kurdish threat perception due to the presence of PKK safe havens in both countries. For Washington, however, the Kurdish presence in these countries turned into a militarily strategic, tactical and operational advantage in the fight against Saddam Hussein in Iraq, and

ISIS in Syria. Such divergence in threat perception became impossible for Turkey to tolerate in Syria, where US partners were not just Kurdish nationalists, as in the case of Iraq, but members of the PKK.

A second aspect of the Middle East that caused major problems in Turkish-American relations, particularly after 2010, was Turkey's deteriorating relations with Israel. Shortly after coming to power, the Justice and Development Party (AKP) of Recep Tayyip Erdogan enjoyed excellent relations with Tel Aviv. Yet, the Palestinian issue and Erdogan's perception of Hamas as a victim in Gaza changed everything. Ever since the Mavi Marmara flotilla incident in 2010 Turkey and Israel have seen each other as regional rivals (Arbell 2014; Oğuzlu 2010; Balcı and Kardas 2012). Not surprisingly this situation has strong implications for Turkey's image in American politics and particularly in the US Congress where the pro-Israel lobby used to be a strong supporter of Ankara against Greek, Armenian and Kurdish lobbies.

A third dimension of Turkish-American problems emerged in the context of the Arab Spring and the role of the Muslim Brotherhood (MB), particularly in Egypt. The fact that the United States failed to call the toppling of the Muslim Brotherhood government by the Egyptian military a "coup" created deep resentment in Ankara. Turkey's support for the Muslim Brotherhood-oriented political parties during and after the Arab Spring fueled the understandable perception of an Islamist turn in Turkish foreign policy after 2011 (Özkan 2014). The fact that Saudi Arabia, the United Arab Emirates, Egypt and Israel today consider the MB as a terrorist organization with former US Secretary of State Mike Pompeo also being a strong advocate of such a designation, turned the issue into a major irritant in Turkish-American relations. When Turkey itself faced a failed coup attempt in 2016 and the United States refused to extradite Fetullah Gülen, despite Turkey labeling him as the leader of the terrorist network that orchestrated the whole affair, the limits of counterterrorism cooperation as a shared security interest in Turkish-American relations became abundantly clear.

The Kurdish Predicament Between Ankara and Washington

Of all these factors poisoning the strategic partnership, the Kurdish issue is by far the most significant for Ankara. The challenging nature of the problem became clear for the first time in the context of the First Gulf War of 1990–1991. Soon after the liberation of Kuwait, the UN-established no-fly-zone in northern Iraq gradually undermined Turkey's security. Lack of central authority in northern Iraq allowed the PKK to establish training grounds and stage operations against Turkey from the region. US support for the Iraqi Kurds worsened Ankara's concerns about Kurdish separatism during the 1990s, which turned into a truly "lost decade" for Ankara in terms of democratic performance, economic stagnation, systemic instability, diplomatic crisis with Europe and the United States and a soft-coup forcing the AKP's Islamist predecessor, the Welfare Party, out of power. The conspiratorial belief that the United States was behind Kurdish nationalism and terrorism re-emerged during this first decade of the post-Cold War era, in ways that recalled the pre-Cold War Kemalist instincts that blamed British imperialism for the Kurdish insurrections of the 1920s and 1930s.

Turkish concerns over United States-Kurdish cooperation were to play a major role years later in 2003 as Turkey decided not to grant the United States military access to Turkish airspace and bases for the invasion of Iraq. This debacle was the first chapter leading to a breakdown of trust between the two allies. Despite this disaster with the Bush administration, the AKP tried hard to maintain good relations with both Washington and the European Union during its first decade in power. Accession negotiations with the EU began in 2005 in part as a reward for Ankara's positive attitude in Cyprus. Washington, on the other hand, did not punish Turkey for its failure to cooperate in the invasion of Iraq and continued to value Turkey as a democratic model in the Islamic world, as the Bush administration itself pursued a "freedom agenda" aimed at democratization efforts in the Arab world.

One incident in northern Iraq, however, served as a strong reminder that the Kurdish question remained a major bone of contention in Turkish-American relations and was in many ways the harbinger of what would unfold in Syria more than a decade later. On July 4, 2003, US forces in northern Iraq detained 11 Turkish special force members suspected of planning to participate in the assassination of a local Kurdish politician. The soldiers were released after 48 hours, but not before they were hooded and treated as prisoners by the American military causing great humiliation and resentment in Turkey. The Turkish general staff spoke of "the worst crisis of confidence" between Ankara and Washington in more than 50 years, and Foreign Minister Abdullah Gul warned that "this harm cannot be forgotten" (Howard 2003).

The post-invasion chaos in Iraq drove Turkey more deeply toward the Middle East. After the invasion, Ankara's worst fears were realized. Iraq became a breeding ground for international terrorism and descended into sectarian and ethnic violence. Tehran's influence was greatly increased in Iraq and in the region more broadly. The Iraqi Kurds' drive for autonomy—and quest for formal independence—gained momentum. Once believed to have been dissolved, the PKK took up arms again. Beginning in January 2005, the PKK launched repeated attacks on Turkish territory, killing several hundred Turkish security forces. Although the PKK maintained some guerilla and urban presence in Turkey, most Turkish observers believed its main attacks were being organized from sanctuaries in the Kandil Mountains, in northern Iraq.

While Ankara was frustrated with the United States, it did not take very long for American public opinion to turn against the invasion of Iraq as well. The arrival of the Obama administration and the new President's decision to end America's military presence in the country came as a shock to Iraqi Kurds. With the departure of the United States, the Kurdish Regional Government (KRG) in Erbil now had to find ways to improve relations with Ankara. With the Americans out of the way, the Erdogan government was happy to engage the KRG from a position of strength and with an eye on lucrative energy projects. Ankara recognized the KRG and opened a consulate in Erbil in 2010. Diplomatic relations were followed by lucrative economic contracts. In a few years Turkey became a major importer of Kurdish oil and an investor in energy and civilian infrastructure with its highly competent construction companies.

The PKK's presence in this region, however, had the potential to poison the growing economic and political ties between Ankara and Erbil. For reasons having to do with domestic politics, such as the military-civilian balance moving in favor of the AKP, as well as the need for stability and growth in Turkey's own Kurdish regions, Erdogan decided to engage in secret negotiations with the PKK as early as in 2009, in what later came to be known as the Oslo Process. During the talks, both the Turkish security forces and the PKK scaled back their offensive operations. The road to peace between Ankara and the PKK proved predictably complicated with several setbacks between 2009 and 2014.

For instance, the initiative ran aground in the run-up to the Turkish general elections in June 2011. This resulted in a re-escalation of violence that increased casualties to a level not seen in more than a decade (Marcus 2015). By late 2012 it became obvious to both Ankara and the PKK that no clear winner would emerge from a new round of violence. In December 2012, Erdogan announced that Turkey's National Intelligence Organization (MIT) had been holding talks with Abdullah Ocalan, the jailed leader of the PKK, in an attempt to convince the organization to lay down its arms and withdraw from Turkish soil. Unlike previous peace attempts, which were very secretive, this time the media and Ocalan stood at the center of the negotiations. Both parties adopted seemingly softer approaches as the PKK cadres in Europe and Iraq also expressed their support for the ongoing talks (Pope 2014).

Erdogan also seemed intent on pushing the negotiation process forward. He had considerable political capital at his disposal after his electoral victory in 2011 and wanted to deliver peace and quiet in the Kurdish southeast where his party was making major political inroads thanks to new economic investment projects and growing trade relations with Iraqi Kurdistan. The broad outlines of the process included ceasefire declarations by the PKK, the release of hostages and prisoner activists and the withdrawal of PKK militants into northern Iraq after laying down their arms. In return, the Turkish government was expected to craft legislation to overhaul the definition of terrorism and move forward with a new democratic constitution improving minority rights and furthering administrative decentralization. As part of settlement talks, the PKK declared a ceasefire in March 2013 and began its withdrawal from Turkey toward camps in northern Iraq. For the first time in its modern history Turkey appeared so close to a democratic solution to its most intractable conflict.

While Turkey pursued a Kurdish peace process at home, the Middle East witnessed significant upheaval with the Arab Spring. The revolution in Tunis led to a wave of mass mobilization in Egypt and the unimaginable happened in a few months as the regime of Hosni Mubarak collapsed after a tenure that had lasted 30 years. The regime of Libyan dictator Gaddafi also disintegrated as the country descended into civil war. Ankara embraced the Tunisian and Egyptian revolutions without reservation. After some hesitation due to financial interests and investments in Libya, Erdogan also decided to support regime change and NATO-led operations in Libya.

THE SYRIAN QUAGMIRE

Syria, however, was where the rubber hit the road for Turkey. Damascus was the crown jewel in the AKP's "zero problems with neighbors" policy of economic, political, diplomatic and cultural engagement with the

Middle East. Despite considerable problems in the 1990s during which the Assad regime supported the PKK, relations between Ankara and Damascus began to improve after Syria expelled Abdullah Ocalan in 1999, paving the way to his arrest and imprisonment by Turkish authorities.

Between 2003 and 2010 trade, tourism, cultural and diplomatic relations between Erdogan's Turkey and Bashar al-Assad's Syria witnessed a tremendous growth. Erdogan and Bashar al-Assad saw each other as strategic, economic and diplomatic partners (Bishku 2012). During the AKP's golden years of domestic democratization, economic growth, and good relations with the West and the Middle East, Ankara even mediated between Syria and Israel to secure a lasting peace in the Golan Heights dispute. It was therefore understandable that Erdogan should approach Syria with caution. However, after months of demonstrations, a brutal crackdown by the regime and Ankara's failure to convince Assad to adopt a reformist course, Turkey began supporting the Islamist opposition with the hope that it could tip the balance in favor of regime change. The Turkish expectation was that what had happened in Tunisia, Egypt and Libya would also end up happening in Syria soon. And the arrival of a Muslim Brotherhood-oriented government in Damascus would highly benefit Turkish strategic and economic interests as it did in Egypt.

Regional and domestic dynamics, however, led to sectarianization of the conflict in Syria—a problem that did not exist in the case of other Arab Spring countries in North Africa. Iran and Russia entered the Syrian civil war and the country soon found itself deeply involved in a major quagmire. By 2012, especially after Syria's shooting down of a Turkish fighter and killing two of its pilots, Turkey began to voice support for an international military intervention in Syria. To its dismay, however, neither the United States, nor the EU were interested in that option. Turkey, with Saudi Arabia and Qatar, had to rely on its own resources to change the balance of power on the ground. It did not take long for Ankara to turn into a major military and logistic supporter of Syrian Islamist insurgents. By 2013 Turkey was already a major hub for Syria's exiled opposition and a conduit for the steady stream of foreign jihadi fighters making their way into Syria.

Eventually, Ankara turned a blind eye even to members of ISIS, who slipped in and out of the country and sometimes sought medical treatment there (Stein 2016). All the while, Turkey opened its borders to millions of refugees fleeing the fighting and built vast camps to hold the new arrivals. The gesture was expensive but morally just, Erdogan argued—an act of Sunni compassion and solidarity in the face of the Assad regime's atrocities. That narrative struck a chord with the public and opposition to the refugee influx remained relatively muted. All told, Turkey has hosted 3.6 million Syrian refugees.

In the meantime, Turkey's frustration with the Western reluctance to get militarily involved in Syria continued to grow. Neither Washington nor European countries were interested in establishing a safe zone in northern Syria to support the opposition against Damascus. What came next in 2014 led to a disaster in terms of Turkey's own "Kurdish opening" and its already tense relations with Washington because of Syria. For several years, the Obama administration resisted calls to play a direct role in the Syrian war, preferring instead to provide funding and training for some rebel groups. But President Barack Obama changed his mind as the Islamic State took advantage of the chaos of the war to capture vast swaths of Syrian and Iraqi territory.

By mid-2014, the US military decided to airdrop weapons to Kurdish militias, the strongest of which was the People's Protection Units, known by its Kurdish initials, the YPG. From the US perspective, the US action came after months of failed efforts to convince Ankara to do more against ISIS and at a critical juncture when the YPG was waging a war against ISIS in the northern Syrian town of Kobane on the Turkish border. In the eyes of Washington, the YPG was by far the most effective local force and the most reliable partner against ISIS. From the Turkish perspective, however, Washington was now officially in bed with the PKK. The YPG was nothing less than the Syrian affiliate of the same terrorist movement Turkey has been fighting since the early 1980s. Under these conditions, any hope of pursuing the Kurdish peace process at home also naturally vanished, as talks with the PKK collapsed and Ankara's war against Kurdish insurgents resumed with new intensity a year later. By mid-2015, the AKP returned to the old paradigm of an alarmist security-first approach, feeling betrayed by its NATO ally's decision to arm its arch enemy. The frustration was mutual since Washington knew Turkey was working closely with jihadist networks close to ISIS (Zaman 2015; Jenkins 2018; Gürsel 2015; Talley 2019).

In short, Syria now represented not only the near death of the Turkish-American alliance but also the termination of any prospect of Turkish peace with the PKK. Up until this point it was arguably possible for Ankara and Washington to compartmentalize their problems in the Middle East. Differences on issues such as the Israeli-Palestinian dispute, the military coup in Egypt toppling the Muslim Brotherhood, or even differences vis-à-vis Iran and Iraq paled into insignificance when compared with Syria, where the problem was no longer that Ankara and Washington did not share the same threat perception any more. They were now actively supporting each other's existential enemies. The pretense of a strategic partnership was no longer possible.

The Russia entry in the Syrian civil war in 2015 made things worse for Turkey, as Moscow came to the rescue of Damascus. The risk of a Turkish-Russian confrontation came perilously close after Turkey downed a Russian jet for violating its airspace in late 2015. Shortly after the incident, as Moscow vowed to retaliate, a panicked Turkey called for a NATO emergency meeting hoping for contingency plans in preparation of collective defense. What Ankara received instead was some token words of solidarity and a call for calm and de-escalation. Ankara felt even more neglected when Germany and the United States declared they would not change their earlier plans to withdraw Patriot batteries deployed in Turkey for scheduled maintenance.

Ankara understandably felt sidelined as its security concerns were not taken seriously, just when it feared a Russian military retaliation. All this strengthened the view in Ankara that the US-led alliance was not committed to Turkey's defense (Emmott et al. 2015). In the meantime, Russia announced economic sanctions against Turkey. Moscow ended commercial and charter flights between the two countries, imposed a ban on Russian businesses hiring any new Turkish nationals, placed import restrictions on certain Turkish goods and on Russian tourists traveling to Turkey. Bilateral relations between the two countries showed some signs of improvement in June 2016 only after Erdogan expressed his regrets for the downing of the Russian jet in a letter that Putin accepted as an apology (Luhn and Black 2016).

Just one month after the relative improvement in Turkish-Russian ties, things went from bad to worse in Turkish-American relations when the Erdogan government survived a bizarrely botched coup attempt by a clique within the Turkish military that apparently acted in defiance of the chain of command. Erdogan immediately blamed the US-based cleric Fethullah Gülen for orchestrating the coup and launched a massive purge within not only the military and civilian bureaucracy but in all civil society, as well as in business and educational institutions. In Ankara's view, the United States was not fast and clear enough in condemning the coup attempt whereas Russian President Vladimir Putin called Erdogan immediately and offered Russian Special Forces deployed in a nearby Greek island. Ankara has been demanding Gülen's extradition ever since. The United States has refused the request so far on the grounds that the decision is up to the courts and that Turkish authorities have failed to produce hard evidence tying Gülen to the coup attempt. For Turks, this US stance on Gülen only confirms the conspiratorial view that Washington itself was behind the coup.

Shortly after the failed coup, the Turkish military launched its first operation into northern Syria with the goal of clearing a border area from both ISIS and YPG forces. Erdogan has turned increasingly autocratic and nationalistic since 2016. He has changed the Turkish political system into a one-man rule, presidential regime with the 2017 referendum and intensified his crackdown on Kurdish, liberal, Gülenist opposition forces as the backsliding in Turkish democracy has reached unprecedented levels. The Turkish army continued to launch military operations into northern Syria in 2018 and 2019, dealing a blow to Kurdish aspirations for self-administration and coming close to a military confrontation with US special forces training their YPG partners against ISIS. In the last few years, Turkey has effectively carved up its own zones of control in critical parts of northern Syria and joined Iran and Russia in diplomatic talks in the framework of the Astana process for a political solution to the Syrian conflict (Bechev 2018).

In the meantime, Turkish-American relations continued to worsen. In 2018 Ankara purchased the S-400 Russian missile defense system, despite clear warnings from the United States that such weapons would not be not interoperable with NATO systems and that Turkey would face economic and military sanctions if it moved ahead with the order. After the delivery of the S-400s to Turkey in 2019, Turkey was officially cut out of the F-35 warplane program and the same year, when Turkey launched its third and most comprehensive military operation in northern Syria, the US Treasury imposed targeted and temporary sanctions against the Turkish Ministry of Defense. Finally, in December 2020 the departing Trump administration imposed military sanctions on Turkey's defense industry in the framework of the Countering America's Adversaries Through Sanctions Act. Turkish-American relations are likely to hit a new low point under the incoming Biden administration. As a candidate, former Vice-President and now President Joe Biden called

Erdogan an autocrat, criticized his policy toward Kurds, and advocated working with the Turkish opposition (Champion and Wadhams 2020).

CONCLUSION: A EURASIAN FUTURE FOR TURKEY?

Delivery of the S400 missiles and Turkey's decision to test the system in the summer of 2020 was indeed a watershed moment in Turkey's relations with both NATO and the United States (Stein and Hamilton 2020). Turkey-Russia relations could evolve into a strategic partnership in the future if Turkey's relations with the West are further strained. Ankara is not at this point yet, since its relations with Moscow remain fragile. Despite cooperation in Syria, Turkey and Russia are on opposing fronts, with Russia backing the Assad regime and Turkey still supporting what is left of the Syrian opposition. The Syrian province of Idlib, which is the last remaining Islamist stronghold, remains a flashpoint in Turkey-Russia cooperation. It is also important to remember that Turkey and Russia are also in opposing camps in a series of regional flash points ranging from Libya to the Caucasus.

Turkey and Russia may today only have a marriage of convenience. Yet, it is hard to avoid the impression that Ankara and Washington are heading toward divorce. Given the growing level of distrust between Ankara and Washington on critical issues ranging from the S-400s to Syrian Kurds and Fetullah Gülen it would be naïve for analysts not to take the potential for a Eurasianist Turkish foreign policy seriously. If current trends of anti-Western nationalism and authoritarianism continue, Ankara will start officially questioning its place within the transatlantic alliance. This Turkish quest for strategic autonomy does not bode well for Turkey's relations with Washington, the European Union and NATO.

Today, Syria, the Kurdish question and ISIS have turned into a nightmare for the Turkish-American alliance. Only time will show if the two countries again find ways to restore a once-strategic partnership. At the moment crisis management and damage control appear the most realistic scenario. As Erdogan declared on the third anniversary of the failed coup of July 15: "Despite our political and military pacts with the Western alliance, the fact is that once again the biggest threats we face are from them" (Gazete Duvar 2019). As long as Turkey's threat perception remains Kurdish separatism and the United States maintains its support for Syrian Kurds, there is no realistic reason to be optimistic. The reason is simple: If there is one issue that creates more alarm than

Kurdish nationalism in Turkey, it is Kurdish nationalism with Washington's military support behind it. And Syria is the place where this Turkish nightmare turned into a Kurdish dream.

REFERENCES

Arbell, Dan. 2014. "The U.S.-Turkey-Israel Triangle." Brookings Analysis Paper 34, October 6. https://www.brookings.edu/research/the-u-s-turkey-israel-tri angle/. Accessed on 7 April 2021.

Balcı, Ali, and Tuncay Kardas. 2012. "The Changing Dynamics of Turkey's Relations with Israel: An Analysis of 'Securitization'." *Insight Turkey* 14 (2, Spring): 99–120.

Bechev, Dimitar. 2018. "Russia and Turkey: The Promise and the Limits of Partnership." In *Russia's Return to the Middle East: Building Sandcastles*, edited by Nicu Popescu and Stanislav Secrieru, 95–101. Paris: European Union Institute for Security Studies.

Bilgel, Fırat, and Burhan Can Karahasan. 2017. "The Economic Costs of Separatist Terrorism in Turkey." *Journal of Conflict Resolution* 61 (2): 457–479.

Bishku, Michael. 2012. "Turkish-Syrian Relations: A Checkered History." *Middle East Policy Council* 19 (3, Fall).

Bolukbasi, Suha. 1993. "The Johnson Letter Revisited." *Middle Eastern Studies* 29 (3).

Champion, Marc, and Nick Wadhams. 2020. "Erdogan Is Getting Ready for Four Rocky Years of Biden." *Bloomberg*, November 24. https://www.blo omberg.com/news/articles/2020-11-24/erdogan-gets-ready-for-a-rocky-four-years-of-biden. Accessed on 7 April 2021.

Duvar, Gazete. 2019. "Erdoğan: S-400 tarihimizin en önemli anlaşması." July 14.

Emmott, Robin, Sabine Siebold, and Phil Stewart. 2015. "Turkey Urges NATO to Keep Up Its Patriot Defenses." *Reuters*, October 8. https://www.reuters.com/article/us-mideast-crisis-syria-nato/turkey-urges-nato-to-keep-up-its-pat riot-defenses-idUSKCN0S20HJ20151008. Accessed on 7 April 2021.

Gursel, Kadri. 2015. "Turkish Daily Exposes Weapons Transfer to ISIS." *Al Monitor*, September 1.

Howard, Michael. 2003. "US Arrest of Soldiers Infuriates Turkey." *The Guardian*, July 7.

Jenkins, Gareth. 2018. "Yesterday's Wars: The Cause and Consequences of Turkish Inaction Against the Islamic State." *Turkey Analyst* 7 (18).

Jung, Dietrich. 2003. "The Sevres Syndrome: Turkish Foreign Policy and Its Historical Legacies." *American Diplomacy*, August 2003. https://americand

iplomacy.web.unc.edu/2003/08/the-sevres-syndrome/. Accessed on 7 April 2021.

Luhn, Alec, and Ian Black. 2016. "Erdogan Has Apologised for Downing of Russian Jet, Kremlin Says." *The Guardian*, June 27. https://www.thegua rdian.com/world/2016/jun/27/kremlin-says-erdogan-apologises-russian-jet-turkish. (Page not available anymore).

Mandıracı, Berkay. 2016. "Turkey's PKK Conflict: The Death Toll." *International Crisis Group*, July 2016.

Marcus, Aliza. 2015. "Turkey's Kurdish Guerrillas Are Ready for War." *Foreign Policy*, August 31.

Oğuzlu, Tarık. 2010. "The Changing Dynamics of Turkey-Israel Relations: A Structural Realist Account." *Mediterranean Politics* 15 (2): 273–288.

Olson, Robert. 1989. *The Emergence of Kurdish Nationalism and the Sheikh Said Rebellion*. Austin: University of Texas Press.

Özkan, Behlül. 2014. "Turkey, Davutoglu, and the Idea of Pan-Islamism." *Survival* 56 (4): 119–114.

Parris, Mark. 2008. "Toward a Successful Turkey Policy: Suggestions for the Next Administration." (Unpublished Manuscript).

Pope, Hugh. 2014. "Turkey and the PKK: Saving the Peace Process." *International Crisis Group*, November 6. https://www.crisisgroup.org/europe-cen tral-asia/western-europemediterranean/turkey/turkey-and-pkk-saving-peace-process. Accessed on 7 April 2021.

Reuters. 2021. "U.S. Secretary of State Nominee Calls Turkey a "So-Called Strategic Partner." January 19. https://www.reuters.com/article/usa-biden-state-turkey/u-s-secretary-of-state-nominee-calls-nato-ally-turkey-a-so-called-strategic-partner-idUSL1N2JU2Z6. Accessed on 7 April 2021.

Shapiro, Jeremy, and Asli Aydintasbas. 2020. "Biden and Erdogan Are Trapped in a Fantasy World." *Foreign Policy*, January 6. https://foreignpolicy.com/2021/01/06/biden-america-and-erdogan-turkey-are-trapped-in-a-double-fan tasy/. Accessed on 7 April 2021.

Soylu, Ragıp. 2019. "Anti-US Sentiment in Turkey Reaches a New High, Poll Shows." *Middle East Eye*, February 1. https://www.middleeasteye.net/news/anti-us-sentiment-turkey-reaches-new-high-poll-shows. Accessed on 7 April 2021.

Stein, Aaron. 2016. "Islamic State Networks in Turkey: Recruitment for the Caliphate." *Atlantic Council*, Issue Brief.

Stein, Aaron, and Robert Hamilton. 2020. "How America's Experience with Pakistan Can Help it Deal with Turkey." *War on the Rocks*, August 25.

Talley, Ian. 2019. "U.S. Backlists Four Turkish Companies for Aiding ISIS." *The Wall Street Journal*, November 18. https://www.wsj.com/articles/u-s-blackl ists-four-turkish-companies-for-aiding-isis-11574110776. Accessed on 7 April 2021.

Taşpınar, Ömer. 2005. *Kurdish Nationalism and Political Islam: Kemalist Identity in Transition.* London: Routledge.

Tobakov, Igor. 2017. "Neo-Ottomanism Versus Neo-Eurasianism?: Nationalism and Symbolic Geography in Postimperial Turkey and Russia." *Mediterranean Quarterly* 28 (2): 125–145.

Yavuz, Hakan, and Bayram Balci. 2018. *Turkey's July 15th Coup: What Happened and Why.* Utah Series in Middle East Studies. Salt Lake City: The University of Utah Press.

Zaman, Amberin. 2015. "Captured Fighter Details Islamic State's Turkey Connection." *Al Monitor*, June 17.

CHAPTER 13

By Way of a Conclusion

Michel Duclos

Much less knowledgeable than the authors of the preceding chapters, I am aware of the immense honor that was bestowed on me when I was asked to conclude this book. I will try to accomplish this task with the humility that is appropriate for one who is just a simple practitioner of diplomacy and, moreover, a generalist.

Let us begin with a question: Is there not something artificial in talking about a "triangle" of Turkey-Iran-Russia? To a certain extent, yes there is. Firstly, because it is difficult to imagine in this way three countries, three former empires, which have been marked by a long history of rivalry and conflicts that has left behind it reflexes of deep distrust.

Then because Turkey and Iran are not, if we can put it this way, playing in the same league as Russia. This is a global power, undoubtedly downgraded but retaining a particular status on account of its nuclear arsenal, its seat as a permanent member of the Security Council and lastly its fierce determination to keep its "rank" on the international stage. Iran and Turkey are regional powers, as are Saudi Arabia, Egypt and Israel. Geographical proximity and a strong historical tradition have made Russia

M. Duclos (✉)
Institut Montaigne, Paris, France

B. Balci and N. Monceau (eds.), *Turkey, Russia and Iran in the Middle East*, The Sciences Po Series in International Relations and Political Economy, https://doi.org/10.1007/978-3-030-80291-2_13

235

a regional actor, but one that remains an external power, with global ambitions besides.

Might we say, in the current world context—marked in particular by the diffusion of power and the hybrid character of conflicts—that this distinction between external powers and regional ones is tending to become blurred? In part, this is in fact true, at least in some specific areas of tensions. But above all there are three more immediate reasons that justify us speaking of a Turkey-Russia-Iran triangle.

First reason: The unending Syrian conflict has, de facto, brought the three actors together. We will come back to this point, but we should already note what is obvious: The three accomplices entered the Syrian game with different aims, that at the outset were compatible for Russians and Iranians, but completely opposed regarding Turkey and the other two. However, for several years already they had found ways of working together in the context of what is called the Astana Process.

Second reason: In the region the Russia-Turkey-Iran triangle faces another one, made up of Israel, the USA and some of the Gulf States (Saudi Arabia and the United Arab Emirates), united around the aim of containing Iran and also of countering political Islam, notably in its "Muslim Brotherhood" manifestation that is backed by Mr Erdogan's Turkey. It has escaped no-one's notice that Russia's cooperation with Turkey and Iran does not make it the enemy of Saudi Arabia and even less of Israel. Similarly, the USA, close to Saudi Arabia and Israel, has remained allied with Turkey within the Atlantic Alliance.

Third reason: Our three actors are revisionist, or even revanchist powers, impelled by a strong anti-Western resentment. This resentment—in the guise of state anti-Americanism—is part of the genetic code of the Islamic Republic of Iran; it has been strenuously cultivated by President Putin and his colleagues in the Kremlin to shore up the nationalist pillar of their regimes; it has doubtless always existed in Turkey, but once again, in the hands of Recep Tayyip Erdogan (RTE), it has become a tool for the mobilization of several layers of Turkish opinion.

We thus come to the point where we ask a second quite simple question: How did things get to this point? Let us not go back to the deepest of roots, as a historian may do, but let us identify three immediate causes, for the benefit of the present argument.

First, the end of the Cold War, of which we might say that the current Russia-Turkey-Iran triangle is emblematic. Since the end of the 1990s we have shifted into a world where yesteryear's reflexes of "bloc vs bloc" have been progressively erased, no doubt with some discrepancies depending on the regions of the world. Concerning the Near East, the major event was obviously the US invasion of Iraq in 2003, the significant consequences of which are well known. The Iraqi adventure of the Bush administration would have been difficult to image in a Cold War context: The Americans would have shown themselves to be more cautious.

A more modest element seems to be equally significant: In the case of this attack on Iraq by the USA, the Turkish parliament refused to allow American troops to cross through Turkish territory (the story goes that Prime Minister Erdogan was in fact favorable). The discipline of the Cold War period was no longer in effect. A short while afterward, the Turkish government allied itself with Brazil to find (or so it believed) a solution to the issue of Iranian nuclear power—that its American and European allies rejected.

After the end of the Cold War, came the eruption of the Arab Spring or Springs. The wave of uprisings that shook the Near East unsettled the politics of states in the region as well as that of outside actors and deeply influenced relations between the different actors. At the start of the rebellions, the upper echelons in Iran and the Justice and Development Party (AKP) circles were full of hope: The people, they thought, are shaking off the yoke of secularist dictators and will turn toward political Islam. The Supreme Leader of Iran quickly changed his mind when he realized—doubtless under the influence of the Revolutionary Guards—that his ally al-Assad, whose faction was the only entry point into Syria for Iran, risked being overthrown. On the other hand, Erdogan noticed with horror that al-Assad was not following his advice and was massacring his people. And above all, he took as a terrible personal failure—an affront ever since he believed that the Western powers were in favor—the coup d'état in Egypt on July 3, 2013, that overthrew President Morsi, his partner within the international Muslim Brotherhood. For Erdogan's Turkey, the Arab Spring was a sizeable trauma: His model of government had been on the brink of becoming the norm in a certain number of countries and then was eliminated everywhere. At about the same time, on the domestic front, the Gezi Park movement was developing.

In Moscow, while the experts had correctly analyzed the economic and social reasons behind the unrest, in the Arab Spring the Kremlin only saw a Western plot backing the Islamists in order to proceed to a series of regime changes. Iran and Russia found themselves on a counter-revolutionary line; the scenario was different for Turkey: hostility toward al-Assad but also directed at Marshal Sisi; bitter rivalry with certain Gulf states, notably the United Arab Emirates, over the issue of political Islam. The Westerners did not really have a proper policy (relations between the USA and Egypt, for example, never regained the closeness they had enjoyed before the Arab Spring). In sum, in the eyes of the region's governments, Russia seemed to be the only major external power with a clear strategy that, fundamentally, was in support of the regimes in place.

Vladimir Putin knew perfectly well how to get this message across to President Erdogan during the attempted coup d'état of July 15, 2016, when Turkey's Western allies lamentably dragged their feet.

Lastly, but not least, the third factor: the American withdrawal. We can discuss the scope of this withdrawal endlessly; we can talk until we lose sight of the reasons for this (the shale gas revolution, the weariness over external military interventions, etc.). The view within the countries of the region was that although they had not properly quit (they kept a size-able military presence in the area) thenceforward the USA was reluctant to keep a regional *Pax Americana* in place. The feeble American reaction to the Houthi attacks on Saudi Arabia in summer 2019 is a striking illustration of this.

It seems to us that the combination of these three phenomena—the end of the Cold War, the Arab Springs, the way the American with-drawal was perceived—resulted in three consequences. In the first place, there was an "autonomization" of the regional actors: The Saudis and the Emiratis threw themselves into the Yemen adventure with no safety net, Turkey sent its army into Syria, each one goes it alone with their Iraqi policy, their Syrian policy and soon their Libyan policy, etc.

Secondly, regional disorders and way the American retreat was perceived offered Russia a window of opportunity to make its grand return. After invading Georgia in 2008, the Russians devoted a great deal of effort to modernizing their army. From 2011 to 2012 Vladimir Putin made the strategic decision to confront the West. The Ukrainian affair in 2014 meant he had burnt his boats regarding Westerners. He continued on his path by sending planes into Syria in September 2015. From that, he gained immense prestige throughout the entire region that was trans-formed into a capacity to influence extending well beyond the region. Unlike Barack Obama he had understood that the Near East remains one of the major measures of power in the world.

In the third place, the power vacuum left by the weakening of state power and the American disengagement signaled that the time had come for the rise in power of different terrorist movements: Al-Qaeda, Daesh and others.

On this last point, there is a bitter paradox to be noted. The anti-terrorist fight could have been the common cause, a factor of rapprochement between the powers involved in the Near East. But it never was. The issue of terrorism has instead hardened oppositions for what was seen as terrorism by one side was rarely the same for the others. Daesh certainly provoked a certain mobilization, a general movement in principle but, in fact above all, the Russians fought the moderate pro-Western groups in Syria, the Americans viewed Hezbollah and its followers in Iraq as terrorists while in Iran they were allies; Turkey was above all obsessed by the threat of the Kurdistan Workers' Party (PKK) and its Syrian branch, the Democratic Union Party (PYD), all the while being suspected of compromise with some Islamist groups and even with Daesh. A conspiracist view of things arouses thoughts of the Iranians but also of many Russians for whom the only terrorism is that perpetrated by the Sunni *takfiri* with underground backing from the CIA in the way it had earlier supported the *Mujahidin* in Afghanistan against the USSR. On the other hand, Western intelligence services accuse Iran of sheltering Al-Qaeda leaders.

It is in this context that the conflict in Syria should be read, as suggested in our book *La Longue Nuit Syrienne* (*The Long Syrian Night*) (Duclos 2019).

In Damascus, in the second half of the 2000s, conditions seem to have converged for the country to experience riots, rebellions even, for demographic, economic and social reasons, to which, thanks to modern means of communication, was added the increasingly visible contrast between, on the one hand, the corruption and the wealth of the elites, close to the palace, and on the other hand the pauperization of the population suffering from high levels of unemployment. Nevertheless, it was the context of the Arab Springs that triggered the uprising and gave it the political impetus that marked it. The religious fragmentation of the country and the monstrous perversity of Bashar al-Assad's regime caused the uprising to mutate into civil war, that from 2013 onward was divided more and more along religious lines. As we know, first the Iranians then the Russians gave decisive support to the Damascus regime. The Turks, the Americans, the Europeans, and certain Gulf states helped the opposition armed groups to different degrees. The Syrian conflict thus took on the shape of a globalized civil war.

One of the traits of this globalized civil war was that it acted as a catalyst for the rise in power of authoritarian regimes, just as the Spanish Civil War in the 1930s had served as a testing ground for the emergence of totalitarian powers. Iran saw its role in the region increase through its proxies. As already stated, the Russians regained global status. Erdogan's regime was already on the road to radicalization, but the Syrian drama hastened the process. Moreover, through terrorism and the influxes of refugees, governments such as Kaczynski's in Poland and Orban's in Hungary as well as diverse populist nationalists like Salvini in Italy also benefited from a greater profile among confused European opinions. Conversely, liberal democracies have paled in comparison and the USA and Europe seem incapable of influencing events and are reluctant to use force. Secondly, their attention exclusively focused on combatting Daesh has left room for other players in the Syrian drama—Turkey, Russia and Iran (as well as Israel, whose role will always be ambiguous: hostile to Iranian aims but approving with regard to both father and son al-Assad).

In the Syrian affair, Russia has always taken care to eliminate any possibility of a role for the United Nations, on this point shoring up obstruction by the Damascus regime. After the fall of Aleppo in December 2016, with Western players definitively removed from the game and the international community having shown its powerlessness, Turkey on one side, with Russia and Iran on the other, were the only ones left in the game. Russian diplomacy displayed some remarkable creativity: It invented (early 2017) the Astana format that, in the guise of an agreement on "de-escalation zones", allowed the three actors to manage their differences by coming together in agreement on the equivalent of zones of influence, or even, in the best of cases, in a co-piloting of the crisis. The Astana club has come through some rocky moments at times of very high tension, particularly between Turkey and Russia (about Idlib since 2018 in particular), but it is still there.

Can such a partnership, that is so clearly shaky, continue over the long term? Is it sustainable as we now say? Can it go beyond the situation that caused its creation, which was the management of the Syrian conflict? That is at the very heart of the question underpinning this book. We will offer to shed our own light by means of a daring analogy: The Turkey-Russia-Iran team is in a way a reminder of how the Entente Cordiale was formed between the UK and France at the beginning of the twentieth century. Let us reassure the reader: We understand the limits of the analogy and we will come back to this later on.

What we would like to note, in just a few words, is that the historic hostility between the French and the British is used as being largely similar to the remembered antagonisms that underpin the present distrust between Turks, Russians, and Iranians. At the dawn of the twentieth century, the two major colonial empires that were still expanding were engaged in a fierce contest and they came close to war over the Fashoda incident (1898). What their statesmen decided was not to sign an alliance, which was unimaginable at the time, but to work toward the sensible management of the risks of escalation within the differences between their nations. And that was because they were both experiencing a common threat, that happened to be the growing ambitions of Germany. The motivations behind Astana are therefore not so different from the design of the Entente Cordiale. Without prolonging the metaphor, we can however note among the points of resemblance that despite their conflictual relations France and the UK have not waged war on each other since 1815 (Waterloo); the Turks and the Iranians have been at peace since 1639 (the Treaty of Qasr-i-Shirin or Zuhab).

The hypothesis that we may form is thus that partners who are a priori deeply mistrustful or even hostile can come to an understanding to limit the potential damage caused by their disagreements, especially if the environment imposes a certain solidarity on them. The lesson of the Entente Cordiale is that in such a scenario the partners in question can little by little get to know each other, understand each other better and somehow tame each other, to the point where they find themselves on the same side when the time comes for the ultimate test (1914, in the case of the Entente Cordiale).

If we transpose the Entente Cordiale experience to the Astana triangle, will we be witness to a strengthening of the partnership despite the maintained areas of competition? Or, on the contrary, will potentially diverging interests between the three necessarily shatter the triangle? We will not make a complete list here of the possible diverging interests, but in passing, we can note Russian ambitions in Libya and elsewhere, Turkish ambitions in the Caucasus and Central Asia as well as in Iraq and Lebanon, as well as Iranian ambitions over the whole zone. For instance, the new Turkish-Ukrainian relation is difficult for Moscow to stomach. Is it not inevitable that there will be a misstep at some point in these triangular relations that basically remain transactional?

This is where the analogy with the Entente Cordiale—a risky analogy, we agree—reaches its limits. In the Astana trio, several asymmetries can be observed that did not exist between the British and French empires at the beginning of the twentieth century.

First of all, there is asymmetry in the bilateral relations within the Astana trio: For Russia, Iran is just one partner among many (less important than Israel, for example); Russia is one of the very few powers on which, for security issues, Tehran can rely; Turkey depends on Russia from an economic or in any case from an energy point of view while Russia basically does not depend on Turkey; as we demonstrated in our collective work *L'Iran et ses voisins* (*Iran and its neighbors*) (Therme 2020), Iranians and Turks have a long shared history of hostility but also of reciprocal understanding encouraged by a certain economic interdependence.

Equally, there is asymmetry in terms of regimes. The idea of an Entente Cordiale was behind the first approaches made by Louis Philippe then again during the Second Empire. If it became a reality at the start of the twentieth century, it was because an affinity had grown between the regimes of the British monarchy and the Third Republic, two parliamentary democracies. Between the three Astana regimes, there is certainly a connivance between authoritarians and the anti-West creed that has been mentioned, both of those factors contributing to ease relations, even though they may be rough (thinking of the Putin-Erdogan dialogue in particular). It remains that the Islamic Republic has its own canons of governance and it is not a personalized dictatorship. Erdogan's presidentialism seems fairly unlikely to become stabilized for it depends greatly on the personal equation of the new Sultan; no-one knows how the Putinian regime will evolve. The "ideological glue" between the three is possibly questionable.

This is all the more so since in the Russian-Turkish relationship there is a charm whose spell might be broken: The pleasure for Mr Putin—who is very "Cold War" minded, in fact—of driving a wedge between Turkey and the Atlantic Alliance, is reinforced by the blackmail that Erdogan is applying to the Allies ("hold me back or there'll be a calamity").

Finally, there is asymmetry in the respective geopolitical roles of the Astana three. Will Russia, a global power, as we have already said, not find itself drawn into China's orbit in the context of a new global bipolarization? For Iran, as for Turkey, is not this bipolarization an opportunity to create for itself margins of maneuver? If we retain this hypothesis then a priori Turkey is better placed than Iran. It already enjoys a special status, that of being a member of NATO wherein it can, with no major risk at present, be somewhat unfaithful to the Atlantic Alliance. Its economy depends heavily on the European Union but the EU has never succeeded in instrumentalizing this dependency. Iran is more constricted in its international game by the options forced on it by the ideological foundations of its regime. On the regional plan in particular, Turkey remains a fickle power that might change partners, as it has done in the past; the Islamic Republic does not really have an alternative strategy, except maybe for a difficult reconciliation with the West.

All in all then, the future of the triangular relationship between Turkey, Russia, and Iran depends on the trio's internal dynamics, on the evolution of the regimes concerned, on the regional strategies that each chooses, and finally on the capacity of external actors—the members of the "other trio" that we have mentioned (The Gulf states, Israel, the USA) plus Europe and China—to interfere in the development of the triangle. For many observers, it is this external actors parameter that will be the most determining, particularly the attitude of America and its European allies.

It would be wise therefore to be content with this very open conclusion, but that is truly banal and even tautological. Maybe the reader wishes for a more precise prognosis. So, in order not to disappoint them, and without however claiming a role as the Delphic Oracle, which we are not capable of playing, there are three possible scenarios on offer, that may be worthy of stimulating reflection.

- First scenario: A regional stabilization based on a balance between Turkey and Iran. This is a scenario envisaged by some circles in Tehran.

This presumes that the USA goes right to the end of its policy of withdrawal. We should note that the Abraham Accords—the normalization of relations between Israel and a certain number of Arab states and in particular those in the Gulf—can be read as a kind of insurance against such a development. For this first scenario to function it would also be necessary for the coalitions of the "anti-Iranians" in the region to collapse, in other words that the internal contradictions of the alternative triangle that we have identified (USA, Gulf states, Israel) are stronger than the desire to cooperate. Under such conditions, a Tehran-Ankara axis might in fact be imagined, providing that the Turks and the Iranians settle their disagreement in Syria and manage their sore points in Iraq, Lebanon and possibly elsewhere.

The strength of this scenario is precisely that a "policy mix" wherein regional order is preserved and competing appetites are regulated could in fact lead Iran and Turkey to become closer (this is not the tendency at the time of writing). Such a rapprochement would help to structure the Near East if the USA and Russia adopted a more distant attitude with regard to the region, preoccupied as they are by other priorities, yet all the while maintaining a certain guarantee of security including for the USA with regard to those Gulf states marginalized by cooperation between Iran and Turkey. Israel would doubtless be a major obstacle, unless there are internal developments that are hard to imagine. Another unknown is the attitude of China that has become the leading economic partner of all the states in the region. It thus could have an interest in favoring regional peace where the USA plays no major part. It could also act to ensure persistent instability that would oblige America to remain focalized on the Near East to the detriment of its "pivot" toward Asia.

Those who support an evolution of a "Tehran-Ankara" type axis—in Iran but also elsewhere, including in Europe—put forward a historic-culturalist argument: In a zone where the states have all been created recently, the two natural anchor points for any regional order would be the two countries that are the heirs of the Ottomans and the Sasanians, who possess the structures of a state and have a tradition in the wielding of power. In the Turkey-Russia-Iran triangle, it would thus be the Turkey-Iran side that would end up setting the pace—Russia remaining an external power.

- Second scenario: The triangle breaks down under the strain of the return of a Western-oriented coalition taking the region in hand. Russia is foiled, at least to some degree: It maintains its positions, notably in Syria, but it loses its current central place. This is the solution that Washington and its allies should seek to implement.

In such a hypothesis, either Iran is marginalized because the coalition of its opponents imposes itself (the somber side of the scenario); either it is neutralized or even better "normalized", which is conceivable if the nuclear issue is finally sorted, and this procures a détente in the regional situation (rosy-colored view of the scenario). The other major variable allowing the emergence of this second scenario is a repositioning for Turkey. As we have already suggested, the return of successful relations between Turkey and Israel, or between Turkey and other regional states (Egypt) is not impossible. Above all, the USA has the political cards in hand and Europe has the economic cards when it comes to finding a new kind of relation with Turkey anyway, whatever the fate of Recep Tayyip Erdogan and his party, the AKP.

Does the nature of Erdogan's regime—the nationalist character of its orientation, his addiction to expansionism, etc.—make it impossible for there to be any arrangement between the West and Turkey while the new Sultan is in place? Is an issue such as that surrounding the Syrian Kurds insurmountable? Are the Americans and the Europeans capable of adopting a more dynamic position of dissuasion / commitment regarding Ankara than has been the case so far? These are in fact serious unknowns and opposite them must probably be placed the decreasing returns on Turkish investment in Russia and moreover the Russian investment in the region. If this second scenario turned out to be the one that prevailed, Russia-Turkey relations and Russia-Iran relations would continue but with a lower profile than is currently the case, the question of the Turkey-Iran relation remains central to the region.

- Third scenario: The perpetuation of the current triangle, with balances and imbalances in perpetual recomposition, even if the "Astana Process" seems to be stalled for the moment.

What gives importance to this scenario is the Syrian deadlock and the probability that for a long time yet Syria will remain a failed state with no perspective of a political solution, which will entail the bankruptcy trustees—Turkey, Russia and Iran—remaining in cahoots. What also makes this scenario credible is the difficulty in imagining the implementation of certain conditions that the preceding scenarios suppose such as a dual Russian-American withdrawal from regional affairs or a significant breakthrough in the relations between Iran and the West.

The third scenario is the most unstable of the three. It may be the one that Russia prefers since a certain instability accommodates its strategic role in the region. One is tempted to say that it is the most likely. Insofar as it leaves the three protagonists face to face it is also the one in which the reasons for discord between Russia, Turkey, and Iran would find themselves exacerbated over the months or even the years to come. Only temporary measures last, as the saying goes. It is doubtful however that Russian-Turkish arrangements over Idlib or the simmering rivalry between Turkey and Iran, for example, could last eternally. Moreover, it is to be expected that the regime in Damascus has some surprises in store, even for its protectors. Thus, the third scenario seems to be the most likely but not the most durable. Return to square one.

Translation by Moya Jones

REFERENCES

Duclos, Michel. 2019. *La longue nuit syrienne*. Paris: L'Observatoire.
Therme, Clément. 2020. *L'Iran et ses rivaux, entre nation et revolution*. Paris: Editions Passés Composés.

Index

247